The Garden of Truth

Also by SEYYED HOSSEIN NASR

A Young Muslim's Guide to the Modern World
An Introduction to Islamic Cosmological Doctrines
Ideals and Realities of Islam
Islam: Religion, History, and Civilization
Islam and the Plight of Modern Man
Islamic Art and Spirituality
Islamic Life and Thought
Islamic Philosophy from Its Origin to the Present
Islamic Science: An Illustrated Study
Knowledge and the Sacred
Man and Nature: The Spiritual Crisis of Modern Man
Muhammad: Man of God
The Pilgrimage of Life and the Wisdom of Rumi
Poems of the Way
Religion and the Order of Nature
Science and Civilization in Islam
Sufi Essays
The Islamic Intellectual Tradition in Persia
The Heart of Islam
The Need for Sacred Science
Three Muslim Sages
Traditional Islam in the Modern World

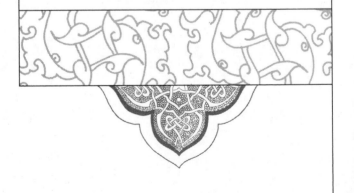

The Garden of Truth

The Vision and Promise of Sufism, Islam's Mystical Tradition

SEYYED HOSSEIN NASR

HarperOne
A Division of HarperCollins*Publishers*

HarperOne

Maps by Topaz Inc.

FIRST EDITION

Library of Congress Cataloging-in-Publication Data

Nasr, Seyyed Hossein.
The garden of truth : the vision and practice of Sufism / Seyyed Hossein Nasr.—1st ed.
p. cm.
Includes bibliographical references and index.
ISBN: 978-0-06-079722-5
ISBN-10: 0-06-079722-3
1. Sufism—Doctrines. 2. Sufism—Customs and practices. I. Title.
BP189.3.N364 2007
297.4—dc22

2007018364

07 08 09 10 11 RRD(H) 10 9 8 7 6 5 4 3 2 1

بسم الله الرحمن الرحيم

In the Name of God, the Infinitely Good, the All-Merciful

CONTENTS

LIST OF TRANSLITERATIONS

Arabic and transliterated Roman characters

ء	ʾ	ط	ṭ	*long vowels*		*Persian letters added to Arabic alphabet*	
ب	b	ظ	ẓ	ای	ā		
ت	t	ع	ʿ	و	ū	پ	p
ث	*th*	غ	*gh*	ي	ī	چ	*ch*
ج	j	ف	f			ژ	*zh*
ح	ḥ	ق	q			گ	g
خ	*kh*	ك	k				
د	d	ل	l				
ذ	*dh*	م	*m*	*short vowels*		*diphthongs*	
ر	r	ن	n	ـَ	a	ـَو	aw
ز	z	ه	h	ـُ	u	ـَي	ai (ay)
س	s	و	w	ـِ	i	ـِيّ	ayy (final form ī)
ش	*sh*	ي	y			ـُوّ	uww (final form ū)
ص	ṣ	ة	ah; at				
ض	ḍ	ال	(article) al- and ʾl				

The Islamic World

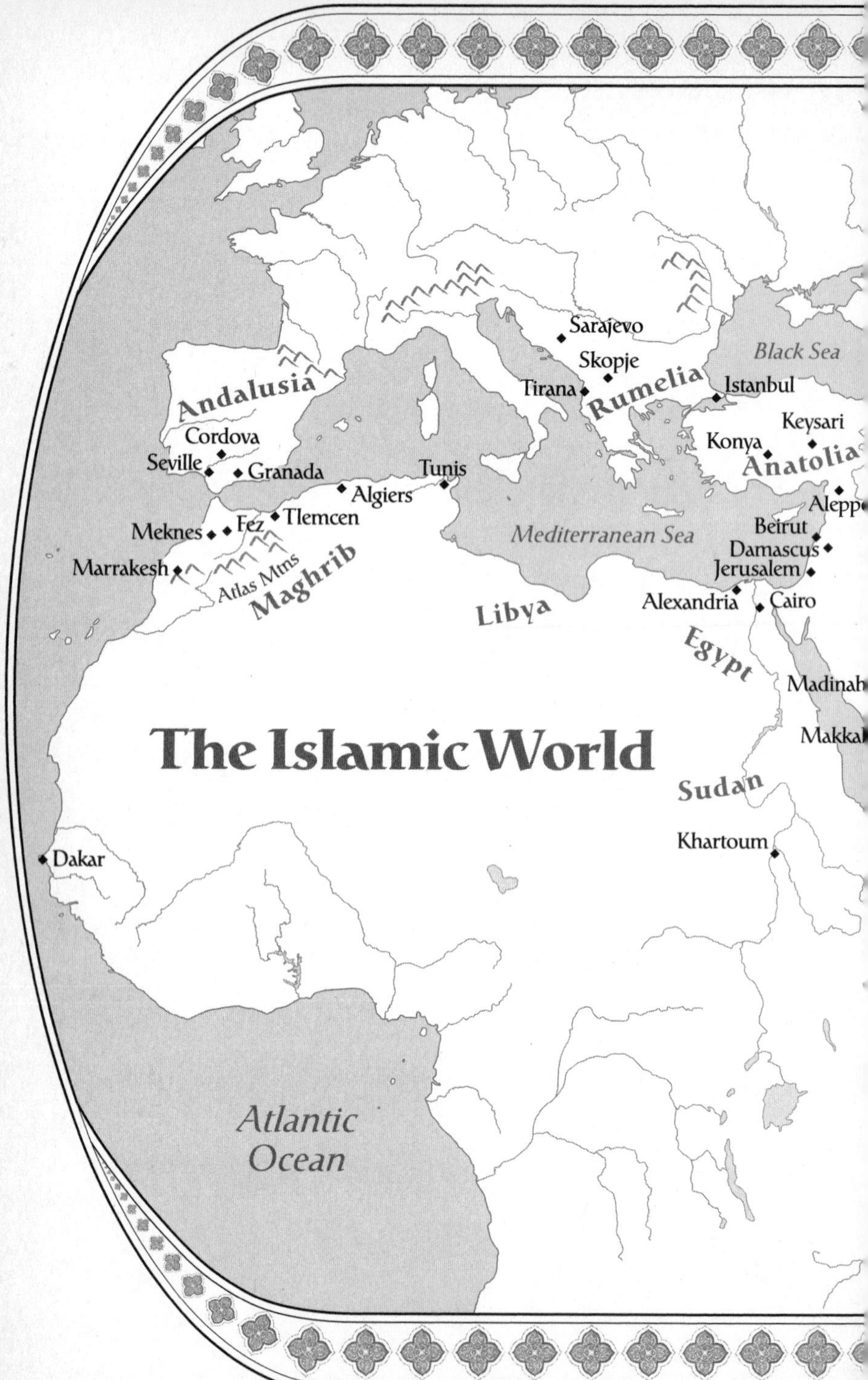

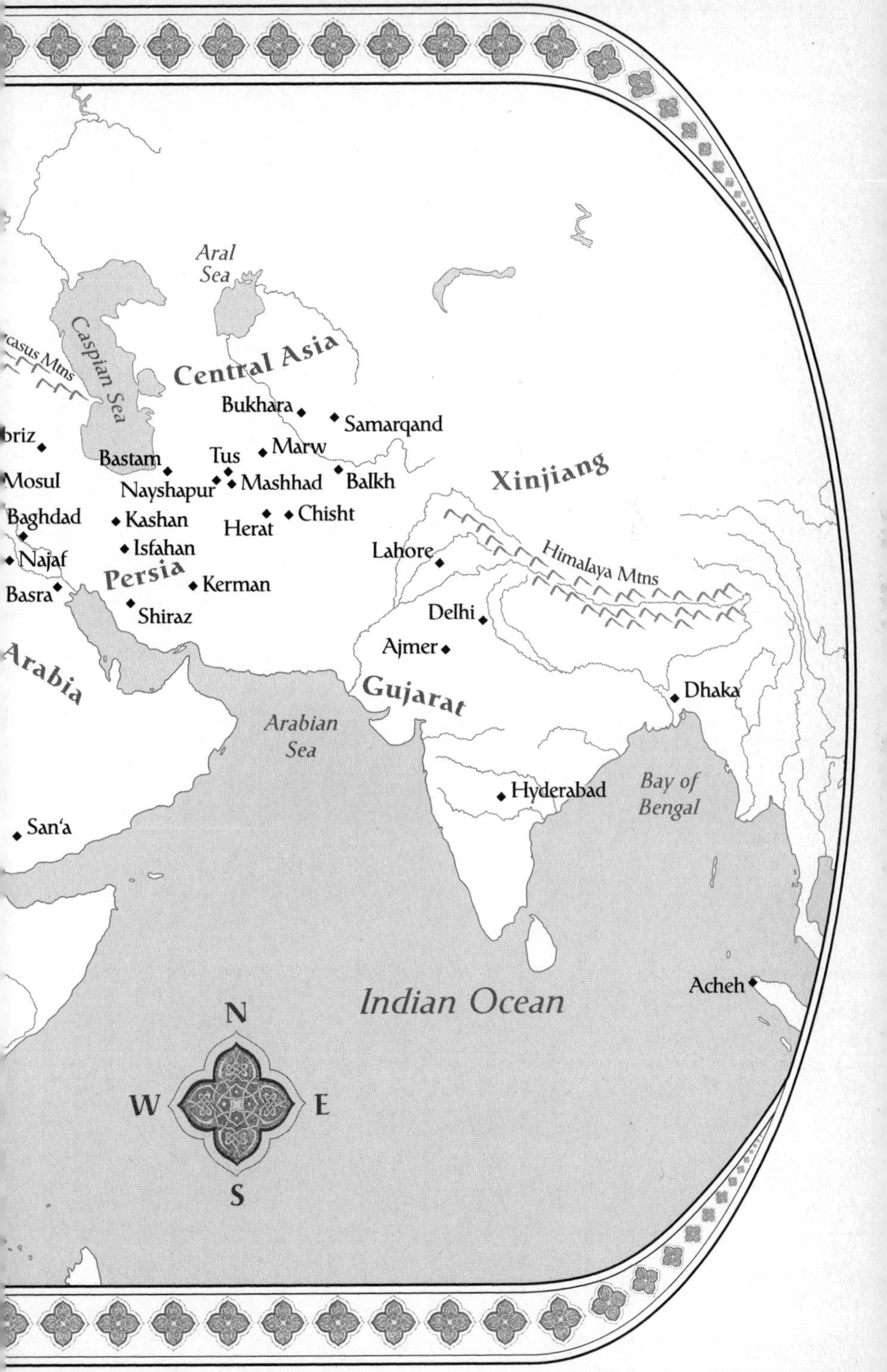
Aral Sea
Caspian Sea
casus Mtns
Central Asia
Bukhara
Samarqand
briz
Marw
Bastam
Tus
Balkh
Mosul
Nayshapur
Mashhad
Xinjiang
Baghdad
Kashan
Herat
Chisht
Isfahan
Lahore
Najaf
Himalaya Mtns
Persia
Kerman
Basra
Shiraz
Delhi
Ajmer
Arabia
Gujarat
Dhaka
Arabian Sea
Hyderabad
Bay of Bengal
San'a
Acheh
Indian Ocean
N
W
E
S

INTRODUCTION

The present book is the result of over fifty years of both scholarly study of and existential participation in Sufism. Providence has made it possible for me to visit many Sufi sites from the Atlantic to the Pacific, to encounter numerous Sufi masters, to participate in almost countless Sufi gatherings, and to read and study many Sufi works and scholarly writings about Sufism by scholars of both East and West. My goal in this book, however, is not to present a history of Sufism or just an academic work on the subject, although I have sought to be scholarly to the best of my ability. My aim is rather to present to the reader a Sufi text written in English and using contemporary language. In purely academic works, one relies only on written sources or field reports based on external observation, whereas this book, while using written historical sources, issues from the lived reality of Sufism, the experience of Sufi spirituality, the all-important centuries-old oral tradition, and truths that are metahistorical. I felt obliged to write this book because I believe that after some two centuries of study of Sufism in the West, with the appearance of many translations, analyses, histories, and some profound expositions of Sufi metaphysics, and given an ever greater interest in Sufism by certain Westerners, it is necessary to write, not just another book about Sufism, but a Sufi book. It is necessary to present the reality of Sufism as did the authorities of old but in a manner accessible to the present-day serious Western seeker or Western-educated Muslim seeker, even if such a person has no previous knowledge of the subject. In this book I have dealt with universal truths of interest to those attracted to the life of the Spirit and in light of the human condition in general, presenting them from within the spiritual and intellectual universe of Sufism while providing a means of access to that universe and revealing some of its riches.

Until a few decades ago a few fine studies of Sufism as well as competent translations of Sufi works were available in European languages, but no introductions to the subject written from within the Sufi tradition. During the last few decades some outstanding works dealing with the heart of Sufism and written from its perspective have appeared, such as *Sufism: Veil and Quintessence* by Frithjof Schuon, *An Introduction to Sufism* by Titus Burckhardt, and *What Is Sufism?* by Martin Lings. All of these exceptional, masterly works presume, however, some knowledge of Sufism as well as of traditional metaphysics. William Chittick's *Sufism: A Brief Introduction,* also written from the Sufi point of view, is more of an introduction but couched in scholarly language, being more about Sufism rather than being a Sufi treatise. Then there are works of Western Islamicists, sympathetic to Sufism but not participants in its practices. Of this genre the well-known book *Mystical Dimensions of Islam* by Annemarie Schimmel stands out, and more recently there has appeared *The Shambhala Guide to Sufism* by Carl Ernst. By contrast, the present book seeks to introduce the reader to the inner teachings of Sufism in the manner of classical Sufi works but in a contemporary language.

Like classical Sufi texts, this work is interspersed with Quranic citations, sayings (*ḥadīths*) of the Prophet of Islam, and poetry. Where not indicated otherwise, the translation of these quotations is my own. The verses of the Quran are of course indicated, but since I learned the *ḥadīths* and many of the poems through oral tradition, no references are given for most of them. Still, to guide the reader to the major scholarly and poetic sources, references are provided for some of the quotations. My hope, however, is that the text will be read by those seeking to study Sufism from within or with a teacher as well as by those drawn to spirituality in general, and not considered simply as a scholarly work.

That is also why the spiritual teachings in this book are addressed directly to the seeker without hiding behind the garb of scholarship.

The title of this book, *The Garden of Truth,* is drawn from the traditional Islamic symbolism of the garden. The traditional Islamic garden is an earthly reflection of Paradise, and the word *paradise* itself comes from the Middle Persian word *pardīs,* meaning garden, and is also the origin of the Arabic word *firdaws,* meaning paradise and garden. Using the symbol of the garden, the Quran refers to Paradise itself as the Garden. Moreover, the Sacred Text speaks of levels of Paradise. The Sufis have drawn from this symbolism and speak of the Garden as designating not only the various levels of paradisal realities but also the Divine Reality beyond Paradise as usually understood. The highest Garden is associated with the absolute Truth, which is one of the Names of the Divine Essence. Hence, we can speak of the Garden of Truth as that reality wherein all the spiritual realities are gathered. The Sufis also speak of the Gardener as God in His absolute and infinite Reality, and of *jannat al-Dhāt,* or Garden of the Divine Essence. I therefore also make occasional use of this symbolism in the pages that follow.

Sufism is a vast reality that provides the means for those who follow its tenets to reach the Garden of Truth. It is the path to the Garden and, on the highest level and in its inner reality, the "content" of the Garden as well as the means of reaching the Presence of the Gardener. The Sufi tradition contains a vast metaphysical and cosmological set of doctrines elaborated over a long period by Sufi teachers and masters of gnosis. It contains methods of spiritual realization that address nearly all the different spiritual possibilities on the levels of action, love, and knowledge. It has preserved over many centuries and going back to the Prophet a regular chain of transmission of initiatic power (*walāyah/wilāyah*) and the grace (*al-barakah*) necessary for the spiritual journey. And above all, it can enable men and women to reach the state of sanctity.

Sufism has manifested itself in vast expanses of time and space, from the first century of Islamic history, that is, the seventh century, to now, and from Senegal and Morocco to Indonesia and China. Sufi orders are found in all Islamic lands as well as in India, China, Russia, non-Muslim Africa, and since the twentieth century in many Western countries. Sufism has also produced in several languages some of the greatest mystical poetry ever written and has created some of the most interiorizing music ever heard. Within the Islamic world it has influenced ethics and social behavior, philosophy, theology, some of the natural sciences, and nearly all the arts from calligraphy and miniature painting to architecture and urban design. It has, moreover, played a crucial role in the encounter and dialogue between Islam and other religions and cultures.

Although attacked since the nineteenth century by both modernists and puritanical reformists in the Islamic world, Sufism is still very much alive in most Muslim countries. Although denatured, diluted, and distorted in certain circles in the West, it is now also present in a serious form in many parts of America and Europe. In both the Islamic world and the West, Sufism will continue to play an important role in bringing about understanding across religious borders, in addition to its central role in providing an authentic spiritual path for those who seek to reach in this life the Garden of Truth and ultimately the Gardener. In the Islamic world Sufism is the most powerful antidote to the religious radicalism called fundamentalism as well as the most important source for responding to the challenges posed for Islam by modernism. In the West it is the most accessible means for understanding Islam in its essential reality. Sufism constitutes also a central link between the spiritual traditions of Islam and the West.

In this book, however, I am concerned not so much with the cultural and civilizational role of Sufism as with the souls of men and women in quest of the Truth. I therefore seek to present the realities of Sufism while keeping in mind the concrete spiritual and intellectual needs of contemporary men and women in both East and West. May the book be a humble guide for those who seek.

In conclusion, I wish to thank the Radius Foundation and Katherine O'Brien for making possible the preparation of the manuscript of this book for publication, and to Eric Brandt, Laurie Dunne, and others at HarperOne who have made its publication possible.

Seyyed Hossein Nasr
Bethesda, Maryland
May 14, 2007

Part One

One

WHAT IT MEANS TO BE HUMAN

Who Are We and What Are We Doing Here?

"Am I not Your Lord?" They said, "Yea, verily we bear witness."
Quran 7:172

After extinction I came out, and I
Eternal now am, though not as I.
And who am I, O I, but I.[1]
'Alī Shushtarī

THE UNAVOIDABLE QUESTION

Wherever we are and in whatever time we happen to live, we cannot avoid asking the basic questions of who we are, where we came from, what we are doing here, and where we are going. In everyone's life, especially when one is young, these basic questions arise in the mind, often with force, and demand answers from us. Many simply push them aside or remain satisfied with established answers provided by others in their family or community. In traditional societies such answers always came from the teachings of religion, and to a great extent they still do for the majority of people in many parts of the world. But there have always been and still are today the few who take the question "who am I?" seriously and existentially and who are not satisfied with answers provided by others. Rather, they seek to find the answers by themselves, trying with their whole being to delve into the inner meaning of religion and wisdom. They continue until they reach the goal and receive a response that provides for them certitude and removes from them the clouds of doubt. In any case, how we choose to live in this world—how we act and think and how we develop the latent possibilities within us—depends totally on the answer we provide for ourselves to this basic question of who we are, for human beings live and act for the most part according to the image they have of themselves.

Sufism addresses the few who yearn for an answer on the deepest level to the question of who they are and in a manner that would touch and transform their whole being. The Sufi path is the means within the Islamic tradition of finding the ultimate answer to this basic question and of discovering our real identity. Throughout the ages religions have sought to teach us who we are and through their inner teachings to provide the means of "becoming" our True Self. Islam is certainly no exception. It unveils the complete doctrine of our true nature and also the nature of the levels of reality issuing from the One, who alone is ultimately Real, and provides teachings that, if put into practice, lead us back to the One through a path of spiritual effort combined with joy and felicity. The Quran asserts majestically, "Verily we come from God and to Him is our returning"(2:156). The One is of course that Supreme Source and End of all things whom Abraham, Moses, and Christ addressed as the One God and whom the Quran calls by His Name in Arabic, *Allāh*.

It is no accident that the Sacred Law of Islam is called the *Sharī'ah,* which means road. It is a road that all Muslims are obliged to travel if they are to die in a blessed state. For most, however, the journey on this road is limited to the plane of action, the performance of good acts, and faith in the reality of God. Few wish to take a step further to discover the ultimate nature of who they are and carry self-knowledge to its end. Sufism, which is the inner or esoteric dimension of Islam, while beginning with the *Sharī'ah* as the basis of the religious life, seeks to take a further step toward that Truth (*Ḥaqīqah*), which is also the source of the *Sharī'ah.* Sufism, which is also called the *Ṭarīqah,* or the spiritual path, is the divinely ordained means of providing an answer to that ultimate question and leading us to the Truth or *Ḥaqīqah* contained within that answer. The *Sharī'ah* is the circumference of a circle whose radii are the *Ṭuruq* (plural of *Ṭarīqah*) and whose Center is the *Ḥaqīqah* or Truth, that is, the Source of both the Law and Way as well as the Center for one who begins on the circumference, journeys along one of the radii, and finally reaches the Center, which is also his or her own center. To reach the Center means not only being in a blessed state but also reaching the state to which various mysticisms refer as union with God.

The Prophet of Islam said, "Whosoever knows his self, knows his Lord"; that is, self-knowledge leads to knowledge of the Divine. Sufism takes this saying (*ḥadīth*) very seriously and also puts it into practice. It provides, within the spiritual universe of the Islamic tradition, the light necessary to illuminate the dark corners of our soul and the keys to open the doors to the hidden recesses of our being so that we can journey within and know ourselves, this knowledge leading ultimately to the knowledge of God, who resides in our heart/center.

Not only were we created by God, but we have the root of our existence here and now in Him. When we bore witness to His Lordship as mentioned in the Quranic verse, "Am I not your Lord?" the world and all that is in it were not as yet created. Even now we have our pre-eternal existence in the Divine Presence, and we have made an eternal covenant with God, which remains valid beyond the contingencies of our earthly life and beyond the realm of space and time in which we now find ourselves.

The answer to the question "who are we?" is related in a principial manner to our ultimate reality in God, a reality that we have now forgotten as a result of the fall from our original and primordial state and the subsequent decay in the human condition caused by the downward flow of time. We have become forgetful beings, no longer knowing who we are and therefore what our purpose is in this life. But our reality in God, who resides at the depth of our being, is still there. We need to awaken to this reality and to realize our true identity, that is, to know who we really are.

Not everyone wants to awaken from that daydreaming we call ordinary life, but there are those who do. These men and women deeply yearn to discover their true identity, which means not only to discover the reality of God but also to journey on a path that leads to His embrace. Sufism is meant for such a person, and if you are such a person, then it has a message for you, for it is a path of return to your reality in God and indeed to God Himself. It provides the means to awaken us from the dream of forgetfulness of who we are and allow us to enter into and remain in the remembrance of the Divine Reality, which is also the heart of our selves, the Self of all selves. The Sufi path leads from the desert of outwardness, forgetfulness, selfishness, and falsehood to the Garden of Truth, wherein alone we can realize our true identity and come to know who we are. The message of Sufism is perennial because human nature is always human nature, beyond accidental changes of historical epochs and fashions of the day, and also because as long as we are human, the question that each individual faces is "who am I?" The response of Sufism to this perennial question resonates today as it has always done for those whose ears are sensitive to its call and who yearn for illuminative knowledge.

LIFE IS A JOURNEY

According to Sufi metaphysics, and in fact other metaphysical traditions in general, all that exists comes from that Reality which is at once Beyond-Being and Being, and ultimately all things return to that Source. In the language of Islamic thought, including both philosophy and Sufism, the first part of this journey of all beings from the Source is called the "arc of descent" and the second part back to the Source the "arc of ascent." Within this vast cosmic wayfaring we find ourselves here and now on earth as human beings. Moreover, our life here in this world is a journey within that greater cosmic journey of all existents back to the Source of all existence. We are born, we move through time, and we die. For most of us, without knowing who we really are, we move between two great mysteries and unknowns, namely, where we were before we came into this world and where we shall go after death. The answer of materialists and nihilists is that we came from nowhere and we go nowhere; we had no reality before coming into this world, and nothing of our consciousness survives our death. They reduce our existence to simply the physical and terrestrial level and believe that we are merely animals (themselves considered as complicated machines) who have ascended from below, not spiritual beings who have descended from above. But if we are honest with ourselves, we realize that even the concept of matter or corporeality is contained in our consciousness and that therefore when we ask ourselves who we are, we are acting as conscious beings and have to begin with our consciousness. If we are intellectually awake, we realize that we cannot reduce consciousness to that which is itself contained in our consciousness.

Now, no matter how we seek to go back to the origin of our consciousness, we cannot reach its beginning in time, and the question again arises what our consciousness, its origin, and its end are. The spiritual practices of every authentic path, including Sufism, enable those who follow and practice them earnestly and under the appropriate conditions to gain new levels of consciousness and ultimately to become aware that consciousness has no beginning in time (but only in God) because "in the beginning was consciousness," and it has no temporal end because "in the end is consciousness." Once we discover who we are in the spiritual sense, we gain an insight into the mystery of where we came from before the caravan of our earthly life began its journey here below and also into the mystery of where we shall go after the end of this terrestrial journey. Self-knowledge also pierces the veils that limit our ordinary consciousness and ultimately leads to those higher states of consciousness that stand above the world of becoming. We are then able to be aware of our human reality and our ultimate identity beyond the confines of time and space. Sufism makes possible the piercing of these veils as it leads the seeker on an inward journey within the journey on the road of the Sacred Law, or the *Sharī'ah,* which is itself a journey within the journey of life, while life itself is a journey within the journey of all beings in their return to the Source. The Sufi path is an inward journey whose goal is to know who we really are, from where we came, and where we shall go. Its aim is also to know ultimately the nature of Reality, which is also Truth as such.

WHO THEN ARE WE?

As we travel upon this road of self-knowledge with the help of the means provided by tradition—means without which such a journey is in fact impossible—we gain a new perspective concerning every kind of reality with which we had identified at the beginning of our journey. We come to realize that although we are male or female, that attribute does not really define us. There is a deeper reality, one might say an androgynic reality, transcending the male-female dichotomy so that our identity is not determined simply by our gender. Nor are we simply our body and the senses although we often identify ourselves with them. As we travel upon the Sufi path, it also becomes more and more evident that what we call "I" has its existence independent of sense perceptions and the body as a whole although the soul continues to have a consciousness of the body while being also aware through spiritual practice of the possibility of leaving it for higher realms.

Likewise, although we have emotions and psychological states with which we often identify, the spiritual path teaches us that they do not define and determine our identity in the deepest sense. In fact, often we say, "I must control my temper," which demonstrates clearly that there is more than one psychological agent within human beings. As St. Thomas said, confirming Sufi teachings, "*Duo sunt in homine*" ("There are two in man"). The part of us that seeks to control our temper must be distinct and not determined by the part of our soul that is angry and needs to be controlled. Yes, we do experience emotions, but we need not be defined by them. In the same manner, we have an imaginative faculty able to create images, and most of the time ordinary people live in the lower reaches of that world of imaginal forms. Again, we are not determined by those forms, and journeying upon the spiritual path is especially effective in transforming our inner imaginal landscape. As for the power of memory, it is for the most part the repository of images and forms related to earlier experiences of life. Metaphysically speaking, however, it is also related to our atemporal relation to our Source of Being and the intelligible world to which we belonged before our descent here to earth. That is why true knowledge according to Plato is recollection, and in Sufism the steps of the path are identified with stages of the remembrance of the Friend. Most people, however, consider these everyday remembered experiences as a major part of their identity. Yet again, the center of our consciousness, our I, cannot be identified with our ordinary memory. We can forget many things and remain the same human being. The spiritual life may in fact be defined as the practice of techniques that enable us to forget all that we remember about the world of separation and dispersion and to remember the most important thing, which this world has caused us to forget, namely, the one "saving Truth," which is also our inner reality.

Many would say that if we are not determined by our gender, bodies, emotions, imaginative faculties, or memories, then surely we are what we think and are determined by our minds. Here we are reaching a more delicate realm. One can say with Aristotle that man is a rational animal, which means that it is in the nature of the human being to think. Even as great a Sufi figure as the thirteenth-century Persian master, Rūmī, says,

> O Brother, thou art thought itself,
> The rest of thy being is but sinew and bone.
>
> *Mathnawī, 2:278*

But by *thought* Rūmī did not mean simply everyday discursive thought, which skips from one concept to another without the whole being of the person who holds the thought participating in the concept (even if it be true), a thought that does not go beyond the level of mental play. Moreover, conceptual knowledge can be wrong and lead to error, and excessive cerebral activity can distract our consciousness from the center of our being. That is why mystics have also spoken of "unknowing," and more specifically, Sufis have stated explicitly that in order to reach the Truth one has to "tear the veil of thinking." In any case, while we have a mind, our true identity resides in an even deeper level of our being.

This deeper level is the heart/intellect, the heart being the center of the human microcosm and also the organ of unitive knowledge associated with the intellect (in the medieval sense of *intellectus,* or the Greek *nous,* not in its current sense of reason). The heart is also where the Divine Reality resides in men and women, for as the sacred *ḥadīth*[2] asserts, "The Heavens and the earth cannot contain Me, but the heart of my faithful servant does contain Me."

Here, at the very center of the heart where the Divine resides, is found the root of the "I" and the final answer to the question "who am I?" Sufism seeks to lead adepts to the heart, where they find both their true self and their Beloved, and for that reason Sufis are sometimes called "the people of the heart" (*ahl-i dil* in Persian). Of course, the phrase "both their true self and their Beloved" does not mean any ultimate duality, for as Rūmī also said, in the heart there is room for only one I, which is both the root of our true self and the Self as such. Who am I? I am the I that, having traversed all the stages of limited existence from the physical to the mental to the noumenal, has realized its own "nonexistence" and by virtue of this annihilation of the false self has returned to its roots in the Divine Reality and has become a star proximate to the Supernal Sun, which is ultimately the only I. Having passed through the door of nothingness and annihilation, I come to the realization that at the root of my consciousness, of what I call I, resides the only I that can ultimately say I and that ultimately alone is.

Neither this body am I, nor soul,
Nor these fleeting images passing by,
Nor concepts and thoughts, mental images,
Nor yet sentiments and the psyche's labyrinth.
Who then am I? A consciousness without origin,
Not born in time, nor begotten here below.
I am that which was, is and ever shall be,
A jewel in the crown of the Divine Self,
A star in the firmament of the luminous One.

Being human, however, implies a second phase of discovery in light of the first. Having discovered his or her roots in the Divine through the teachings and practices of Sufism, the Sufi then returns to the lower levels of existence, which are again seen as parts of his or her identity but not as they were before. Rather, they are transformed so that each at its own level reflects something of that supernal Reality, which determines our ultimate identity. The heart, having been discovered and its hardened shell melted through spiritual practice, emanates a light that shines upon the mind, which then, rather than jumping aimlessly from one concept to another, becomes an illuminated instrument of the intellect, able to discern true knowledge and distinguish between truth and falsehood, substance and accidents, necessity and contingency, levels of existence, and, most of all, the Absolute and the relative.

It becomes an aid in, rather than a detriment to, self-realization. The same is true of the imaginative faculty, which becomes transformed in such a way as to create imaginal forms reflecting higher rather than lower levels of reality and to facilitate the theophanic contemplation of sacred forms. As for the emotions, rather than being negative and dispersing one's spiritual energies, they become completely transformed into positive energies dominated by love, charity, empathy, and so forth and controlled by virtues, which shall be mentioned later in chapter 5. Our memories are likewise transformed, becoming the treasure-house for the remembrance of the Friend rather than a bleak warehouse filled with trivial and opaque forms, concepts, and images.

We finally come to the body, which in most mystical schools in the West is looked upon primarily as an impediment to the freedom of the spirit. Of course this aspect of the body is real, but another aspect is also very significant and is emphasized strongly by many schools of Sufism. First of all, we have more than one body. We have levels of subtle bodies within us corresponding to all levels of cosmic reality going up to God. Sufism makes possible the awareness of these other bodies and makes clear their role in the spiritual life. Second, as the soul and the psyche become illuminated by the spirit and the real "I" begins to shed its light on the individualized self, the body also becomes transformed by this inner illumination and in fact often becomes itself illuminated. One need only recall in the Christian context the halo in the iconography of saints and the incorruptibility of their bodies; a new and at the same time primordial relation is established in them between spirit, soul, and body. In Sufism the body becomes an outward source of *barakah,* or grace, in the case of those men and women who have come to realize who they really are. The body also becomes a tangible and concrete external form that preserves and reflects the spirit within. It becomes the temple of the spirit.

To the question "who are we?" we can then answer finally that we are latent archetypes embedded in the Divine Reality, which is the ultimate root of every "I," and that through that archetype, which has become existentiated by God, we have existence in all realms of being from the spiritual to the physical, microcosmically and also macrocosmically. We were brought into this world in order to realize who we are and, having discovered that reality, to live accordingly while on earth. But this self-discovery is not possible without inner illumination, the subjective counterpart of objective revelation (upon which the former usually depends, there being occasional exceptions that only prove the rule). In the Islamic tradition, it is primarily Sufism that answers this basic existential question of who we are and through this answer provides guidance for a life full of spiritual felicity, marked by illumination and leading ultimately to deliverance from the bondage of all limitation.

TO BE GOD'S SERVANT

Not only is the root of our "I" immersed in the Divine Essence or "I," which is ultimately the only Essence, all else being Its Self-Disclosure and manifestation, but we also possess a human and individual self created by God, which is real on its own level. To understand fully the reality of being human, we must also understand fully this aspect of our nature as God's servants, to use the language of the Islamic tradition. Our ego must realize its full servanthood, which the Sufis call *'ubūdiyyah,* before the Lord, and we must realize that as servants we can never become the Lord. That is why such great Sufi masters as Abū'l-Ḥasan al-Shādhilī, the thirteenth-century founder of one of the most important Sufi orders, asserts that the desire for union with God itself distances us more than anything else from God. Likewise, the Andalusian sage Ibn 'Arabī, who also lived in the thirteenth century and who spoke so much of the unity of the Real, asserts in a similar manner that the servant (*al-'abd*) remains the servant and the Lord (*al-Rabb*) remains the Lord. But with God's grace, with the affirmation of the Lord, that divine spark within humanity, which is identified with the intellect, can transcend all dualities, including that of servant and Lord, to reach the One, the Divine Essence, which is the root of the "I" of the servant. Without realizing our perfect servitude, however, we cannot realize that ultimate Oneness because without that realization our egos, still asserting their separate existence, would prevent God within from saying "I."

In Arabic, the word *servanthood* (*'ubūdiyyah*) is related etymologically to the word for *worship* (*'ibādah*). The Quran states, "We created man and the *jinn* so that they would worship Us" (51:56); and also "There is no god but I, so worship Me" (21:25). From the Islamic point of view, therefore, the very raison d'être of human existence is to worship God and thereby to realize the perfect state of servanthood, which means also to realize what it means to be fully human. Sufism asks us to delve into the deepest meaning of worship in order to realize this nature of our being as God's perfect servants and also as creatures created by God as His valid interlocutors. In Sufism, humanity is the mirror reflecting all God's Names and Qualities; we are beings created, according to a famous *ḥadīth,* "in the image (*ṣūrah*) of God," *image* meaning here not form in the ordinary sense, for God is formless, but rather reflection of the Divine Names and Qualities. Sufism also understands "in order to worship me" to mean "in order to know me," a knowledge (*ma'rifah*) that is possible only through the realization of our perfect servanthood. That realization means etymologically not only obeying God as our master, but also realizing that all things ultimately belong to God and that in ourselves we are nothing but the poor (*faqīr*), the term *faqīr* being in fact one of the most common names for a follower of the Sufi path. The Persian term *darwīsh,* which entered the English language as *dervish,* implies the same truth. It means humbling oneself before the threshold of the Divine Reality. The highest meaning of servanthood is in fact the realization of our "nothingness" before God. It is only by passing through this gate of "annihilation," or what the Sufis call *fanā',* that we are able to gain subsistence, *baqā',* in God and to reach the root of our "I" and also therefore the Divine. Human beings qua human beings cannot enter the Divine sanctuary, but there is within us a reality that is already Divine. To be fully human is to realize our perfect servitude and to remove the veil of separative existence through spiritual practice so that God, transcendent and immanent within us, can utter "I."

A COMMENTARY ON THE OPENING CHAPTER (*AL-FĀTIḤAH*) OF THE QURAN

Sufism looks upon all Islamic acts of worship from the point of view of actualization of perfect servanthood, which makes possible for us to realize, through faith, acts of worship and spiritual practices leading to intellectual and illuminative understanding, who we really are, and who God is. All acts of worship are for the purpose of remembering God and drawing nigh unto Him or, more precisely, realizing this already existing nearness and intimacy, for as the Quran says, "If my servants ask about me [O Muḥammad], (tell them) I am indeed near" (2:186). Nowhere is this Sufi view of worship, which leads to both self-knowledge and knowledge of God combined with love and devotion, more evident than in Sufi commentaries upon the opening chapter of the Quran, called *sūrah al-Fātiḥah,* which is repeated over and over in the daily canonical prayers that Muslims perform five times a day throughout their lives after reaching adolescence. Such commentaries have been written by many spiritual authorities over the ages to the present day.

The text of the chapter, which is the first *sūrah* of the Quran, is as follows:

> In the Name of God—the Infinitely Good, the All-Merciful
> Praise be to God, the Lord of the worlds,
> the Infinitely Good, the All-Merciful,
> Master of the Day of Judgment.
> Thee we worship, and in Thee we seek help.
> Guide us upon the straight path,
> the path of those on whom Thy Grace is,
> not those on whom Thine anger is,
> nor those who are astray.[3]
>
> *Quran 1:1–7*

Let us try to study this chapter from the point of view of the significance of worship in relation to the human state. But before doing so, it is important to mention that every word and letter of the Quran in the original Arabic has not only an outward but also an inward meaning, including a numerical symbolism, similar to what one finds in the *gematria* associated with the Kabbalah and Hasidism. Moreover, the Quran has many levels (seven, according to some) of inner meaning, of which the highest is, according to the Sufis, known only to God. Sufi commentaries, which are called *ta'wīl,* that is, spiritual hermeneutics, are not humanly contrived meanings but rather the exposition of meanings already contained in the Sacred Text but hidden from the eye of outwardness. The word *ta'wīl* means to take something back to its origin, and in fact spiritual hermeneutics, in unveiling the inner meaning of the Sacred Text, also takes it back to its origin, for manifestation implies going from the inward to the outward so that metaphysically speaking the inner and the origin are ultimately the same reality.

Coming back to the *Fātiḥah,* I shall provide a commentary based on one aspect of the inner reality of this text related to the question of what it means to be human and not, of course, addressing all aspects and levels of its inner meaning (about which Sufis over the ages have written numerous commentaries, some of them book length). Like all other chapters of the Quran save one, the *Fātiḥah* begins with the formula "In the Name of God—the Infinitely Good, the All-Merciful." Now God has many Names, but the two Names *al-Raḥmān* and *al-Raḥīm,* the Infinitely Good and the All-Merciful, are the gates through which the revelation of the Quran pours forth for the guidance of human beings. *Al-Raḥmān,* which is a Name of the Divine Essence, is also the Divine Name that the Sufis associate with the existentiation of the cosmos itself. They believe that God breathed His Goodness, which is also Mercy, upon the latent archetypes residing in the Divine Intellect and Divine Knowledge and that through this "Breath of the Compassionate or the Infinitely Good" (*nafas al-Raḥmān*) the world came into being. Therefore, were it not for God's infinite Goodness and Mercy, nothing would have come into existence, including us, nor would there be a revelation to guide us out of the labyrinth of our ego and psyche toward full self-knowledge leading to the knowledge of God and of His creation and our ultimate deliverance from all limitation. The formula at the beginning of the first chapter of the Quran, which is called *basmalah* in Arabic, not only consecrates the Sacred Text but also establishes the metaphysically necessary basis for the descent of the revelation and its reception.

The text of the chapter itself begins with "Praise be to God," and this statement is on behalf of human beings although here it is uttered by God. The word for praise is *al-ḥamd,* and the attitude inherent in it constitutes an essential aspect of being truly human. The Quran asserts in several verses that all things praise God, but the praise by men and women is of special significance because human beings have been given the possibility of not praising God and of not being thankful to Him. The term *al-ḥamd^u li'Llāh,* or "praise be to God," which also implies gratefulness to Him, is so significant that it penetrates the daily life of all Muslims. Its constant repetition in daily discourse creates a perpetual attitude of praise of God and thanksgiving. Traditional Islamic sources assert that on the Day of Judgment all Muslims who have followed their religion faithfully will assemble under the "flag of praise" (*liwā' al-ḥamd*) carried by the Prophet.

In Sufism *ḥamd* and the inner attitude associated with it are central. Followers of the Path are expected to be always grateful to God and to praise Him no matter what their circumstances. According to a Sufi story, one day a master and his disciples were sitting together. The master asked one of the disciples, "What are the conditions under which we should say *al-ḥamdu li'Llāh?*" The disciple replied, "Whenever one receives bounty or a gift from God one should say *al-ḥamdu li'Llāh.*" The master responded, "What then is the difference between you and the dog sitting in front of us? If I throw him a piece of meat, he wags his tale in gratitude and praise of God. And when I do not do so, he simply sits there awaiting something from me." The master added, "A *darwīsh* is a person who, if he receives a gift or bounty from God, says '*al-ḥamdu li'Llāh*' and if he receives nothing and is in the greatest state of difficulty and need, he still says '*al-ḥamdu li'Llāh.*'" The attitude of praising God and being always grateful to Him, with the awareness that in ourselves we are poor and God is the Rich from whom all blessings flow—from the life we have to the air we breathe to the food we eat to the earth upon which we walk—is necessary for being truly human. It is a significant component of our humanity and is a basic way for us to realize who we are and to reach the state of perfect servanthood.

The greatest gift of God to us, however, is His Word or revelation, which enables us to return to Him. "Praise be to God" at the beginning of the *Fātiḥah* may be understood in the sense that we praise God and are grateful to Him for being worthy of receiving His revelation, and we say *al-ḥamdu li'Llāh* because God has created us as human beings and spoken to us, that He has placed us in a state in which we *can* say consciously *al-ḥamdu li'Llāh*. The grandeur of the human state is not in that human beings can make complicated machines or conceptualize complex theories, but in that men and women are worthy of being addressed by God and being considered worthy of receiving His revelation and guidance. This opening *al-ḥamdu li'Llāh* may be said to be not only an opening for the rest of the Quranic revelation that follows, but above all gratefulness for our being human. To be human is to be capable of hearing the Word of God and being led back to Him. The fact that in the Islamic rites each Muslim—man and woman—stands directly before God in the daily prayers without any intermediary indicates from the Sufi point of view not only that each Muslim has a priestly function but also that there is a nexus linking each soul directly to God. As Rūmī says,

> There is a connection, without diminution, without comparison,
> Between the Lord of the soul and the soul of human beings.
>
> *Mathnawī, 4:761*

One answer that the Sufis give to the question about human nature is that the human person, the *anthropōs* (including the male and the female), is a being created to be able to be addressed by God and to address Him in turn, consciously and with free will. Our relation to God, which means also the Divine Self at the center of our being, determines who we really are and what we are meant to be. We can each start with the question "who am I?" and if we search enough be led step by step to the Sufi answer that we are beings who can address God directly by praising Him and being grateful to Him, that is, by saying *al-ḥamd*[u] *li'Llāh,* and in turn be worthy of being addressed by Him and consequently to reach Him, and to realize that ultimately He is the only I.

This verse of the *Fātiḥah* continues by speaking of *Allāh* as the Lord of the worlds. This means metaphysically and cosmologically that God is the master of all space and that we are beings situated in one of many worlds, in all of which He is the Lord. To say "Lord of the worlds" is to realize that space is not simply quantitative extension measurable in Cartesian coordinates. Rather, it is symbolically the realm of Divine Presence, which permeates all places in which we live and move and have our being in this and in all other worlds. This verse speaks of *worlds* in the plural, which means, first of all, that reality is not limited to this world and, second, that there is no world—that is, other states of being, not worlds of modern science fiction—into which we can journey in soul and spirit in which the lordship of God is not the central reality. There is no extraterritoriality with respect to God's dominion, His laws, and our responsibility to Him as human beings, as beings defined by our having responded to Him even before the creation of the world when He asked us "Am I not your Lord?" with a resounding affirmation. To be fully human is to realize our servitude toward God and to be always aware of this lordship wherever, in whichever world, we happen to be.

The *Fātiḥah* follows with the repetition of "the Infinitely Good, the All-Merciful" to remind us that all the worlds in which God is Lord are also filled with His Goodness, Mercy, and Compassion. Moreover, since this verse is followed by the one concerning time, it might be said that the repetition of *al-Raḥmān* and *al-Raḥīm* is the means for us to be reminded that although our lives are bound by the conditions of space and time, it is the presence of Divine Goodness and Mercy that stands between these two parameters and constitutes the reality in which we actually live and have our being.

The next verse, "Master of the Day of Judgment," concerns the flow of time at the end of which there is death and meeting with God. To be aware of our human condition is to realize that we are on a journey in this life, which ends with death followed by resurrection, and that we are destined for the unavoidable meeting with God, which means that although we die, we are also immortal. The profound reality of our consciousness cannot be eradicated by the accident of bodily death. The verse speaks not only of the Day beyond all days, but also of Judgment. This eschatological assertion is of the utmost significance for our life here on earth. It reveals the grandeur of the human state and the fact that actions in this life on earth have consequences beyond the life of this world.

Now, these are matters widely accepted by people of faith everywhere. The Sufis take a further step, however, and seek to die and be resurrected here and now and to experience the encounter with God while still here in this world through spiritual practices and by climbing the ladder of perfection. In the deepest sense those who have already achieved the goal have already died, been resurrected, met the Master of the Day of Judgment, been judged by the Supreme Judge, and rest in the Paradise of Divine Proximity. The Prophet of Islam was once asked about death and resurrection. The Prophet answered, "Look at me; I have died and been resurrected many times."

If we put aside the opening *basmalah,* the first three verses of this seven-verse opening chapter of the Quran deal with the nature of God while having consequences for the human state. The fourth and middle verse, "Thee we worship, and in Thee we seek help," concerns the human state itself in relation to God. The raison d'être of being human, as already mentioned, is to worship God and to seek His help in realizing our utter dependence upon the Divine Reality. The normal human being is a being who worships the Divine in whatever form It might be, as the long history of various human societies—excluding the secularized part of the contemporary world, which is an anomaly—reveals. For Sufis, worship (*'ibādah*) is not merely one of the activities of human beings, it is the activity defining the state of servitude (*'ubūdiyyah*) and therefore of being human. Moreover, in Sufism the highest form of worship is knowledge of God, which is always combined with love. According to a sacred *ḥadīth,* God asserts through the mouth of the Prophet, "I was a Hidden Treasure; I desired (or loved) to be known. Therefore I created the world so that I would be known." This famous *ḥadīth,* so often cited in classical Sufi texts, has many meanings, the most evident of which is that knowing God is the purpose of creation. To worship God through *ma'rifah* or unitive knowledge is therefore the fulfillment of the very purpose of creation and the highest form of worship. The definition of *iḥsān* or virtue, which is that of Sufism itself, is "To worship (or adore) God as if thou seest Him and if Thou seest Him not, then He seeth Thee." This sacred *ḥadīth* refers to the same truth, for vision is directly related to knowledge.

As for seeking His help, of course all believers ask for God's help in time of need. The Sufis, however, are those who realize that, being poor in the ontological and spiritual sense, they are always in need of God and dependent upon His help. The earnest prayer, "in Thee we seek help," also strengthens our reliance upon God and our awareness that ultimately He alone can help us. To be fully human is to be constantly aware of this dependence and reliance, or *tawakkul,* about which classical Sufi texts speak again and again.

Standing before God who is Infinitely Good and All-Merciful, who is the master of space and time, whom men and women worship and whose help they seek, what does the servant ask from the Lord? It is to be guided upon the straight path. The last three verses of the *Fātiḥah* contain in brevity the complete doctrine of human salvation and our existential situation vis-à-vis the reality of Universal Existence. These verses specify three possibilities: the straight path, which is "the path of those on whom Thy grace is"; the path of "those on whom Thine anger is"; and the path of "those who go astray." In relation to the Divine Reality, which is both transcendent and immanent at the center of our being as the Self, there are only three paths one can follow. The first is to march upward toward that Reality, the second to descend away from It, and the third is to neither ascend nor descend but to go horizontally, sideways, drawing spiritually neither closer to nor farther away in relation to the vertical axis of existence. Our existential situation can be further clarified by recourse to geometrical symbolism. We are situated at the point of the intersection of the vertical and horizontal axes of a cross. We have a choice to ascend the vertical axis and be among those "on whom Thy grace is," or to descend on the same axis into ever lower states of being as one of those "on whom Thine anger is." Finally, we can wander along the horizontal line of the cross among "those who go astray." Eschatologically these three possibilities correspond from a certain perspective to the paradisal, infernal, and purgatorial states.

While the cross is a symbol that ordinary Muslims do not take in its Christian sense, since Islam does not identify the cross with the death of Christ, there does exist in Islamic esoteric teachings, both Sufi and Shi'ite, an elaborate doctrine of the metaphysical significance of this symbol and its relation to the reality of the Universal Man, which will be discussed shortly. In any case, the Sufi understanding of the inner meaning of the *Fātiḥah* reveals this existential situation, one of whose spatial symbolisms is the cross, of the human being as he or she stands before God.

All Muslims believe in the central significance of the straight path (*al-ṣirāṭ al-mustaqīm*), and Islam itself has been called by some the religion of the straight path. This basic Quranic image and symbol has many aspects and diverse meanings. As far as the path of life is concerned, the Sufis ask what this straight path is, and when told that it is the path that leads to God, they seek to follow it to its end while in this life. They want to climb the vertical axis of the cross, like the ladder of Jacob, to Heaven here and now. For Sufism, "the straight path" is ultimately the *Ṭarīqah* or the Sufi path itself, which begins with the *Sharī'ah* or Divine Law. It is the path of return to the Source or the *Ḥaqīqah,* of which we have already spoken. For them the "straight path" is also the path of ascent.

To repeat the *Fātiḥah* at least seventeen times a day in the various daily canonical prayers combined with movements and other words that complement its meaning and to be aware of its inner significance, some of which we have outlined here, is to realize true servanthood before God. For the Sufi it is to realize what it means to be truly human. With the aid of the Quran, which plays such a central role in all of Islam including Sufism, the person of inner vision comes to realize the significance of being God's servant, which leads ultimately to the realization of our annihilation before Him (*fanā'*) and subsistence in Him (*baqā'*). In this way the human being becomes aware of the ideal to which he or she must dedicate all of life.

THE UNIVERSAL MAN

In classical Sufism the answer to the question, "what does it mean to be human?" is contained fully in the doctrine of what is usually translated as the Universal or Perfect Man (*al-insān al-kāmil*), whose detailed exposition is to be found in the writings of such famous authorities as

Ibn ʻArabī and the fourteenth-century Persian master who lived in the Yemen, ʻAbd al-Karīm al-Jīlī, the author of the most famous work in Arabic bearing this title. The idea of Universal Man, which some have also called Perfect Man, is so central to Sufism that one of the greatest Western scholars of Sufism, Louis Massignon, called it "the privileged myth of Islam."

We find in Greek philosophy the idea of *anthropōs teleios,* which can be understood as "perfect man," and some have traced the philosophical formulation of this idea by Sufis to the Greek and more specifically Neoplatonic sources. But even if Sufis used certain theoretical formulations drawn from such sources, the reality they were describing did not come from earlier philosophical texts. The Universal Man is a reality independent of any philosophical descriptions of it. On the basis of the Quran and the teachings of the Prophet, the Sufis were able to experience the reality of the Universal Man, which after several centuries came to be described in doctrinal fashion by Ibn ʻArabī and others.

In any case, according to the Sufis the Universal Man is the reality containing all the levels of existence other than God. It includes all the latent possibilities in each of those levels—a reality that, in those who have actualized it within themselves whether they be male or female, has become fully realized. The Universal Man is the androgynic prototype of the human state, both male and female, and also the prototype of the cosmos. That is why there exists a correspondence between the microcosm and the macrocosm. The Universal Man is like a mirror before God, reflecting all His Names and Qualities, and is also able to contemplate God through eyes that are illuminated by the light of God. He or she contemplates God's creation through God's eyes. The Universal Man possesses both active and passive perfections, and such well-known religious symbols as the Seal of Solomon and the Crescent symbolize the wedding of these twin perfections in both men and women.

In the human world the Universal Man finds its exemplars in the prophets and the great saints. Its function is both revelatory and initiatic. To become truly human is to realize, with the help of those who have already realized the state of perfection, the reality of the Universal Man, which we all are potentially. Realization means reaching the state of the Universal Man. It means returning to our primordial state (*al-fiṭrah*) and ultimately to our reality in God with the guidance of those who have already realized to one degree or another the state of the

Universal Man. To realize the state of the Universal Man is in turn to become the veritable servant of the Lord, to be aware of our central state in this world as His vicegerent (*khalīfah*), to realize our *fanā'*, and finally, through this annihilation of the ego, to reach with the light of the intellect within us the Supreme Essence, which alone is ultimately real.

WHAT ARE WE DOING HERE, AND WHAT SHOULD WE BE DOING HERE?

What most of us are doing here in this world is living in a daydream called ordinary life, in the state of forgetting what Christ called the one thing necessary, that is, the Divine Reality. And we are in such a state because we have forgotten who we are. All we need to do is to wake up and realize our primordial nature, which is always there although buried deeply within many layers of the dross of forgetfulness. The Prophet said, "Man is asleep and when he dies he awakens." Sufism is meant for those who want to wake up, who accept dying to the ego here and now in order to discover the Self of all selves and to be consumed in the process in the fire of Divine Love.

Since we all die, it is better to seek to wake up now under conditions that involve our free will and intelligence rather than in a situation in which we are helpless. This initiatic death is the beginning of the spiritual path. In answer to the question, "what should we be doing here?" the Sufis, like sages of other traditions, say that we should take full advantage of the precious state of being human, wake up to the reality of our prototype as Universal Man, and seek to walk, while we still can, through the door that opens to the inner chamber of our heart and also to the Divine Presence. That opportunity will not always be there, for our next breath may be our last. If we do not pass through that door now, which opens into more inward or, to use the objective symbol, higher levels of being, leading finally to the Reality which is the Source and End of all, that door, which will close at the moment of death, may not be open to us tomorrow. We have no guarantee that we will continue in the state we possess as human beings in this world once we reach posthumous states of being. That is why Rūmī, echoing the saying of the Prophet, "Die before you die," suggests to those with ears to hear and eyes to see,

Go die, O man of honor, before you die,
So that you will not suffer the pangs of death,
Die in such a way as to enter the abode of light,
Not the death that places you in the grave.

What we should be doing here is discovering who we really are while we can. Now this process, which requires death to our "selves" and the piercing of the walls of our ego to penetrate into our heart, is not possible without the spiritual master, who already knows what it means to be fully human and who has realized this knowledge himself or herself through journeying across the mountains and valleys of microcosmic existence to reach the One. As we shall see later in this book, in Sufism the prototype of this spiritual guide is ultimately the Prophet himself, and all Sufi masters are his representatives in this realm of initiatic guidance. As the fully realized Universal Man and beloved of God, the Prophet was given the initiatic power, called *walāyah/wilāyah* in Arabic, that makes it possible for us to awaken from our earthly daydreaming and to fulfill the ultimate raison d'être of being human, that is, loving and knowing God, which means realizing the perfect state of servanthood combined with intimacy with the Divine and, through the transparency of our outer self, allowing God within us "to know" Himself.

TO BECOME SOMEONE; TO BECOME NO ONE

From the Sufi point of view only the person who has reached the center of his or her being and knows who he or she really is can be considered fully human and be really someone. In fact, the cap that members of many Sufi orders wear is often called the crown of poverty (*tāj-i faqr* in Persian), and those human beings who have realized fully what it means to be human are the real royalty of this world. They are princes among human beings for, as some old masters have said, they are the ones who cannot choose because God has already chosen for them. It was once asked of that supreme prince of the Sufis of Khurasan, Bāyazīd Basṭāmī, who lived in the ninth century, "What do you want?" He answered, "I want not to want." Such people, who have realized what it really means to be human, are in the state of perfect servitude and proximity, a state in which their will is surrendered to the Will of God. It is they who are really someone in this world even if not noticed by those with only outward-looking eyes.

In Arabic and Persian the word *rajul* (pl. *rijāl*) means not only man/men but also outstanding figures whether in the field of science, religion, or politics. One speaks of the political *rijāl* of a particular country or era as well as the *rijāl al-ghayb,* literally, absent or invisible figures, who constitute an important part of the Sufi universe. In Sufism, those who have walked with determination upon the Sufi path and performed that crucial spiritual battle against their negative tendencies, or what is called the greater *jihād,* are considered the real *rijāl* of this world. They are the people who are someone in the eyes of God, whatever their station in society. The word *rijāl* carries a masculine gender, but lest one think it refers simply to the male gender, it is important to recount the famous Sufi tradition according to which on the Day of Judgment when all human beings are standing before God, He will say, "The *rijāl* [in the spiritual sense] step forward." And the first person to step forward will be the Virgin Mary. It is by virtue of coming to know ourselves and therefore our Lord that we become really someone beyond all transient honors and distinctions with which fallen human beings seek to distinguish themselves. And in becoming someone spiritually and in the eyes of God, we fulfill the purpose of human existence.

Paradoxically, however, to become someone spiritually means also ultimately to become no one. It is in the end to transcend all particularities and realize the Self within all selves, to become not this person or that person but personhood as such, which also means becoming the perfect mirror of the Divine. To return to the symbol of the sun, it is also to pierce with the light of the intellect all veils of duality and otherness to return to the Sun of the Self, which is the origin of all selves and the source of the intellect shining within those who have realized the state of perfect servanthood. It is in light of return to the Self that many Sufis have spoken, often in ecstatic language, of having gone beyond name, color and race, country, and even the formal aspects of religion, beyond faith and infidelity, to become no one and yet someone in the highest sense of the term. A sonnet (*ghazal*) attributed to one of the exalted masters of Sufism, who remains someone of the greatest importance even today and yet became no one, expresses the reality of this final state of being human, the state of realizing the unity beyond all dualities, the one Formless reality beyond all formal distinctions:

What is to be done, O Muslims, for I know myself not,
Neither a Christian am I, nor Jew, nor Magian nor Muslim.
Neither of the East am I nor West, nor of the land, nor sea;
Nor of nature's quarry, nor of heavens circling above.
I am not made of earth or water, not of wind or fire;
Nor am I of the Divine Throne nor of floor carpeting,
Nor of the realm of the cosmos, nor of minerals.
I am not from India, nor China, nor Bulgaria, nor Turkistan;
I am not from the kingdom of the two Iraqs, nor from the earth
of Khorasan.
Neither of this world am I nor the next; nor of heaven nor hell;
Nor from Adam nor Eve nor of Eden, nor paradise or its porter.
My place is the placeless, my mark the markless;
Not either body nor soul for I am myself the Beloved.[4]

Rūmī, Dīwān-i Shams-i Tabrīzī

To be human in the full sense is to be able to realize the Truth and become fully immersed in its light. It is to be drawn so intimately into the bosom of the Beloved that one could say with Rūmī, I am no longer in this body or soul but have "become" the Beloved. And this Beloved is the eternally Living, in whose Life alone do we find eternal life and felicity beyond the gates of the death of the ego and the obliteration of all that separates us from transcendent and immanent Reality, which is also our Self, the very center of our being.

Truly I am a wondrous thing
For him who sees me:
Lover and Beloved, both am I,
There is no second.
O seeker of the essential Truth,
Thine eye's film hides it.
Return unto thyself, take note:
None is but thee.
All good, all knowledge springs from thee;
In thee's the Secret.[5]

'Alī Shushtarī

Part Two

Two

TRUTH

The Knowledge That Illuminates and Delivers from the Bondage of Ignorance

Truth hath come and falsehood hath vanished away.
Verily, falsehood is ever certain to vanish.
Quran 17:81

Then you shall know the Truth, and the Truth shall make you free.
The Gospel according to John 8:32, NIV

One with Thee make me, O my One,
  through Oneness
Faithed in sincerity no path can reach.
I am the Truth, and Truth, for Truth, is Truth,
Robed in Its Essence, thus beyond separation.[1]
Ḥallāj

The famous tenth-century Sufi Manṣūr al-Ḥallāj uttered *anā'l-Ḥaqq,* that is, "I am the Truth" or "I am the Real," and paid for it with his life, for many misconstrued the real import of these words. These words have nevertheless echoed like an ever-repeated refrain through the annals of Sufism during the past millennium. What is this Truth of which Ḥallāj spoke, for which he paid with his life, and that all Sufis have sought to attain, considering its attainment to be the supreme goal of human life? The term *ḥaqq* used by Ḥallāj is a Quranic term. It means both truth and reality and is in fact a Name of God, who is usually referred to in Sufi literature alternatively as *Allāh* or *al-Ḥaqq,* for God is both absolute Truth and absolute Reality. The term *ḥaqīqah,* which is derived from it, refers at once to the Truth and to truth in whatever context and at any level of reality with which one is concerned. In the same way that the word *realization* contains the term *real,* spiritual realization in Sufism is called *taḥaqquq* (from the word *ḥaqq*), and the accomplished Sufi is called *muḥaqqiq* in the lexicon of figures such as the "supreme master" Muḥyī al-Dīn ibn 'Arabī, whose teachings have dominated much of Sufism for the past seven centuries.

According to Sufism, the supreme goal of human life is to attain Truth, which is also Reality, the source of all reality, and whose attainment, as also stated by Christ, makes us free, delivering us from the bondage of ignorance. Although deeply involved with love and also on a certain level with action, Sufism is at the highest level a path of knowledge (*ma'rifah* in Arabic and *'irfān* in Persian), a knowledge that is illuminative and unitive, a knowledge whose highest object is the Truth as such, that is, God, and subsequently the knowledge of things in relation to God. There is such a thing as the Truth, and it can be known. This is the first of all certitudes, from which flow all other certitudes of human life. The knowledge of the Truth is like the light of the sun while love is like the heat that always accompanies that light.

In the Quran we read, "Moses said to his household: Verily, beyond all doubt I have seen a fire. I will bring you tidings of it or I will bring you a flaming brand that ye may warm yourselves" (Quran 27:6).[2] To bring tidings of the fire, to see a firebrand, and to be warmed (which could also be translated as being burned) by the fire in this Quranic verse symbolize the three stages of attaining certainty of the Truth, which is symbolized here by fire. To use the traditional accounts of the levels of certainty, there is first of all the lore or science of certainty (*'ilm al-yaqīn*), which is like hearing a description of fire from a reliable source and gaining certainty from this description. This is usually called the lore of certainty, but it also means certainty of lore or on the level of lore. Then there is the eye of certainty, or in a sense the certainty of seeing (*'ayn al-yaqīn*), which is like seeing the fire and gaining certainty of its existence through direct vision. Finally, there is the truth of certainty (*ḥaqq al-yaqīn*)—or again what can also be understood as certainty of truth—which is like being consumed by the fire and gaining the highest certainty of it by "becoming" the fire. The goal of the life of the spiritual person is to ascend this ladder of certainty until he or she is consumed by the fire of the Truth, to which some Christian mystics refer as being consumed in God.

In a famous verse Rūmī says:

> The result of my life is contained in but three words:
> I was unripe, I ripened, and I was consumed.

He is referring here to the same reality. There is first of all the certainty that there is such a thing as the Truth. Furthermore, on the basis of this first certainty, one can advance to higher levels of certainty of the Truth until one is consumed by It and one enters the Garden of Truth Itself.

THE CENTRALITY OF GNOSIS TO SUFISM

Christ said, "In my Father's house are many mansions" (John 14:2). This saying has of course several meanings. One of them is that there are many religions that lead to God. It also means that there are different types of spiritual paths, some based on sacrifice and selfless action, some on faith and devotion, some on love, and some on knowledge. Since Islam is the religion of unity, its inner dimension, which is Sufism, integrates these different possibilities within itself. But also since Islam is based ultimately on the knowledge of the Oneness of God, the way of knowledge is central to the Sufi path although, as already stated, this knowledge is always combined with love, faith, and correct action. That is why many of those who know in a unitive and illuminative manner and who are called gnostics (in the original sense of the term and not as a Christian heresy) have often composed the most sublime mystical love poetry. The knowledge of which Sufism speaks is not mental knowledge but a light that illuminates the beholder of this knowledge and in fact all around it and finally returns the human being to its Source, the Supernal Sun. On the highest level, the subject as well as the object of this knowledge is God. The gnostic in Sufism is called *al-'ārif^u bi'Llāh,* one who knows *by* God and not one who knows God, for ultimately it is only the Divine Spark within us that can know the Divine. Our duty is to remove the veils within that prevent such a unitive knowledge from taking place.

The Prophet has said, "Knowledge is Light," and one can add that the Quran speaks of God being the Light of the heavens and the earth. Now, existence itself is a ray of light that issues from the Divine Sun. Knowledge is therefore also being. The more one knows in a principial manner, and not only discursively, the more one *is.* On the highest level the knower, knowledge, and the known are one. To know the Truth with one's whole being is ultimately to "become the Truth," to realize that the root of our "I" is the Divine Self Itself, who alone can ultimately utter "I." It was not the individual ego of al-Ḥallāj who uttered *anā'l-Ḥaqq*. That would be blasphemy, and that is how those ignorant around him who did not understand interpreted it. In reality, one who does not utter *anā'l-Ḥaqq* is still living as a polytheist and idol worshipper, positing his or her own ego as a reality separate from God as *al-Ḥaqq* and idolizing that ever-changing and evanescent ego as well as the world as a divinity. In any case, the quest for the Truth lies at the heart of Sufism, and the goal of the adept is to be able to ascend the levels of certitude until one's separate existence is consumed by the Truth and one is given access to the Garden of Truth.

SUFI DOCTRINE AND ITS FUNCTION IN THE SPIRITUAL LIFE

The description and theoretical exposition of the Truth is contained in Sufi doctrine while the realization of the Truth is possible only through spiritual practice. Sufi doctrine, which is also called theoretical gnosis (*al-taṣawwuf al-'ilmī* in Arabic and *'irfān-i naẓarī* in Persian), is itself the fruit of spiritual realization and not simply philosophical speculation (for more discussion, see appendix 1). It is presented to those in quest of the Truth as a map of the structure of reality and the road that is to be followed to transcend the cosmic labyrinth. One might say that the Sufi masters first climbed the cosmic mountain and then flew into the sky of the Divine Presence and after that, upon descending, drew a map for other climbers who wished to reach the summit and fly to the Beyond. Sufi doctrine is like the lore of certainty and its realization the truth of certainty. From the operative point of view, the doctrine is presented and then its truths realized, but in reality it is the realization of the truths of the path that have made it possible in the first place for master expositors of Sufi doctrine to formulate their teachings and guide men and women on their journey to the One. Theoretical gnosis appears as a *theoria,* in the original Greek sense of vision, of the Truth, but in fact it issues from consummation by that Truth. Only then can it act as guide for those who wish to reach that Truth. Sufi doctrine or theoretical gnosis seems to begin with the mind, but for its full understanding it must be accompanied by practice, which involves the whole of one's being and requires faith. Through this process what appears at first as a concept in the mind becomes a luminous presence that transforms one's whole being, further informing the theory or doctrine.

Sufi doctrine is in a sense both the beginning and end of the Sufi path. It is the beginning because it presents to the seeker, before he or she undertakes the spiritual quest, the basic truths concerning the nature of reality and finally the crowning Truth concerning Ultimate Reality as such. It is the end because the goal of Sufism is the attainment of that gnosis or *ma'rifah,* described theoretically in texts of Sufi doctrine but now realized with one's whole being. The lore of certainty in which we hear about the fire of truth cannot but lead, ultimately, through our quest after the fire, to discovering it and being consumed by it.

In traditional Islamic society most disciples were introduced to only certain essential elements of Sufi doctrine, and gradually as they progressed upon the path, more and more doctrine was taught to them. The great expositions of Sufi doctrine by such figures as Ibn 'Arabī, and later followers of his school such as Ṣadr al-Dīn Qunyawī, 'Abd al-Razzāq Kāshānī, Dā'ūd Qayṣarī, 'Abd al-Karīm al-Jīlī, Ibn Turkah Iṣfahānī, 'Abd al-Ghaniy al-Nābulusī, and many others were certainly available but studied only by a few among the larger groups of adherents of Sufism. The tradition itself, the Quran along with its inspired commentaries, the sayings of the Prophet (*Ḥadīth*) and of many sages and saints, traditional literature, and other sources, provided for those embarking upon the path a homogeneous religious and intellectual ambience and the basic elements of the Truth necessary to attain the goal.

Today we no longer live in such a situation, even in many parts of the Islamic world. Especially in the West, most people no longer hold a homogeneous spiritual and metaphysical worldview from which one can begin. To make Sufism understood to Westerners in such a situation, it is therefore necessary, even more so than in traditional Islamic circles, to begin with a fuller exposition of Sufi doctrine. This in turn involves not only presenting these doctrines but also clearing the ground of errors that prevent the mind from understanding the doctrines involved. In a world in which agnosticism and skepticism were very rare, one did not have to remove such errors before speaking of the existence of God. Today, obviously, the situation is very different.

Ideally, therefore, it would be necessary to clear the ground of all prevalent errors, according to the Sufi point of view and authentic metaphysics in general, such as secular humanism, rationalism, empiricism, behaviorism, deconstructionism, and so forth, which clutter the minds of so many men and women today. Only then can one present to them the Truth, which Sufi doctrine seeks to expound and explain. But that is not practically feasible here, and it would require another book. I shall therefore present the main aspects of Sufi doctrine with the presumption that those who read this book are already in quest of something beyond the fashionable "isms" of the day and that through their intelligence they will understand, at least on the theoretical level, what this doctrine entails. For those who remain rooted in the modern and now postmodern mind-set in which Truth itself in its absolute sense is denied and metaphysics is not even considered a possibility, what is said about the Truth here can at least make them better acquainted with the worldview that underlies and defines Sufism in its diverse manifestations. Nevertheless, whenever necessary, reference will be made to errors that prevent the truths of Sufism from being comprehended.

THE DIVINE REALITY

The highest truth is the truth of the Highest, and the knowledge of the Supreme Reality is supreme knowledge. Although this principial knowledge is at the heart and within the very substance of the intellect, the Supreme Principle cannot be known in the ordinary manner of knowing to which our minds have become habituated. It cannot be comprehended by the mind because the very term *comprehend* is derived from a Latin word meaning to encompass and to embrace, but the Divine Reality is Infinite and cannot be encompassed by anything. The only way to know It is to plunge into the Sea of Divinity, to swim in the Ocean of the Godhead, to use the well-known image of Meister Eckhart. Our intellect is like an arrow that can reach the sun and is given the power by God to anticipate the knowledge gained by this "union." That is why we are able to speak about God and even make the assertion in an apophatic manner that God in His Essence is beyond all that we can say of Him. At the heart of Sufi doctrine and theoretical gnosis stands the Reality, which is unutterable and yet makes all metaphysical uttering possible and, furthermore, manifests Itself in categories that can be known in a kathaphatic manner, that is, in positive categories. The subject of Sufi metaphysics is said in classical texts to be the unconditioned absolute Reality, which is not even conditioned by absoluteness. Yet this metaphysics begins and ends with the truth of this Supreme Reality because It is the Origin and End of all things and Its realization the supreme goal of human life. As mentioned in the previous chapter, the Supreme Principle is both the absolutely transcendent Reality and the absolutely immanent Self, who determines the ultimate reality of human beings and defines what it means to be human.

The Divine Essence, or what is referred to in Christian theology as Ipseity, called *al-Dhāt* in Arabic, is beyond all determination and definition and corresponds to what certain Christian mystics call the Godhead or the Divine Ground. It is the Essence of the Divine Order or God. The Islamic term for God, *Allāh,* denotes the Divine Essence as well as the Divine Names and Qualities, which make creation and manifestation possible. The Name *Allāh* denotes at once Godhead and God as the Divine Person and Creator. It contains, therefore, both the impersonal and personal aspects of the Divinity. *Allāh* is God understood in the full metaphysical understanding of the term and not according to particular confessional and theological definitions. *Allāh* is Reality, which is at once absolute, infinite, and pure goodness and perfection. God is the Absolute, the One before whom no relativity may even be said to exist. He is the Infinite in that in Him are to be found all possibilities. It must be remembered here that the words *possibility, potentiality,* and *potency* are all related etymologically. This truth is an indication of the fact that possibility and the power to bring all existents into being are related in the Divine Order. God is also infinite and absolute goodness and perfection as well as the source of all goodness and perfection in the created order.

Sufi metaphysics has used several symbolic languages to express the truths with which it is concerned, including symbols connected to light, to the features of the human face, and to love, but most of all it has relied on the revelation by God in the Quran of His Names and Qualities. There is subsequently in Sufism the very important science of the Divine Names, which Muslims believe have been revealed directly by God as a means of unveiling His Nature, to the extent that He has wished, to the Prophet and through him to the followers of His last revelation. This science has both a theoretical and a practical import. Theoretically it depicts a metaphysical vision of the Divinity and the cosmology that flows from it, and practically it makes possible access to the Divinity for it is through the Names of God—the sacred Names revealed by God in the Quran concerning Himself—that men and women are able to return to God and to realize who they really are. To call God by His "Beautiful Names," to use the Quranic terminology, results in receiving His answer since He Himself has revealed these Names as His Names; it results in drawing nigh unto Him.

In this science a distinction is made first of all between God's Essence, His Names and Qualities, and His Acts (*al-Dhāt, al-Asmā',* and *al-Ṣifāt* and *al-Af'āl* in Arabic). Although the Essence Itself is beyond all names and determinations, being the black light, which is black because of the intensity of its luminosity, certain Names pertain to It and It alone and never to His Acts, which constitute His creation; such Names include *huwa* (the Essence), *al-Raḥmān* (the all-Good), *al-Raḥīm* (the infinitely Merciful), and *al-Aḥad* (the One). Then there is the level of the Names and Qualities, which are the first Self-Determinations or Self-Entifications (*ta'ayyun*) of the Essence. At this level are Names pertaining to various Divine Qualities such as generosity (*karāmah*) with the corresponding Name *al-Karīm* (the Generous), or the Quality of knowing (*'ilm*), of which the corresponding Divine Name is *al-'Alīm* (the Knower). Finally, there are Names such as *al-Khāliq,* meaning Creator, pertaining to God's Acts, which are the foundations of His creation; in the deepest sense, creation is not only a result of a Divine Act but the whole created order an Act of God itself.

At the level of the Essence there is absolute oneness, but on the level of the Names and Qualities multiplicity is introduced although without destroying in any way the Divine Unity, since each Name and Quality is a self-determination of the Essence. Furthermore, it is at the stage of the Names and Qualities that the first basic duality, that is, the archetype of the feminine/masculine duality in the human and cosmic orders (the yin/yang of the Chinese tradition) appears. The Names are divided into those of Majesty (*jalāl*), the source of the masculine, and those of Beauty (*jamāl*), the source of the feminine. God is at once just and forgiving, wrathful and merciful, although as it is written on the Divine Throne, according to a sacred saying of the Prophet quoted often by Sufis, "Verily My Mercy precedeth My Wrath." This *ḥadīth* means that although God is just and is wrathful toward evildoers, His Mercy comes before His Justice and He forgives those who have committed evil acts yet turn to Him in earnestness and with their whole being. Were it not for this ordering of the Names in the Divine Order, there would be no positive dualities observable in creation such as the male/female or yin/yang distinctions. Such dualities must, however, be distinguished from false dualisms, such as gods of good and evil, which one finds in certain dualistic religions, for the dualism implied in the ordering of the Divine Names in Islam does not in any way detract from the Oneness of the Divine Principle. The whole universe comes into being through the interplay of the various determinations of the Divine Names and Qualities. The Names of God are not simply words in the ordinary sense but realities, each of which reflects an aspect of the Divine Reality. Moreover, in every religion each Name that plays both a cosmological and salvific role is sanctified through revelation by the Reality to which the Name refers. For example, in Hinduism we have the sound *Om* and on another level the names Śiva and Viṣṇu, which correspond in the Hindu universe to the Names and corresponding Qualities of God in Islam. In any case, the science of the Names is, according to the Sufis, the key for knowledge of ourselves, of the world, and ultimately of God as well as the means of return to our Origin.

THE ONENESS OF BEING

The Sufi science of the Divine Reality cannot be fully understood without discussing the famous doctrine of the "transcendent oneness or unity of being" (*waḥdat al-wujūd*), which has been so often misconstrued by Westerners and also by some modernized as well as exoteric Muslims as pantheism. To understand this doctrine, which many have called the crowning jewel of Sufism, it is necessary to turn our attention first to the universal hierarchy of reality. There is first of all the Ultimate Reality, which is the Beyond-Being and which some have called Non-Being, that is, a reality that transcends even Being taken as a positive category. It can be symbolized by that darkness or black light standing above and not below light and its polarizations by a prism into various colors. It is the aspect of the Divinity that is above as well as within the creative aspect of God and does not participate in the creative act. It corresponds metaphysically to the Void or *śunyata* in Buddhism and to the supreme Tao, which cannot be named in Far Eastern doctrines. The first determination of Beyond-Being is Being, the ontological principle, which is God in His aspect as Person and Creator, the reality we address as Thou and our Lord. Then there is the Logos *in divinis,* to be distinguished from the created Logos. This Logos *in divinis* is at once the origin of universal existence and of all prophetic functions. Christianity states that it was by the Word (that is, the Logos) that all things were made and that Christ was the Logos. A similar doctrine can be found in Sufism, where the Prophet is identified, in his inner reality as the Muhammadan Reality (*al-ḥaqīqat al-muḥammadiyyah*), with the Word or Logos. As far as levels of being are concerned, we can speak of Beyond-Being, Being, and Universal Existence, which embraces and gives reality to the existence of all things. It is by virtue of the act of existentiation or what the Quran calls the command "Be!" (*kun!*) that everything in the universe has come into being. Multiplicity has appeared, but inwardly it still bears the imprint of unity.

The truth of the oneness of Being can be fully known only by being experienced spiritually. When the veil of the ego is removed within the human being, the inner Divine Spark sees and knows the Divine everywhere behind the veils of multiplicity. God becomes the eye with which the human being sees, and the human being becomes the eye with which God sees the world. In reality God is the light with which we see all things. That is why we cannot see Him in the ordinary sense. As Maḥmūd Shabistarī, the fourteenth-century Persian Sufi poet, said in a celebrated verse in his *Rose Garden of Divine Mysteries:*

Thou art like the eye and He the light of the eye,
Who has ever been able to see with the eye that with which the eye sees?[3]

It is also possible to have an intellectual participation in seizing this truth through proper metaphysical preparation. That is why there are extensive works of Sufi doctrine and theoretical gnosis such as those of Shams al-Dīn Fanārī and Ibn Turkah Iṣfahānī, to which we shall turn in appendix 1, as well as writings of philosophers and theosophers such as Ṣadr al-Dīn Shīrāzī that deal extensively with the doctrine of the oneness of Being, which can in fact be interpreted in several ways. The meaning of *waḥdat al-wujūd,* if not the actual expression, can be found in sources ranging from certain Quranic verses, such as "Whithersoever ye turn there is the Face of God" (2:115), to certain sayings of the Prophet, such as "I am Aḥmad without the *m*" (meaning *Aḥad* or the One, referring to the inner oneness of the Prophet with the Source of all being). It is also the theme of many poems, some of which are among the greatest masterpieces of Sufi poetry. As for its full exposition, it must be sought in works of Sufi metaphysics. In any case, to understand even the theoretical meaning of the oneness of Being on any level requires a certain intellectual intuition as well as intellectual preparation, in addition to Divine grace, while only the saint who has reached the end of the Sufi path and become drowned in the Ocean of Divinity can know its meaning fully and in the ultimate sense.

Only a person of the spiritual rank of Ibn 'Arabī could have sung:

We were letters, exalted! not yet uttered,
Held aloft in the keep of the Highest of Summits,
I Therein am Thou, and we are Thou,
And Thou art He, and All is in He is He—
Ask of any that so far hath reached.[4]

To speak of being is to speak of reality. Now if God is *al-Ḥaqq,* that is, the Absolute Truth and Absolute Reality or Absolute Being—which in this case may be said to embrace both Beyond-Being and Being—and He is at the same time *al-Aḥad,* the One, there cannot be two independent realities. That would ultimately involve dualism in the principial order and the negation of both the oneness and the absoluteness of God. Although it may appear so outwardly, there cannot therefore be but one Being; all beings must issue from and ultimately be nothing other than Being. Complete ontological otherness would imply a form of dualism and posit a thing to be real independent of God or, to speak more philosophically, to possess a being completely other than the Absolute Being. Every creature has a face turned to God, which is also the Face of God turned to that creature, bestowing being upon that creature; and each creature has a face turned to the world and has an essence in itself, which makes it what it is in itself. This is what the Islamic philosophers call the quiddity or essence of an existent, as opposed to its existence, and the Sufis refer to the highest level of this reality as its immutable archetype (*'ayn thābit*). The latter is literally "nothing" in that it has no existence in itself. Everything that exists does so as the result of God's existentiation of its archetype. Every creature is ultimately the manifestation of the Face of God and Its reflections through the immutable archetypes upon the mirror of nothingness. When the Quran asserts, "Everything perisheth save His Face" (28:88), the Sufis understand this truth as referring not to some future eschatological event but to the here and now. At this very moment, which is also the eternal now, everything is nonexistent and has perished in itself save the Face of God, and right now in whichever direction one turns there is His Face, if one could only see. To understand this reality is to realize the meaning of the oneness of Being.

The world appears to us as multiplicity, and the goal of the spiritual life is to ascend from this multiplicity to unity, to see the One in the many and the many integrated into the One. Now the doctrine of the oneness of Being does not negate the reality of multiplicity. Nor does it claim that God is the world and the world in its totality is God, a position held by pantheists. How could a metaphysics that speaks so categorically of the transcendence of God be accused of pantheism? What the Sufis assert is not that God is the world, but that the world is mysteriously plunged in God, to use a formulation of Frithjof Schuon. Existence is a manifestation of Being, and all existence issues from and belongs to Being in the same way that the rays of the sun are finally nothing but the sun.

Some Sufis and Islamic philosophers have interpreted the doctrine of the oneness of Being to mean that all levels of being come from the one Being, that all the rays of light emanate from the sun, while many

Sufis claim that on the highest level of understanding there is in fact only the one and absolute Being. Viewed from within the sun, there is nothing but the sun. So, many masters of gnosis have asserted that when you gain a clear understanding of the nature of things, to quote the famous *Treatise of Unity* (*al-Risālat al-aḥadiyyah*), "you do not see in this world or the next aught beside God."[5] Everything in the universe is a mirror in which is reflected determinations of the One Essence, the Absolute Being and Reality, which alone is, the alpha and omega of all existence and also the single Reality and Being here and now of all things that appear to us as independent objects and realities. To realize this truth fully is to be able to see God everywhere. It is to realize the supreme goal of human life by returning to our pre-existential reality in the Divine.

CREATION AND THE MANIFESTED ORDER

Although there is metaphysically only one Ultimate Reality, the Beyond-Being, of which the first Self-Determination is Being, on the level of relativity we have the world of multiplicity, in fact, many worlds ranging from the archangelic to the material, all of which are manifestations and Self-Determinations of the One. Those very Sufis who spoke of the oneness of Being as the highest understanding of the Truth also asserted that there are grades and levels (*marātib* in Sufi texts) of being, which constitute the many worlds that separate us from the One. They even asserted and continue to assert that the person who does not believe in the multiple states or grades of being, or what is known as the great chain of being, is an "infidel" and lost to the world of faith. To be human living on this terrestrial plane of existence and to believe in God as the Absolute Being necessitates accepting the hierarchy in between. All religions in fact emphasize this cosmic hierarchy in one way or another, as we see in texts as far apart as the writings of Dionysius the Areopagite and Tibetan Buddhists on cosmology. The truth of the matter is that, on the one hand, we have a universal hierarchy linking each lower state of being to a higher one, from the carpeting on earth (*al-farsh*) to the Divine Throne (*al-'arsh*)—that is, symbolically speaking, from the lowest to the highest order of universal existence, to repeat a famous Sufi dictum—and on the other hand, each existent, by virtue of its existence, also has a direct link to Being. On the human level it might be said that while we occupy a particular level of existence, with animals and plants below and angels and archangels above us, as medieval Christian cosmology also asserted, we also have a direct link with God beyond all intermediary agencies. Both of these realities are part and parcel of the structure of the manifested or created order and also play a major role in the spiritual life.

It might be asked, why are there levels of being? Why did the One have to manifest the many, or in theological terms, why did God create the world? This basic metaphysical question has been posed in different religious climes, and each religion has provided its own response, usually couched in mythical or symbolic language. For example, Hinduism speaks of *līlā* or "divine play" as the reason for creation of the world—and of the many worlds comprising the totality of the cosmos, a totality not confined to its lowest part, the material plane, as many Western people today identify it.

Metaphysically speaking, the Divine Principle, as already stated, is at once absolute and infinite. Now the Infinite must include all possibilities, including the possibility of negating Itself. The realization of this possibility is manifestation, that is, all the levels of reality besides the Divine Principle that appear to exist as distinct realities by virtue of their separation from the Principle. Also, the Divine Principle is absolute goodness, and as St. Augustine said, it is in the nature of the good to give of itself in the same way that it is in the nature of light to emanate rays and to illuminate what is around it. To speak of God, understood by the gnostics, is also to speak of the world as His creation. Metaphysically we speak of *manifestation* or *emanation*, such as the emanation of the rays of the sun from the sun. When God is envisaged in His personal aspect, we then speak of *creation*. The Sufis do not see any contradiction whatsoever between the two. Moreover, in speaking of creation and the reason for it, while they repeat the saying, "There was God and there was nothing with Him," to emphasize the total independence of the Divine Principle, its absoluteness and infinitude, they add, "And it is now as it was," that is, metaphysically and on the highest level there is here and now only the One, and the only truth to be realized at the end of the path is the oneness of Being.

Let us come back, however, to the Islamic and more particularly Sufi explanation for the creation of the world. A famous "sacred saying" of the Prophet already cited tells us, "I was a 'Hidden Treasure'; I loved to be known; therefore I created the world so that I would be known." Three basic elements to this saying are of cardinal importance for the Sufi understanding of the meaning and ontological status of creation. First of all, the purpose of creation is God's Self-Knowledge through Self-Manifestation and Self-Disclosure. The Self-Disclosure is made possible through the reflections of God's Names and Qualities upon what Sufis call "the mirror of nothingness." Now a mirror is a surface that reflects what is placed before it, and in itself the surface is "nothing," that is, it has no form of its own. Since there cannot be any being independent of God, what we see as the cosmos therefore cannot but be a reflection of God's Names and Qualities upon what is ontologically "nothing," like a mirror. Of course, some could also say that the cosmos, not to speak of founders of religions, is an incarnation and descent of the Divine Reality. Sufism, while accepting the idea of descent, does not, in accord with the Islamic tradition as a whole, consider as legitimate the idea of incarnation and therefore speaks not of incarnation but rather of the theophany of the Divine Names through their reflection in the myriad mirrors of "nothingness" comprising the cosmos. The purpose of creation is knowledge, and therefore for us to know God, which means ultimately God within our hearts knowing Himself, is to fulfill the purpose of creation.

Second, this saying of the Prophet tells us that God "loved" (*aḥbabtu* in the Arabic version of the *ḥadīth* and often translated as willed or wanted) to be known. Therefore, *ḥubb* or love runs through the arteries of the universe (love to which we shall turn fully in the next chapter). Third, God is the "Hidden Treasure," the source of all creation. From the inward point of view there is not only creation by God but also creation *in* God, as Kabbalistic doctrines and certain Christian metaphysicians (such as Erigena, also known as Eriugena) also assert. The archetype of all creation is in God Himself, in the "Hidden Treasure," and nothing can exist that did not have a pre-existential reality in that "Hidden Treasure." That is why the Quran asserts that the spiritual root of all things is in the Hand of God. Although creation appears to us as a separate reality, inwardly its very reality is rooted in the "Hidden Treasure." The world is not only creation but more inwardly manifestation and Self-Disclosure of the Divine Principle. It is not only a result of the Divine Will but also the "flow" of manifestation from the Divine Nature.

Ibn 'Arabī once asserted that God created the mirror so that we could speak of His relation to His creation. From the Sufi point of view, if we accept the idea of incarnation, then Reality becomes incarnated in the spatiotemporal domain and is affected by the contingencies of this domain. Islam is based on the Absolute and not any of Its determinations or manifestations, even if it be *avātaric,* that is, related to Divine incarnation, as we find in Christianity and Hinduism. Theophanic reflection in the mirror of nonexistence, however, implies that while the image in the mirror reflects the Reality before it and provides an "image" corresponding to that Reality, that Reality is not affected by the reflection or the mirror and no change would occur to it if the mirror were to be broken. Creation is thereby seen by Sufis as myriads of reflections or theophanies (*tajalliyyāt*) of the Divine Names and Qualities in their multifarious combinations.

Classical texts of Sufi doctrine explain the process of creation further by mentioning that there is first of all the determination or Self-Entification of the Divine Names and Qualities into the realm of the immutable archetypes (*al-a'yān al-thābitah*) of all of creation. This is called the most sacred effusion (*al-fayḍ al-aqdas*). Then God breathes through the "breath of the All-Good and Compassionate" (*nafas al-Raḥmān*) upon the immutable archetypes, and from this second effusion, called *al-fayḍ al-muqaddas,* or sacred effusion, results all that exists. The human process of speaking symbolizes this creative act on its own level. We have words in our minds. In the act of speaking, our breath blows upon our vocal chords and manifests those words in external speech. As far as the universe is concerned, everything in it is the result of the *nafas al-Raḥmān*. The very substance and existence of everything is, therefore, ultimately the Breath of God in God's aspect of compassion and mercy. Esoterically speaking, all things by virtue of their existence, which is ultimately the Divine Breath, praise God, as the Quran asserts. They speak in silence of the mystery of existence, but most of us do not have the necessary power of hearing to grasp their silent words. As Rūmī says:

> If only existence had a tongue,
> So that it would lift the veils from existents.
>
> *Mathnawī, 3:4728*

The great mystery of existence is that it veils God by what is none other than Him. As Ibn 'Arabī said, "Glory be unto Him who hides Himself by that which is none other than He." This truth is explicitly stated in the Quran, where it is mentioned, "He [God] is the First and the Last, and the Outward and the Inward and He knows infinitely all things" (57:3). It is not difficult for a person of faith to understand that God is the Alpha and Omega of all reality, that all things come from Him and return to Him. As we know, Christ also spoke of himself as the alpha and the omega. It is also not difficult to understand that God is the Inward, the inner reality of all things. But how can God be the Outward? This is the most difficult aspect of the relation between God and creation to understand. Once a fairly advanced Sufi went to a great master and told him that he could understand that God is the First and the Last as well as the Inward. But he asked the master, "How can God be the Outward?" The master put him in a spiritual retreat (*khalwah*) and told him to invoke the Divine Name *Allāh* until this truth became manifested and clear to him. The disciple followed the instructions. After some two weeks in which he continuously invoked God's Supreme Name, suddenly the walls of the room in which he was holding the spiritual retreat began to invoke *Allāh* and he heard the invocation all around him. As he wrote later, he then understood what it meant to assert that God is also the Outward. The moral of this story is that the in-depth understanding of the truth that God veils Himself by what is none other than God can come only from spiritual realization.

The Sufis also speak of creation not only as an act in the past but also as a continuous process. This is what is called the renewal of creation at every instant. At every moment the universe is absorbed into the Principle and recreated. The relation of the world with God is therefore not based solely on a temporal event called creation "at the beginning." That "beginning" is also the ever-renewed present moment. Although from one point of view creation is old, from another it is fresh and new. God's act of existentiation is ever present, and in fact existence is not so much a state as an act, as the existentiating command of God, "Be!" This doctrine is of great significance not only for cosmology but also for the spiritual life. In the same way that each breath we take rejuvenates and makes possible the continuation of our life, the Divine Breath is renewed at every moment, making possible our and the cosmos's continuous existence in what appears to us as duration. This duration is, however, nothing but the repetition of the "now" within which creation is renewed. In a deeper sense, every tree that we observe in the garden comes freshly from God's creative act.

THE CONTEMPLATION OF CREATION

The elaborate teachings of Sufism concerning manifestation are necessary to complete the metaphysical and cosmological doctrines concerning the nature of reality. As well, they provide both the theoretical background for the contemplation of nature and cosmic realities as means of reaching the Metacosmic Reality and also give us a map to help us journey through the cosmos to the Reality beyond all manifestation. Not all Sufis were given, however, to the contemplation of nature. Some, like the eighth-century woman Sufi saint of Basra, Rābi'ah al-'Adawiyyah, were concerned solely with God, beyond Paradise and hell, beyond prophets, and saints and the grandeur of God's creation. Many others who also emphasized the love of God or pure unity did not concern themselves with the contemplation of nature and study of the cosmic hierarchy, but many did, including some of the greatest gnostics and metaphysicians, such as Ibn 'Arabī and Rūmī. In any case, the contemplation of nature is an important part of Sufi doctrine and practice, and explaining the esoteric significance of the manifested order and natural world is an integral element of the exposition of Truth.

Since in Islam the revelation came in the form of a sacred book, many Muslim sages have looked upon nature as a book of God, as did many of their Jewish and Christian counterparts. The cosmos is in fact God's first and primordial revelation. There is an eternal and archetypal Quran, which is the archetype of both the book revealed to the Prophet of Islam as the Quran and the cosmos, which many Sufis in fact call the cosmic Quran. In the same way that each letter, word, and sentence of the Quran revealed in Arabic comes from God and conveys a message from Him, each phenomenon of nature is also a sign from Heaven. In fact, in the Quran both the phenomena of nature and the verses of the Quran are called *āyāt,* or symbols and signs, each conveying a meaning beyond itself. Every *āyah,* besides its outward meaning, has a symbolic and inward significance. Every cosmic phenomenon is both a fact and a symbol of a noumenon. In a profound sense modern science, being concerned with phenomena only as facts and not as symbols of noumena, is like religious literalism in the interpretation of scripture. Sufism has always rejected both kinds of literalism and has provided over the centuries both esoteric interpretations of the Quran and the most profound "philosophy of nature" based on esoteric commentary upon the cosmic book. This "philosophy of nature" is of the utmost significance in this day and age when, because of sheer outwardness and literalism in both science and much of religion, we human beings have become destroyers of nature rather than its protectors and channels of grace. The inner meaning of the cosmic book has become hidden from us.

Sufis contemplate nature, seeing in its forms, life, and rhythms spiritual realities that are of the greatest importance not only in themselves but also for us as wayfarers on the path to spiritual perfection. For the sage every tree is a reflection of the tree of Paradise, every mountain a symbol of transcendence, the water of every flowing stream a symbol of Divine Mercy, the wind a mark of the Spirit. The eagle flying above symbolizes the human spirit perfected through spiritual practice flying to the Divine Throne, and the fish swimming in the deep is the symbol of the soul immersing itself in the ocean of Infinitude. The universe is constituted of theophanies; the cosmos is a set of symbols to be contemplated and a means to reach the Symbolized, a book to be read and understood in both its outward and inward meanings. Once one has read the cosmic book, one can set it aside and stand before the Author of the Book of Existence. One of the meanings of the Quranic reference to the scrolls being rolled up at the end of time is precisely the end to the reading of the book of nature for the Sufi who, having passed beyond the cosmos, experiences death to the world and resurrection in the Spirit, that is, his or her own eschaton.

THE UNIVERSAL HIERARCHY: THE GRADES OF BEING

As already mentioned, all traditions speak of the grades of being albeit in different languages and symbols, as can be seen in worlds as far apart as Hinduism and Judaism. Even Buddhism, which speaks of existence as *samsāra,* presents to its followers, at least in the Mahayāna and Vajrayāna Schools, vast hierarchies of Buddhas, bodhisattvas, demons, and so forth. Sufi doctrine is no exception in its emphasis upon the doctrine of the multiple states of being, which constitutes a central teaching of the perennial philosophy. The Islamic universe, based on the words of the Quran and *Ḥadīth,* is comprised of immense worlds extending from the material realm to the Divine Presence. Today modern science speaks of the vastness of the cosmos but only in a quantitative manner; it deals with only one level of cosmic existence, no matter how many zeros it adds to distances in galactic and interstellar space and periods of cosmic time. But the whole of the material universe, no matter how extended its physical dimensions might be, is like a speck of dust before the grandeur of the world of the Spirit.

According to a saying of the Prophet, there are seventy thousand veils of light and darkness that separate us from God, and they constitute the universe. This large number refers to the immensity of the cosmos beyond its material level of existence. The Sufi doctrine of the universal hierarchy and grades of being summarizes in an intelligible fashion this reality and provides several different cosmological schemes through which the main levels of being can be envisaged. Before turning to these levels, however, it is important to mention something about the symbolism of the veil (*ḥijāb*), which plays a central role in Sufi metaphysics, similar to that of *māyā* in Hinduism, especially in the school of Advaita Vedanta, whose teachings about the nature of reality are similar in basic ways to the doctrine of the "oneness of Being" of Sufism. Because Christian metaphysical teachings, even in their most profound traditional formulations, rarely speak of the concept of *ḥijāb* or *māyā*, an appropriate term has not existed in European languages for such a concept, and with Hinduism becoming more familiar to Westerners after the Second World War, the term *māyā* has entered into the English language, where it is usually understood to mean illusion or irreality.

The Advaita Vedanta states that only *Ātman*, or the Divine Self, the Divine Ipseity, is Real and everything else is *māyā*, not ultimately real. But this does not mean that *māyā* is simple illusion. The relative is not as real as the Absolute, but the relative does possess relative reality on its own level. It is only from the point of view of *Ātman* that nothing else is real. *Māyā* was in fact translated by the great traditional authority on Hinduism, Ananda K. Coomaraswamy, as "creativity," which of necessity implies separation from the Source and therefore a lower level of reality. The Sufi doctrine of *ḥijāb* or veil is very similar to that of *māyā*. In essence, there are levels of reality or being ordered in such a manner that the lower is less real than the higher, which is veiled from it. The higher contains all that is positively real in the lower, but the lower does not possess the same degree of being or the same level of reality and perfection as the higher.

A veil or *ḥijāb* not only veils but also reveals something through that very act of veiling. We can see the example of this principle in the veils of Muslim women that are also called *ḥijāb*. If there were no cosmic veils, the lower levels of reality would be consumed in the higher ones. A colored glass limits the light of the sun but also allows enough to go through to constitute the next order of luminosity. While every level of being is veiled from the one above, it also symbolizes what is above it to the extent of the reality of the lower level. On each level of being, existents both veil and reveal realities belonging to a higher level of existence. Sufism speaks of the outward (*al-ẓāhir*) and the inward (*al-bāṭin*) not only in relation to God but also concerning creatures. It also speaks of the visible or present (*'ālam al-shahādah*) and invisible or absent worlds (*'ālam al-ghayb*). Some, like Rūmī, also speak of form (*ṣūrah*), which in this case means outward aspect and not the Aristotelian *forma*, and inner meaning (*ma'nā*), which also signifies essence.

The goal of the spiritual life is to be able to lift up the veil of outwardness so as to behold the inward and subsequently come to know the outward in light of the inward. Spiritual realization enables us to see the outwardly invisible within the visible. It makes possible the journey from outward form to inner meaning, what in Islam is called *ta'wīl* or spiritual hermeneutics, in such a manner that the veil itself becomes transparent, revealing the reality within and beyond it. But that is only possible if we are able to penetrate into our own center and to lift the veils within, to become interiorized, to gain inner vision. As the celebrated eleventh-century Persian philosopher and poet Nāṣir-i Khusraw said:

> See with the eye of inwardness the inner reality of the world,
> For with the outward looking eye thou canst never see the
> inward.[6]

No one can enter the Garden of Truth who has not become trained in casting aside the veil (*kashf al-maḥjūb*) and seeing beyond the veil that which it veils and yet reveals. Remarkably enough, what is always ultimately revealed is the Presence of the One, the single Essence reflected in the myriads of mirrors of nonexistence. The multiple states of being do not negate the oneness of Being at all for at all levels there is but the radiance of the one Face of the Beloved; there is ultimately but a single Divine Reality.

The fundamental states of reality may be summarized in many ways, as we see in different Sufi texts. In simple terms they can be enumerated as one, the corporeal; two, the psychological and the imaginal; three, the angelic and archangelic, which is also the world of intelligences and archetypes; four, the Divine Names and Qualities; and finally, five, the Divine Essence. From the ontological point of view, one can speak of Beyond-Being, Being, and the Logos *in divinis,* identified also with the existentiating Principle, the "Word" by which all things were made, and, finally, the realm of separative existence. As for the Spirit (*al-Rūḥ* in Arabic), it may be said to be at the border between the Divine and created orders. Each of these levels in the hierarchy is itself comprised of grades and stages, as for example the various grades of the imaginal world, not to be confused with the illusory and the imaginary (which in the ordinary usage of the term is associated with the unreal while the imaginal world is real on its own level), and the hierarchy of the angels as well as the archangelic world, with which Christians are very familiar. But each grade of being or level of reality is finally nothing but Divine Presence. In fact, being and presence are ultimately the same as far as Sufi metaphysics is concerned. That is why one of the well-known versions of Sufi cosmology speaks only of presences and, going back to Ibn 'Arabī, categorizes all of reality in Five Divine Presences.

The Five Divine Presences, which are another way to indicate the hierarchy of being, are enumerated and described by Ibn 'Arabī as follows: one, *Hāhūt,* the "level" of the Supreme Essence of the Divinity; two, *Lāhūt,* the level of the Divine Names and Qualities and Being as the ontological principle of creation (this level also contains the uncreated Logos or Intellect); three, *Jabarūt,* the archangelic level and the higher paradisal worlds as well as the created Logos; four, *malakūt,* the subtle domain and the imaginal world standing immediately above this world but stretching to the paradisal realm; and five, *nāsūt* or *mulk,* which corresponds to the human, material, and terrestrial world. There are many complicated issues as far as this and other Sufi cosmological schemes are concerned, issues into which we will not delve here in our summary presentation. (For example, some Sufis speak of Six Presences interpreted somewhat differently.) What is important to realize, however, is that in all these schemes, all levels of being (*wujūd*) are also presence (*ḥuḍūr*), presence of the one single Divine Reality. Every level of existence, all that constitutes the many levels of the universe, all the creatures from the fish in the sea to the birds of Paradise are nothing but the Self-Disclosure of God. As the Sufis say, "There is no one in the house but the Master of the house."

THE HUMAN MICROCOSM

There is a correspondence between the human being and all the levels of universal existence, all the stages of the cosmos understood in the traditional sense, and even the Divine Reality beyond the cosmos. That is why to know oneself fully is to know God, as the famous saying of the already-cited Prophet asserts: "The person who knows himself/herself knows his/her Lord." Moreover, to know oneself fully is also to gain access to all the levels of reality Self-Disclosed by God. According to an Arabic saying, "The human being is the symbol of all of existence" (*al-insān[u] ramz al-wujūd*). That is why we can know the world and in fact all levels of cosmic reality beyond the corporeal. The metaphysical knowledge of the human state is an integral aspect of that truth whose knowledge delivers us from the bondage of ignorance and leads to that supreme knowledge that transcends all of manifestation, that illuminates and leads us to ultimate freedom and deliverance.

This doctrine of the correspondence between the human microcosm and the cosmic macrocosm is found in all the authentic expressions of the perennial philosophy, as one sees, for example, in Greek and Christian Hermeticism and Jewish and Christian Kabbalah. In the Islamic tradition it is found implicitly in certain verses of the Quran, such as the one in chapter 2 that states that God taught Adam the names of all things, for to know a name, as traditionally understood, means also to have an ontological correspondence to the being that is named. It is stated more explicitly in some of the poems of 'Alī ibn Ṭālib, the cousin and son-in-law of the Prophet, the fourth caliph of Sunnism, and the first Imam of Shi'ism, who was also the fountainhead of Sufism. In one of the famous poems attributed to him it is said,

> Thou thinkest thou art a small body,
> But no, in thee the macrocosm is contained.

Later on, Sufis elaborated this doctrine in numerous ways. In fact, the doctrine of the Universal Man (*al-insān al-kāmil)*, discussed in the last chapter, includes the microcosm-macrocosm correspondence in an essential way.

We are not merely bodies and not merely bodies and emotions. Nor does humanity consist simply of mind and body, as envisaged in

Cartesian dualism. This latter dualism, which arose in the West, truncates the human reality, which in the simplest form is tripartite, composed of body, soul, and spirit, the *corpus, anima,* and *spiritus* of the medieval Christian thinkers and the *hylé, psyche,* and *pneuma* of many Greek philosophical schools upon which the medieval doctrine was based. But even this tripartite traditional division summarizes a more complex situation. According to Sufi metaphysics, we have a reality on the corporeal level, which is the most outward aspect of our being. Above that level we have a psychological reality, which itself partakes of many grades. Then we have an imaginal faculty corresponding to the imaginal level of cosmic existence, which is related to the world of the psyche; then a mind, which is a reflection of the intellect; then the intellect itself (identified in essence and on the highest level with spirit) on the human level with several degrees and again corresponding to the cosmic and also metacosmic intelligible orders. And finally at the center of our being resides the Divine, the Self of all selves.

To each of these levels of reality correspond faculties that can know that particular level in itself and in relation to higher and lower states of being, for ultimately knowledge is being. Let us recall that, as Aristotle said, we know according to our mode of being; furthermore, what we know affects our state of being. It might be said that we are what we know and we know according to who we are, that is, according to the level of reality actualized in us. We have the external faculties of sight, touch, hearing, smell, and taste with which we know the corporeal world in its outwardness. We have psychological modes of knowing, such as emotions, which lead us to awareness of certain things. We have an imaginal faculty of knowing by virtue of which we can know the imaginal world, as is evidenced when we perceive inwardly an imaginal form that has an external correspondence. Then we have reason, which can know the rational patterns of existence but not the noumenal reality of things. Above that faculty resides the intellect, whose seat is the heart and with the help of which we can know the spiritual and intelligible realities as well as the inward aspects of external reality. It is through this faculty, dormant in most people, that we can gain a vision of spiritual realities. Sufis refer to this faculty as the "eye of the heart," and Hindus call it the "third eye." Finally, there is the Divine Spark or the Divine Intellect reflected at the center of our being, in our heart of hearts, by which we can know God, but by God. This principial heart-knowledge leads not only to the knowledge of all things in their essence but also to the knowledge of all orders of reality other than the Divine in light of that Supreme Knowledge. Illuminative knowledge concerns primarily knowledge of the Light of lights, to quote the language of the twelfth-century Persian Sufi and philosopher, Suhrawardī, but it also casts light upon all other modes of knowing and turns the objects of knowledge from fact to symbol, from opacity to light, from veil to transparent manifestation of inward reality. That knowledge to which the Prophet referred as light is not of course information or conceptual knowledge but the knowledge that illuminates both the subject that knows and the object that is known.

Usually when we think of the body, we limit it to only the physical body and speak of our senses as the means whereby through the body we know and interact with our physical ambience. But many Sufis also speak of multiple bodies within us, each with its own faculties. From this point of view one can say that we have a physical body, a subtle and imaginal body in the psychological and imaginal worlds, an intelligible body, and ultimately a purely spiritual and sacred body. Each body possesses its own faculties of knowing in the same way that our physical body possesses the five external senses. And except for the gross, physical body, all of the other bodies are immortal and survive death. In resurrection all of these bodies, including the physical, are integrated into their archetypal reality.

We are all, male and female, potentially the Universal Man here and now, and not in some temporal future, as some false interpreters of traditional doctrines assert. They believe that through some kind of process in time or progress and evolution there will appear the *Übermensch* or superman in some golden tomorrow. This dangerous notion is nothing but a demonic distortion of traditional doctrines. As we have existence here and now on earth, so also do we have a reality right now on the higher levels of existence, ascending all the way to our principial reality *in divinis,* to our archetype in God before the creation of the world. To become fully human means to actualize all these possibilities within us through knowledge, love, correct action, and virtue. The goal of the Sufi path is to return to our primordial archetype in God. This is the meaning of the enigmatic Sufi saying, "The Sufi is not created." *Sufi* in this saying means not just one who follows the path of Sufism, but one who has already reached the end of the path and returned to and realized that reality that we were and are, here and now, beyond all confines of time and space and before the creation of the world, in the Divine Reality.

THE REALITY OF EVIL AND THE NEED FOR GUIDANCE

With all the debate now raging in America between the Christian view of original sin and fallen humanity and the goodness of human nature according to what some call a modern version of Gnosticism, it is imperative, in discussing the truth according to Sufism, to deal with the question of evil and the necessity for Divine Guidance. It must be emphasized that Sufi treatises are not simply "self-realization kits" to be handed out to those who wish to realize the Supreme Self within on the basis of their own efforts and without Divine Succor. Islam does not believe in original sin, but it does emphasize our fall from our primordial state, that primordial nature we still bear deep within ourselves. We are separated from this nature by layers of forgetfulness and imperfection, by veils that can be removed only with God's Help. And it is precisely these veils, or ontological separation from our Source, that result in what theologically is called evil. It is to these veils with which we usually associate ourselves and our existence that the Sufi saint of Basra, Rābi'ah, was referring when she said, "Alas my son, thine existence is a sin wherewith no other sin can be compared."[7]

Metaphysically one can explain the reality of evil as separation from the absolute Good. Let us remember the saying of that supreme Christian poet, Dante, who said that hell is separation from God. As mentioned above, the Divine is at once the Absolute, the Infinite, and the All-Good. And let us not forget that *infinite* means containing all possibilities, including that of self-negation; as mentioned already, it is in the nature of the good to give of itself as it is in the nature of light to irradiate. This emanation, which constitutes all the levels of existence below the Absolute Being, also implies distancing and separation, gradual dimming of the light and appearance of shadows. Positively, the reality of the world issues from the One Reality, but to use the very term *world* implies already separation from God. As the Kabbalists have said, the Divine had to "withdraw" from Its full Plenitude to create a "space" for creation. What we call evil is the result of this withdrawal and separation. That is why evil does not have the same ontological status as the good in the same way that darkness does not have the same ontological status as light. The so-called problem of theodicy—that is, how could a good God create a world in which there is evil?—is the result of ignorance of the nature of God and the world and lack of knowledge of the doctrine of veil or *māyā*. This so-called problem, which has driven many a modern Westerner away from Christianity and in some cases from Judaism, has been discussed in depth by many non-Western philosophers, theologians, and mystics belonging to other religions. Countless souls in traditional societies have observed evil and misery surrounding them, but such experiences have hardly ever drawn Muslims, Hindus, or Buddhists, to name just a few examples, away from religion and the world of faith. Observing evil in a world created by God who is good has not had the same religious consequences for them as it has had for many in the modern West and of course did not have the same consequences for those in the traditional West, whose reactions to this problem were similar in many ways to those of people today in most non-Western cultures.

From the point of view of the Divine Reality, there is no evil because there is nothing to be separated from the Source of the Good, but for human beings living in the domain of relativity, evil is as real as that domain, although creation in its ontological reality is good since it comes from God. This is demonstrated by the overwhelming beauty of the natural order. That is why both the Bible and the Quran assert the goodness of His creation and the fact that goodness always predominates ultimately over evil. Furthermore, the infernal, purgatorial, and paradisal states are real although located in the domain of relativity but each with very different characteristics. The problem of evil becomes intractable when we absolutize the relative and fail to distinguish between the existential reality of a thing, which comes from the Act of Being, and its "apparent" separative existence. To speak of a world without evil is to fail to understand what the world is and to confuse the Absolute and the relative, the Essence and its veils, or to use the language of Hinduism, *Ātman* and *māyā*.

Some Sufis have said that there is no evil but only goodness and beauty. Such statements must be understood in the context of the state of consciousness from which they were speaking, the state that allowed them to see the Face of God everywhere. Everything has a face turned inward to God beyond all blemish and evil and a face turned outward. The Sufis who have denied evil have gazed upon that face of inwardness and have seen the outward face of things in light of that inner reality. Otherwise, if Sufism had denied evil, there would be no need for Sufism itself because the role of Sufism is to overcome the imperfections and evil tendencies of the soul, called "*nafs* inciting to evil" in the Quran and subsequently by the Sufis. On the existential level of the ordinary soul, they are as real as the soul itself. To transcend evil and to behold only the good and the beautiful, one must transcend one's own ego or this *nafs*. The overwhelming beauty of God's creation and the ultimate triumph of the good, whatever transient phenomena of an evil nature may hold sway in the short run, is itself proof of the existential inequality between good and evil, the beautiful and the ugly. Sufis seek to cling to the good and the beautiful even amid what appears sometimes in life as predominance of the evil and the ugly. They hold fast to the Truth even when surrounded by error and falsehood, being anchored in the certainty that the Truth, which is always good and beautiful in the metaphysical sense, shall finally prevail. The Sufis would be the first to agree with the medieval Latin adage *vincit omnia veritas,* the Truth shall always triumph.

To overcome the imperfections of the soul and the abode of evil cannot be accomplished by fallen humanity without help. If there are exceptions, they only prove the rule, and one must never forget that "The Spirit bloweth where it listeth." Putting such exceptions aside, the rule and principle is that human beings are in need of Divine Guidance to remember who they are, to be able to slay the dragon within. Through His Mercy God has therefore sent prophets throughout history to guide human beings to the One. Moreover, this guidance has two levels, the first concerned with prophecy (*nubuwwah*), which is for the guidance of the whole of a human collectivity and all members of the society for which the revelation is intended, and the second with inner and initiatic guidance (*walāyah/wilāyah*) for the few who aspire to spiritual perfection. This reality in Islam is the source, foundation, and continuous inner spiritual power that makes traveling upon the Sufi path possible. Moreover, access to *walāyah/wilāyah* is only possible within the reality of *nubuwwah*. That is why it is not possible to follow the Sufi path, or *Ṭarīqah,* without following the injunctions and teachings of Islamic Law, or *Sharī'ah,* which is meant for the whole of the Islamic community, including the Sufis.

THE KNOWLEDGE OF THE TRUTH AND DELIVERANCE

Knowledge of the Truth is ultimately not only a theoretical understanding of concepts. It is above all a knowledge that is combined with faith and involves all that we are. It is efficacious if it transforms our whole being and transmutes our soul. It must therefore involve our whole being. We must know not only with our senses and mind, but above all with our heart, which is our center. The knowledge that delivers and frees is one that removes the veils of separation that have caused us to forget our real identity. It is a knowledge that removes forgetfulness of that Divine Reality, which is the source of all things as well as residing at the center of our being, the Self of our self. To understand fully the Truth is to "become" that Truth. It is to cease to be what we are and become what we have always been, are, and shall be in the Divine Reality. To enter the Garden of Truth has as its condition transcending our limitations and becoming freed of the fetters of limited existence and the prison of ignorance. This is both the necessary condition for entering the Garden and the result of entering that Garden. Truth, when actualized through spiritual practice, delivers us from that prison and renders us free in the highest sense of the term. Metaphysical and cosmological truths outlined in this chapter are, according to the Sufis, a *theoria* or vision of the Real as well as a road map to guide us through the cosmic labyrinth to the Abode of the Infinite and the Eternal. They provide keys to open the doors to the expanses of the Divine Empyrean, that is, the highest celestial firmament. Once realized through Divine Guidance, these truths reveal themselves as not only knowledge of the Real but Reality in Itself and in Its manifestations, for truth *is* reality, knowledge *is* being.

In one of his prayers the Prophet of Islam said, "O Lord, show us things as they really are." To attain the stage of realizing the answer to this prayer, which means to see things in their metaphysical transparency, as symbols and not only as facts, as reflections of God's Names and Qualities, as the Self-Disclosure of God rather than as veils, we must know who we are, which in turn means that we must know God and all things, including ourselves *by* God and through Him. Such a knowledge of necessity involves all that we are. It involves love and beauty, faith and righteous action. Its attainment requires spiritual discipline and following the Path, which the Sufis call the *Ṭarīqah*. The Truth is at once the beginning and end of the Path. Its theoretical knowledge, that is, its beginning, enables us to know who we are, where we came from, and where we should be going. Its realization, which must also be combined with love and beauty and which is the end and the goal of our life, brings access to the Garden, whose entry is the ultimate purpose of human existence.

> The book of the Sufi is not the black ink of written words,
> It is none other than an unblemished heart like snow.[8]

Three

LOVE AND BEAUTY

The Fire That Attracts and Consumes, the Peace That Calms and Liberates

He loves them and they love Him.
Quran 5:54

To God belong the most beautiful Names.
Quran 7:180

God, ever mighty and majestic is He, says: "O child of Adam, it is thy right from Me that I be a lover for thee. So, by My right from thee, be for Me a lover."[1]
Ḥadīth

God is beautiful and He loves beauty.
Ḥadīth

The intelligent are the turning point of the
  protractor of existence,
But love knows that they are confounded in
  this circle.
Ḥāfiẓ, Dīwān

THE ROLE OF LOVE AND BEAUTY IN THE SPIRITUAL LIFE

Journeying on the road to the Garden of Truth requires not only acquiring and realizing unitive knowledge, but also being immersed in love and attracted to beauty at its highest level. God has made possible for us human beings to gain access to Him not only through knowledge but also through love and beauty. The Garden is the Garden of Truth, but it is also the Garden of Love, whose Beauty is above and beyond all that we can imagine or have experienced as lovable and beautiful here on earth. The Gardener is also the Beloved, who must not only be known but also loved and contemplated in Her infinite beauty, which consumes the beholder and leads to the ecstasy of union as well as ultimate peace. Men and women experience all kinds of love and behold many beautiful objects in this life here below, but most do not reach the Garden of Truth through such experiences. We must therefore ask ourselves what love and beauty are in the context of Sufism and why the Sufis, who emphasize so much principial and illuminative knowledge, speak so much of love and beauty, which are inextricably bound to each other.

Before answering these questions, it is of great value to quote a sacred saying of the Prophet concerning the relation of knowledge and love:

> Who seeketh Me findeth Me.
> Who findeth Me knoweth Me.
> Who knoweth Me loveth Me.
> Who loveth Me, him I love.
> Whom I love, him I slay.
> Whom I slay, him must I requite.
> Whom I requite, Myself am his requital.[2]

The path to the Truth results in discovery of the Truth, which means knowledge of It. Moreover, the Truth is such that one cannot know It without loving It. And that love leads finally to the embrace of God, Who in turn loves those among His servants who love Him. In the metaphysical sense, however, it is God's love that precedes human love, as we shall see below.

THE NATURE OF LOVE

What good does it do to write about love? One has to experience love in order to understand what it is. As Rūmī said, when it comes to describing the nature of love, the pen breaks and ceases to write. Nevertheless, although dealing with words and concepts, writing about love can awaken a certain awareness in the mind and soul of the reader, which in turn can cause him or her to become prepared to experience love on some level. But love itself cannot be reduced to its description no matter how lucid and poetic, while at the same time words that have come from those who have really loved can bring about recollection and awaken within some people the love that resides within the soul of all men and women. The fire of love can become kindled through appropriate words if the substance of the soul is ready to burn in the fire of love, without which life becomes deprived of value, for again to quote Rūmī: "Whoever does not possess this fire, let him not exist."[3]

Let us start with the metaphysics of love. Love is part and parcel of reality. It is that which attracts beings to each other and to their Source. It is none other than the fire whose light illuminates and whose heat enlivens the heart and bestows life. It is also the storm that can turn the soul upside down and uproot ordinary existence. Love is life but can also be death. It involves yearning and pain of separation as well as the ecstasy of union. Love is also inseparable from existence in its modes. Not only in Christianity is God considered to be love, but according to the Quran also one of His Names is Love or *al-Wadūd*. And since love is part of the Divine Nature, all of existence, which issues from Him, is permeated by love. God is the light of the heavens and the earth, as the Quran asserts. The luminosity of this light is related to knowledge and its warmth to love. There is no realm of existence in which love is not found, save from a certain point of view on the human level, where God has given us the free will to love or not to love; but even on the human plane it can be said that even those who do not love God or the neighbor still love themselves. As far as the cosmos is concerned, love can be seen everywhere if only we become aware of its reality. The branches of trees grow in the direction of light because of love, and animals take care of their young as a result of love. Even the heavens move because of the force of love, which we reduce to the mere physical and quantitative and call gravity. As Dante wrote at the very end of the *Divine Comedy,* the ultimate spiritual union involves the experience and realization of "*l'amor che move il sole e l'altre stelle,*" that is, "the love that moves the sun and the other stars."[4]

Love flows in the arteries of the universe, as does grace, and we as human beings can and do love, the object of our love ranging from an earthly creature, particularly a person, to God Himself. But as already mentioned, in reality love originates with God and not with us. In his two basic commandments Christ ordered his followers first to love God who loves his creation and then to love the neighbor. The Quran provides the metaphysical basis of this love by asserting that God will bring a people "whom He loves and they love Him" (5:54). This verse, which has been quoted many times by Sufis writing about love, makes clear that first of all God loves His creation and as a consequence of this love we can love Him. Moreover, as the two commandments of Christ state, the love of God has primacy over the love of the neighbor, which means all creatures and not only human beings.

There are therefore, from the human point of view, stages of love understood metaphysically and as explained by the Sufis. There is first of all the love of God for Himself and then His Love for His creatures, including us, as a result of which love permeates the very substance of beings in all levels of existence. Subsequently, there is our love for the Divine, and finally there is our love for other beings, which for those who believe is derived from the love for God. This spiritual understanding of love therefore transcends the love of the ego for itself, a false love that has become habitual in most men and women. Only through this hierarchy and the relation between its various levels can the spiritual and transformative power of love, which can even transform the love of the ego for itself to the love for God and the other, be understood. But there is a further element of a more subtle nature involving the instrument as well as the content of revelation binding us to God. Can one love God as a Christian without loving Christ? The answer is quite obvious. The same truth holds for Islam, where the love for the Prophet is a prerequisite for the love of God. One might summarize this truth as follows: to love God, He must first love us, and God does not love the person who does not love His prophet or messenger and his message.

Since love originates in God and issues from Him, real love in this world is ultimately none other than the love for God. Early Christians spoke of *agape* and *eros* to distinguish divine and human or cosmic love, and this distinction is still central to much of Christian theology, especially Catholic theology. The Sufis take a different route. They do not draw a sharp distinction between *agape* and *eros,* considering the second as a shadow of and also ladder to the first. Rather, they speak of real love (*al-'ishq al-ḥaqīqī*), that is, the love of the human being for God, and metaphorical love (*al-'ishq al-majāzī*), which includes all forms of love that appear to be outside and independent of the bond of love between God and human beings. According to this view, most of what we consider to be love is not real love at all but is love only in the metaphorical sense. Furthermore, there is another hierarchy in love stretching from various levels of metaphorical love to real love, which always involves God and can include the love of someone or something, but in God. Yet even metaphorical love is a glimmer of real love for finally there is but one Love with many grades of manifestation.

Sufis also speak of another form of the gradation and hierarchy of love. They begin with the ordinary human condition and end with the state of the saint. The lowest state of love from this point of view is the love of the ego or the self for itself. This is still love, but because of the imprisoning nature of its object, it becomes stifling and prevents the growth of the soul and the possibility for it to reach higher levels of love. Then there is the love of others, whether they be human beings, animals, or objects such as plants, minerals, and also human artifacts, especially works of art. But this level of love is still limited and finite as well as in most cases transient. Often it brings about an attachment to the world that prevents the soul from experiencing higher levels of love, which must paradoxically also involve detachment from worldliness. Then there is love for the sacred realities, including messengers, revealed books, saints, sacred art, and so forth, which, coming from God, turns the soul to Him, provided human beings remain aware of the Source of all that is sacred. Finally, there is the love for God, the Sacred as such, which is boundless and liberating rather than binding since the object of this love is the Infinite. The highest level of love is the love of God for Himself, and it is this Love that makes all other forms of love possible. In fact, all forms of love are reflections, albeit often faint ones, of this supreme Love.

From the spiritual point of view the levels stated above can all be positive, and each lower level can lead to a higher one rather than being limitative. The love of oneself *can* lead to the awareness of the evanescent and at the same time deceiving nature of the ego and its imprisoning effect, leading the person to search for his or her higher self. The love of others can lead to pain and suffering and help the soul to search for that love that does not perish. The love of the natural world can lead to a sense of wonder in the wisdom of God and love for the Creator of the creatures who are the objects of our love. As for the love of sacred objects, theophanies and the like, they almost always lead to the love of the Being Who is the source of the grace and beauty present in them. The hierarchy of love can therefore be seen both as a ladder for ascent to the Divine Empyrean and as description of ever greater limitation and imprisonment of the soul as one descends to the lower levels of the hierarchy.

THE SPIRITUAL SIGNIFICANCE OF HUMAN LOVE

To have truly loved is to have truly lived, and the person who goes through life without having loved has not really lived a fully human life. This belief of the Sufis points to the important truth that not only is love part of life, it also plays a very significant spiritual role in our inner development. As already mentioned, the power of love is transformative. It has an alchemical effect upon the soul and can transmute its very substance. The alchemical wedding between sulfur and mercury that produces various concrete substances (according to alchemy) symbolizes the inner transformation that the embrace of love brings about in the soul, enabling it to gain union in a concrete manner with the Spirit.

A human being can experience many forms of love. We can love our parents, children, and relatives. We can love our town, country, and culture. There is love of nature and art. There is love of religion and the sacred, all leading to the love of God. All these forms of love involve going beyond one's ego, performing sacrifice and suffering, giving and giving again. Also all forms of love are signs of a deep yearning in the soul for that pure love that is divine. But there is one kind of love that is the most powerful on the human plane—and not of course in relation to God—and that is love of a man for a woman or of a woman for a man. Conjugal and romantic love is the testing ground for the growth of the soul emotionally and spiritually, and it is related directly to the love and ultimate union between the soul and the Spirit. This assertion does not of course negate the possibility of detachment from such a love for the sake of God, as we see in the celibacy practiced in certain religions.

Real and authentic love in the romantic sense, and not merely sexual attraction, is a form of grace and a gift from Heaven. It rips through our soul like a powerful hurricane, uprooting our usual attachments and habits. It yanks the roots of our soul from the soil of complacency and self-centeredness. It causes joy as well as pain, ecstasy as well as longing. It detaches the soul from other entanglements and attaches it to the object of one's love, even overcoming the mind's scattered thoughts and concentrating the mind on that single object. Something of the absoluteness of the love for God becomes reflected in such a human love that requires utter selflessness and unlimited giving. Such a love, if authentic, does not diminish if the beloved becomes less beautiful outwardly and loses his or her external attractiveness because the object of that love is the person and not his or her attributes, which may be pleasing to the lover at one moment and not so later on. That is why authentic romantic love grows rather than diminishes as time goes on. Such a love is a gift from God to His creatures, whom He created in pairs, as the Quran asserts, and this love cannot in the deepest sense be separated from the love for God and God's love for us. Hence the spiritual significance of human love.

The sexual dimension of love is itself impregnated with spiritual significance. Sexual union is an earthly reflection of a paradisal prototype. The male experiences the Infinite and the female the Absolute in this earthly union, which returns, albeit for a moment, the human being to his or her androgynic wholeness. The bliss of sexual union is also a foretaste of the bliss of the union of the soul with the Spirit, about which Christian Hermeticism as well as certain other schools of Christian mysticism speak. As mentioned above, the soul can of course withdraw from this earthly attraction through asceticism to seek direct wedding to the Spirit, as we see in monasticism and many forms of Christian spirituality, but the sexual union remains spiritually significant, especially in Sufism, which like the rest of Islam sees sexuality as a sacred reality, hence to be governed by the Sacred Law, not as a sinful act simply resulting from the fall. Sexual union can lead to the experience of *fanā'* or annihilation and therefore liberation, however momentary, from the bonds of separative existence and limitations of ordinary consciousness. From the Sufi point of view, the urge for sexual union, which is the most powerful sensuous urge within most human beings, is in reality the search of the soul for union with God, especially when human union is combined with love. Every beloved is ultimately a reflection of the Beloved or *ma'shūq,* as the Sufis say, who is God in His inner reality, a reality to which Sufis often refer in the feminine. The Essence of God is called *al-Dhāt* in Arabic, and it is grammatically feminine in gender. Seen as the Beloved, the inner dimension of the Divine is that feminine Beauty for which the male soul yearns. In His aspect as Creator and Sustainer of creation, however, God is seen as masculine. From the purely metaphysical point of view, the Divine is of course above the male-female distinction in the same way that in Far Eastern doctrines the supreme Tao transcends the dualism of yin and yang.

The Quran uses words derived from the root of *ḥubb* when referring to love. The Sufis also use such terms, but they add to them the term *'ishq,* which implies intense love, and they claim that the Quran, being sacred scripture, does not use this term because of its extremeness and intensity. The word *'ishq,* according to traditional sources, is derived from the name of a vine that twists itself around a tree and presses so hard upon its trunk that the tree dies. This poetic etymology refers to the profound truth that intense love involves death. As Rūmī says, "the Beloved is alive and the lover a dead being," while there is the famous Latin saying *amor est mors,* "love is death." One is reminded here of the famous "Love-Death Song" (*Liebestod*) in Wagner's opera *Tristan und Isolde.*

The great love narratives usually end in death, as we see for example in Western literature in the stories of Tristan and Isolde and Romeo and Juliet. Their deaths are outwardly related to external forces and circumstances but inwardly point to the relation between intense love and death. It is said that for every man there is a woman—and vice versa—who is such a perfect complement that if the two were to meet here on earth the intensity of their love would cause them to die. Human love even below this extreme stage is always combined with some degree of dying—dying to one's ego, to one's desires, to one's preferences for the sake of the other. And this is so because human love is itself a reflection of Divine Love, which we can experience only after the death of our ego, and can lead to the Divine those souls who are fortunate enough to have experienced this love. That is also why legendary love stories are outwardly about human love and inwardly about the love for God and of God and therefore often end in the earthly death of the hero or heroine or both.

There is many such a tale in Sufism, and perhaps the most famous is the story of Laylā and Majnūn. The original story, which has many later versions, was a simple one. A young Arab Bedouin called Qays meets Laylā at a gathering of women. The effect of this meeting upon him is profound. He falls in love with her and sacrifices his camel for the feast. When a man called Manāzil comes to the gathering, the attention of all the women is turned toward him except that of Laylā, who returns Qays's love for her. He then asks for her hand from her father, but her father refuses, saying that she is already betrothed to someone else. In deep anguish and sorrow, Qays loses his mind and reason and goes into the wilderness half-naked to live with wild animals. The appellation Majnūn, meaning crazed or mad, by which he became known, arose from this behavior. His father takes him on pilgrimage to Mecca with the hope that he will be cured, but this experience only intensifies his love for Laylā. When lucid, Majnūn composes some poems expressing his love for her, but he sees her only once more before his death.

On the basis of this anonymous poem, many prose versions were written. They became popular in Arabic literature and later became part of the Persian literary tradition. Perhaps the greatest masterpiece based on this story, but much elaborated, is by the twelfth-century Persian poet Niẓāmī, who turned it into one of the masterpieces of Persian lyric poetry. Sufis such as Aḥmad Ghazzālī, 'Aṭṭār, and Rūmī transformed this tale into an example of Divine and human love as understood in Sufism. Amīr Khusraw, the great fourteenth-century Persian poet of India, also composed a work titled *Laylī and Majnūn* (*Laylī* being the Persian version of *Laylā*) and dedicated it to Niẓām al-Awliyā', the celebrated saint of Delhi. Furthermore, the fifteenth-century Sufi poet Jāmī composed a major work with this title. The story of Laylā and Majnūn became well known also in the literature of not only Arabic but also the Turkish, Kurdish, Pashto, and several other languages. In the Sufi versions of this famous love story, Laylā or Laylī is understood to symbolize the Divine Essence. The name Laylā/Laylī comes from the Arabic word for night (*layl*), and it means the beauty of the night, which is dark, hence its association with the "black light" of the Divine Essence, which is black because of the intensity of its light, standing above visible light, which symbolizes manifestation. As for Majnūn, its usual meaning as one who is mad is seen symbolically. Now, love also involves a kind of madness, and even ordinary human love often goes against logic and common sense and appears to those not stricken by it as a kind of insanity. The person who loves God with all his or her being certainly appears to be afflicted with some form of craziness by those who consider normal the state of indifference toward Divine Love that characterizes much of the public at large. The beautiful story of Laylā and Majnūn is therefore the vehicle for the expression of Divine Love couched in the language of human love.

DIVINE LOVE

It has already been mentioned that God first loves us before we have the possibility of loving Him. This ontological priority must be always remembered. God could have created beings who could not but glorify Him, and He did so in creating the angels. But in the case of human beings, He created persons endowed with free will, beings worthy of loving Him consciously but also capable of not loving Him. There is no such thing as love through coercion. Divine Love is a reality that permeates creation by virtue of the very act of creation by the Divinity who is also Mercy, Compassion, and Love. But from the human side, it is possible not to love God as it is possible to reject His very existence. Life in this world is not only a test of our faith, as the Quran asserts, but also of our love for God and the possibility of reciprocating on our own limited level His love for us. As the sacred saying quoted at the beginning of this chapter asserts, it is the right of men and women that God be a lover for them. On the basis of this reality, God asks us to be a lover for Him in the fullness of our free will.

The great impediment to responding positively to this divine invitation is that there are so many other things that can become objects of our love, starting with our own ego. God is aware of this situation, hence the revelation of religions and the spiritual power contained within them, which can disentangle the love of the soul for the transient and the perishable and turn it toward God. When the Sufis speak of love, or *'ishq,* they are thinking of its liberating and not confining aspect. To love God fully is to possess complete freedom from every other bond, and since God is absolute and infinite, it is to experience absolute and infinite freedom.

In one of his most famous *ghazals,* Ḥāfiẓ, the supreme master of lyric and mystical poetry in the Persian language, sings:

I reveal and am content with my words,
I am the bondsman of love and liberated from both worlds.
I was flying in the sacred Garden, how can I describe
my separation?
How I became ensnared in the trap of this world?
I was an angel and exalted paradise was my abode,
Adam brought me to this monastery of the city of ruins.[5]

Divine Love liberates us from not only this world but also the next, understood in ordinary religious language as a world whose inhabitants are judged and compensated according to good or evil actions in this world. Through Divine Love we are returned to that sacred Garden in which we were in Divine Proximity before our Fall, that sacred Garden which is also the Garden of union above all the purgatorial states, above both infernal and heavenly abodes as usually understood.

MUST ONE LOVE TO REACH THE GARDEN OF TRUTH?

Since the Garden of Truth is reached through illuminative knowledge discussed in the last chapter, it might be asked whether love is a necessary concomitant of the path of gnosis. In order to answer this basic question it is necessary to distinguish between love as emotion and the metaphysical significance of love. There are mystical paths based solely on love that lead human beings, through the use of the emotion of love directed toward God, to God Himself. Most of Christian mysticism is a mysticism of love, as is the Hindu *bhakti marga*. Sufism is not such a path despite the constant talk by most Sufis about love. In Sufism love is the complement of gnosis and is related to the reality of realized knowledge. Of course, some Sufis emphasize love and others knowledge, but both knowledge and love are always present in any integral Sufi teaching, as is the element of action, with which we shall deal in the next chapter. Rūmī was one of the foremost troubadours of love in Sufism, and his *Mathnawī* begins with verses replete with the praise of love, and yet the same book is called "the ocean of gnosis" by those who know his work well. Others, such as his friend Ṣadr al-Dīn Qunyawī, emphasized gnosis but did not neglect love. In any case, the path of Sufism combines knowledge and love, and rarely does one find a person or a school in Sufism whose teachings, even if emphasizing love, would not possess a sapiental dimension and be purely *bhaktic* and of the same genre as much of Christian mysticism and also certain forms of Hindu spirituality.

In answer to the question whether one can reach the Garden of Truth without love, the answer is no, but at the same time it must be emphasized that sentimental piety, although valuable on its own level, is not sufficient by itself for such a task. There must be realized knowledge, but this realization involves the whole of our being and therefore must include the reality of love. Furthermore, love leads to union, and God loves His creatures; therefore, there is no way to reach God without experiencing the fire of that love, which immolates our separative existence and turns us into cinders, from which the immortal soul emerges with a new life. Consequently, it can indeed be said that he or she who has not loved has not lived.

BEAUTY—DIVINE, HUMAN, AND COSMIC

Beauty and love are two aspects of the same reality from a certain point of view, one possessing primarily an active nature and the other a passive one. One is like burning fire and the other a calm and placid lake, although there is a dimension of tranquillity to love once realized and beauty can also be beheld in thunder and lightning. There is a complementarity within the first complementarity, that is, a passive element within the active nature of love and an active element within the passive nature of beauty. One could in fact easily apply the Far Eastern doctrine of the complementarity of yin and yang and the presence of yin in yang and yang in yin to this fundamental relation between love and beauty. In any case, the two are inseparable on a certain level, for how can one not love the beautiful and how can that which we love not be beautiful on some level (and not necessarily only in its external and outward form)?

In the same way that the Quran and *Ḥadīth* speak of love, they also speak of beauty, and in fact the Quran does refer to the Names of God, which reveal His Attributes to us, as being beautiful. As for the collection of *Ḥadīth,* the Prophetic saying "God is beautiful and He loves beauty" is practically the foundation of Islamic aesthetics. Moreover, the Names of Divine Mercy taken together are called the Names of Beauty. The two basic terms used for *beauty* in the foundational sources of Islam in general and Sufism in particular are *ḥusn* or *iḥsān* and *jamāl*. The latter is a Divine Name, as mentioned in the already-cited *ḥadīth*—and is also mentioned in the Quran—while the first concerns both God and human beings as well as the path to Him. *Ḥusn* in Arabic means at once beauty, goodness, and virtue, which is from the Sufi point of view nothing other than the beauty of the soul. Sufism itself is defined as *iḥsān,* which, as described by a sacred *ḥadīth,* is to worship God as if we see Him and, if we see Him not, as if He sees us. The path to the Garden of Truth is covered with forms of beauty that are all theophanies of the Beauty of the Face of the Beloved, and this path cannot be traversed save by one who embellishes his or her soul with beauty. How then do Sufis understand this key reality in the life of the spirit?

Like being, beauty is a universal reality that cannot be delineated, and logical definitions do not embrace all of its reality. One can point to it in contrast to ugliness, but that is not sufficient for in its essence beauty transcends duality, including the duality of ordinary beauty and ugliness, which we experience through our senses. Some sages, however, have sought over the ages to define beauty. One of the most famous is by Plato, who said, "Beauty is the splendor of the Truth." The Sufis would readily accept this assertion except that they would add that since Truth is also Reality in their perspective, as seen in the word *al-ḥaqīqah,* which means both, beauty can be said to be the splendor of Reality itself. All reality issues from the One, Who is the sole absolute Reality, which is also absolute Beauty. As the One manifests the many on various levels of cosmic existence, this absolute Beauty is also manifested along with existence, of which it is the splendor like the aura around the sun. What appears to us as ugly issues from nonexistence parading in the guise of existence. Since existence itself emanates from the Real, whose aura is beauty, what appears as ugliness is the result of the deprivation of the light of Being and the shadow cast as a result of the distancing from the Source of this light.

Sufis also agree fully with Plato when in the *Philebus* he asserts that beauty is part of the reality of things and not dependent upon our subjective appreciation or perception of it. Beauty is part of the objective reality of each being. It is not dependent upon the beholder except to the extent that each beholder perceives beauty according to the particularity of his or her soul and to the extent that his or her soul is beautiful and able to appreciate beauty. But that does not mean that beauty is based simply on our subjective appraisal any more than our ignorance of the geological structure of a mountain due to our lack of knowledge of geology makes that structure subjective. Yes, we must cultivate our eyes and ears to see and hear beauty, and that can only be done, spiritually speaking, provided the soul has been trained and cultivated and made beautiful through the acquiring of virtue. This training is not, however, the only condition as far as appreciation of the universal manifestation of beauty is concerned. It is, of course, also necessary to master the formal language in which certain types of beauty are manifested. A Persian does not usually appreciate the beauty of the *Sanctus* of Bach's Mass in B Minor nor a German the beauty of an Indian *rāg* without training in the formal "language" involved. Yet certain other types of beauty are universal and cut across cultural particularities. For those who appreciate the beauty of nature, the Himalayas manifest incredible majesty and beauty, which human beings appreciate whether they are from Brazil, Nigeria, or Japan. And the beauty of a human being is perceptible wherever that person goes on the globe. Even in the domain of art, where each civilization possesses its own distinct formal language, certain great masterpieces display beauty of a universal order. One need only think of the Chartres Cathedral, the Alhambra, or a Sung painting. In any case, the training of the soul in the formal language of various arts must accompany in many cases the soul's embellishment with inner beauty while God has manifested beauty in such a way that certain other types of it cut across all cultural boundaries as if to remind us that the Beautiful as such belongs to the Formless and transcends the particularities of all formal "languages."

In Sufism aesthetics is not separate from spiritual discipline and ethics. One cannot be carried on the wings of beauty to the freedom of the spiritual world without that discipline and without being aware and loving the absolute Beauty of God for which the soul yearns, whether it is aware of it or not, in its quest of every form of earthly beauty. This quest cannot simply be carried out without ethical and spiritual discipline. As Plotinus, whom Muslims called the *Shaykh,* or spiritual master, of the Greeks, once said, the soul strives after beauty and beauty is a manifestation of that spiritual power that animates all levels of reality. The Sufis agree completely with this view, which once dominated Western aesthetics but was marginalized in the West, along with Neoplatonic teachings on the subject, in the eighteenth century.

How is this beauty after which the soul yearns perceived and experienced? Since beauty resides in the depth of the soul, and at the same time the soul yearns for it, God has made possible its experience through all the faculties, both outward and inward, that belong to the soul. All of our external senses can experience beauty, especially our seeing and hearing faculties. In fact, most of the time when we refer to beauty, it is audible or visible beauty that we have in mind. But the inner faculties of the soul can also perceive beauty that is hidden from the eye of outwardness. The imaginal faculty can perceive beautiful images. The mind can behold the beauty of mathematical forms in the purely mathematical world independent of the material realm. It can also discern harmony, which is inseparable from beauty. The intellect that shines within us can contemplate the beauty of the purely intelligible world and the angelic realms. As for the heart, when its eye is opened, it can behold the Beauty of the Face of the Beloved itself. Through whatever means our consciousness makes contact and becomes aware of objective reality, there is the possibility of experiencing beauty, a quality that permeates all levels and modes of existence.

Although beauty is ubiquitous, whether we are aware of it of not, there is a hierarchy of beauty, as there is of reality, being, and love. The supreme beauty is the beauty of the Supreme Reality; absolute beauty is the beauty of the Absolute. Even the most intense beauty experienced in this world in the beautiful face of a loved one or a supreme work of art or of virgin nature or even the perfume of the soul of a saint is a reflection of divine Beauty. At once absolute and infinite, this Beauty can be experienced but not described in human words, being a truly ineffable reality. This Beauty is the crown of the hierarchy of beauty and at the same time the source of every form of beauty. Below it in the hierarchy stands the beauty of the purely intelligible and angelic worlds and below them the beauty of certain forms in the imaginal world and then of the spatiotemporal realm that reflect the archetypal and intelligible world most directly. This latter category of forms bound by time and space includes, of course, virgin nature as created by the Supreme Artisan and therefore reflecting in a stunning fashion the beauty of its Maker. Sacred art that is based on heavenly inspiration and that makes possible the direct experience of the spiritual world in material forms also belongs to this category.

According to the famous Hermetic saying, "That which is lowest symbolizes that which is highest." This principle also pertains to the experience of beauty. Although the material realm is the lowest in the hierarchy of existence, it reflects the highest realm. The beauty of a material form can therefore reflect the highest beauty and ultimately the Divine Beauty. Many Sufis over the ages have been fully aware of this truth and have looked upon every beautiful form as a reflection of the Beauty of Her Face.

As for human beauty, it is important to clarify where it stands in this hierarchy. Since the human state contains all levels of existence within itself, it might be said that the human being can embrace the whole hierarchy. The human being can possess physical beauty, beauty of character, beauty of soul, beauty of mind and intelligence, and beauty of heart. In the terrestrial realm, human beauty is in fact the highest form of beauty, especially the beauty of the Universal Man, in whom all human possibilities are realized. As for physical beauty of ordinary people, it is God-given, especially when one is young. As we grow older our actions based on our choices and free will become evermore reflected in our outward countenance, and inner beauty, in the case of those who possess such beauty, begins to dominate the outward while the original God-given outward beauty usually fades away. But outer beauty is far from being insignificant. It is in fact a great gift from God, bringing with it much privilege but also great responsibility. The Sufis have often said that contemplating the beauty of the face of a woman by a male Sufi is the most direct means for contemplating Divine Beauty, and the reverse also holds true. Ibn 'Arabī and Shabistarī, for example, write how each feature of the female face reveals a Divine Quality and unveils a Divine Mystery. Ibn 'Arabī writes that while in Mecca he met a young Persian woman and in beholding her face all esoteric knowledge was suddenly revealed to him. In any case, not only are Sufis, both male and female, lovers of God, but they are also lovers of beauty, which is inseparable from the Divine Reality and which, being related to the infinitude of the Divine, brings about total peace and liberates the soul from all fetters of restrictive existence.

Although many Sufis have been incessant pursuers of beauty and beautiful forms, some have warned against this quest for the beautiful if the soul has not readied itself for the total experience of Beauty through beautiful forms by ridding itself of inward imperfections and ugliness. Precisely because beauty attracts the soul, it can also ensnare it and act as a powerful means of distraction from the Source of all beauty. That is why some sages and mystics in all religions have considered beauty to be a double-edged sword and have tried to restrain themselves from appreciating beautiful external forms at a certain stage of the spiritual journey. Such people are called ascetics (*zuhhād* in Islam), and there were many such people in the early history of Sufism before the full flowering of the dimensions of love and knowledge. These figures, in fact, prepared the necessary ground for that flowering. What such saints and seers were doing and saying was that nothing finite should trap the soul and prevent it from its ascent in the degrees of perfection. And so they concentrated only on God as the One beyond all realms of manifestation and all forms.

The danger with which they were concerned relates to the error of taking a finite form of beauty as an independent reality, independent from God as the Source of all beauty. Precisely because of the nature of beauty, it has the power of attracting the soul unto itself in such a way that the soul forgets the Source of this beauty and also the fact that the beauty of all earthly forms is transient. Few people have been distracted from God because of something ugly. Usually what occupies the soul and turns it away from the Garden of Truth is a form that possesses some type of beauty, to which the soul is then attracted. The shadow of the Beauty of Her Face begins to compete in the soul with that absolute Beauty, and through ignorance the soul cannot distinguish between the Real and its reflections. In any case, in the integral vision of Sufism, beauty remains a central reality in the spiritual life. The Garden of Truth is beautiful, and no one can enter it who does not appreciate beauty and who is not inwardly beautiful, who cannot distinguish between beauty and ugliness, which corresponds to discerning the difference between the real and the unreal, the false and the true.

Beauty is inseparable from the real and the true because, like them, it accompanies the reflection of the One in the many. It opens the door of the finite unto the Infinite and frees the soul from the confines of finite forms, although it is manifested in the formal order. Harmony is the result of the reflection of the One in the manifold, and therefore it is closely related to beauty. Objects of beauty possess qualitative harmony associated with such realities as colors. They can also possess not only qualitative but also quantitative harmony. This can be found, for example, in music, which, in addition to the quality of sound, is related quantitatively to measurement and mathematics, disciplines studied in the science of harmonics. Islamic art is characterized by the harmony of proportions, mathematical clarity, and various degrees of symmetry.

In other spiritual worlds the asymmetrical can also be a vehicle for beauty, as one sees in the Zen garden, but in the Sufi perspective symmetry is usually seen as being related to harmony and harmony to beauty. This kind of beauty involves the intelligence, and intelligibility, including the mathematical, is seen as a beautiful quality perceived on a high level. Below it lies sensuous beauty and above it the ineffable beauty of the world transcending all forms. But as already mentioned, all of these levels of beauty are reflections of the supreme Beauty of the Beloved's Face, which we human beings experienced when we were in the Edenic state.

The experience of that beauty still lies deep within the soul. One of the functions of beauty in human life is to bring about remembrance of that celestial Beauty. If understood spiritually, beauty becomes itself the means of recollection and the rediscovery of our true nature as God had created us, the nature we still bear deeply within ourselves although it has been forgotten as a result of our falling into the state of ignorance and no longer knowing who we are. Having become completely exteriorized, we tend to look only at the external form and seek external beauty, whereas the Sufis contemplate, through external forms, their inner meaning and the inward beauty contained therein. As the thirteenth-century Persian Sufi poet Awḥad al-Dīn Kirmānī said,

> So I look with optic eye on earthly face,
> For outward form bears the seal of inner Meaning.
> The world's but form and we must live in forms:
> One cannot outward Meaning see but in form.[6]

According to a *ḥadīth* of the Prophet, God has written beauty upon the face of all things. This is the face that each creature has turned to God. Spiritual realization means seeing this face and the beauty written upon it as well as hearing the beautiful music of the invocation of each creature, which constitutes its very existence. It means seeing forms in their metaphysical transparency and not their outward opacity. That transparency is inseparable from beauty because it is like a window through which the Light of the Infinite and with it a reflection of Its Beauty enters into the very substance of forms, making them vehicles that, through their beauty, carry us to the Formless and to the Source of all beauty.

O Lord Thou knowest that even now and again,
We did not gaze but upon the beauty of Thy Face.
The beautiful in this world are mirrors of Thy Beauty,
We have seen in the mirror the Face of the Exalted King.[7]

To accomplish this end of contemplating Divine Beauty in earthly forms, however, the soul must regain the beauty of its primordial reality, which is none other than *iḥsān* and which therefore means also becoming embellished with the virtues—virtues that beautify the soul and that ultimately belong to God. The beautiful soul is attracted to Divine Beauty as the moth to the candle and does not fail to experience in every earthly beauty that Divine Beauty of the Gardener of the Garden of Truth, an experience that is inseparable from the ultimate goal of human life.

Kings lick the earth whereof the fair are made,
For God hath mingled in the dusty earth
A draught of Beauty from His choicest cup.
'Tis *that,* fond lover—not these lips of clay—
Thou art kissing with a hundred ecstasies,
Think, then, what must it be when undefiled![8]

Rūmī

PEACE

We cannot discuss the spiritual significance of beauty without turning to the subject of peace. Beauty attracts the soul, and therein the soul finds all that it seeks. Why then go elsewhere? Why be agitated? The beholding of beauty involves rest and repose, serenity and peace. In the formal order, as long as the soul is attracted by the beauty of the form in question, it remains in a state of peace, but in many cases the soul is soon confronted with the existential limitation of the form and, finding this limitation stifling, turns its attention elsewhere and in agitation leaves the state of peace. For the Sufi, however, formal beauty is a symbol and reflection of its celestial archetype, which he or she contemplates through the form. Formal beauty thus leads such a person to the countenance of Infinite Beauty, wherein real peace is to be found. In

Infinite Beauty lies no existential limitation, and nothing can disturb the state of experiencing such supreme peace by turning the attention of the soul elsewhere because the soul is in a state where there is in fact no elsewhere to which it could turn. This state is called by some of the Sufis of Central Asia universal peace (*ṣulḥ-i kull*). It is the peace reached when one becomes immersed in the Reality that is beyond all tension and duality, where opposites meet, the *coincidentia oppositorum*.

It is remarkable that the human soul yearns for peace while living in a world full of strife, contention, opposition, struggle, and war. When we ponder the terms *pace*, *shalom*, *shanti*, and *salām* in Christianity, Judaism, Hinduism, and Islam respectively and their ubiquitous usage by the followers of these religions, as well as terms with the same meaning used elsewhere, we become aware of the universality of this yearning. Sufism emphasizes the significance of this yearning within the soul and the importance of realizing the goal of this yearning. But the Sufis insist over and over again that peace cannot be found in the world of opposition and dualism while we remain bound to this world; it can be found only by transcending this world and reaching the Divine Reality, which, being absolute Beauty, is also absolute peace. As Rūmī says:

> Except in the spiritual retreat of the Divine Truth *(ḥaqq)*
> there is no peace.

According to the Quran and a saying of the Prophet, the greeting of the people of Paradise, of the Garden, is *salām*, or peace; hence the ordinary Muslim greeting, *al-salām*[u] *'alaykūm*, or "peace be upon you." Now, the Garden shines with the splendor of beauty, which we beheld before our Fall and the blessed shall experience again after death. Such beauty could not but be combined with peace and tranquillity. The soul that cannot repose in Divine Beauty is not worthy of Paradise. He or she must in fact bring the inward serenity and peace of the soul to the paradisal realm through attaining the spiritual virtues in order to enter the Garden and to be able to benefit from the peace of the realm into which the blessed soul has gained entry. In the same way a blessed soul must add something to the beauty of the paradisal Abode if that person is to be worthy of being there.

In any case, peace (*al-salām*) is on the highest level a Divine Name, and God is both peace itself and the bestower of peace, as He is beautiful and the source of all beauty. The Quran asserts in a verse that plays an important role in Sufi practice, "It is He who made the Divine Peace (*al-sakīnah*) to descend upon the heart of believers" (48:4). This *sakīnah,* which has its correspondence in the *Shekinah* of the Kabbalists, is a peace that is heavenly and is combined with grace, God being its direct source. But we have to be ready to receive this great gift by conforming to the Truth, having faith in and love of God, and turning our soul to the Source of all beauty through acquiring virtue. To behold the Beauty of the Face of the Beloved is inseparable from absolute and unconditional love of That which Itself is absolute and infinite, and it is inseparable from the experiencing of that peace "that surpasseth all understanding."

Let us remember that the spiritual path involves knowledge, on the one hand, and love and beauty, on the other. The consequence of following these paths, however, also results in the attainment of peace for which the soul yearns. Moreover, as we shall see in the next chapter, the paths of knowledge, love, and beauty require correct action and goodness, without which one could neither realize fully divine knowledge nor be able to love God and behold His Beauty with the fullness of one's being. Consequently, without goodness and virtue one cannot attain the peace that on the profoundest level is inseparable from beauty and that we all seek deep in ourselves even amid the din, chaos, and tensions of the world in which we live.

Four

GOODNESS AND HUMAN ACTION

To Do His Will, to Conform to the Divine Norm

As for him who has faith and does wholesome works, his recompense shall be the most beautiful.
Quran 18:88

Thou didst not throw when thou threwest; rather it was God Who threw.
Quran 8:17

Actions are judged according to their intentions.
Ḥadīth

Wine in ferment is a beggar suing for our ferment;
Heaven in revolution is a beggar suing for our
  consciousness.
Wine was intoxicated with us, not we with it;
The body came into being from us, not we from it.
We are as bees and bodies as the honeycomb:
We have made the body, cell by cell, like wax.[1]
Rūmī, Mathnawī

There are two main gates to the Garden of Truth: knowledge and love, although of course God's Mercy knows no bounds and its exact operation within the human order is beyond our ken. Putting aside the exceptional cases of those drawn into the Garden through special Divine Mercy, the gates remain those of knowledge and love. The roads leading to these gates, however, are paved with human action. To exist as a human being is to act, and how we act in this life—whether we perform good or evil actions—affects our soul and its ability to love and know God. Therefore, no spiritual path can neglect the plane of action, and Sufism is no exception. Those who reside in the Garden of Truth know and love God, but they have also lived with virtue and acted in goodness, which is of course a basic quality whose effects are not limited to the plane of action. Had it not been so, action would not be relevant. Goodness in action is therefore an essential component of the perfection we seek and complements the attributes of beauty, love, and knowledge of the Truth identified with those who reside in the Garden of Truth, and identified as well with that Garden and of course ultimately with the Gardener.

The Hindus speak of the three yogas of action, love, and knowledge, or the yogas of *karma, bhakti,* and *jñāna,* as discussed in the Bhagavad Gita, of which only the last two can lead to eternal salvation and release from the bondage of limitation. Likewise, Sufis speak of the fear of God, *al-makhāfah;* love of Him, *al-maḥabbah;* and knowledge of Him, *al-ma'rifah.* There is, however, a difference between Hindu and Islamic eschatological doctrines on this issue. In Islam once one reaches Paradise, even if it be based on virtuous actions rooted in faith and not knowledge and love of God, one does not fall from the paradisal state, as is the case in Hinduism, where if one follows only the path of action or *karma yoga,* once one's good karma is exhausted in the next world, one falls again into the realm of the lower levels of *māyā* associated with cycles of birth and death. In any case, to fear God, in contrast to His creatures, is to love Him and move toward Him, and to love Him is to know Him as far as the Sufi perspective is concerned. That is why a *ḥadīth* states, "The beginning of wisdom is the fear of God," echoing the famous dictum of the apostle Paul. Fear of God deals with the level of action and turns the will of the adept away from evil acts, which have a negative effect upon the soul, and toward goodness and virtue.

GOOD AND EVIL ACTS

In the second chapter, on truth, we discussed the metaphysical doctrine of the reality of evil, which states that evil is the result of separation from the Divine Principle, which alone is absolute goodness, and that separation is the cause of what appears on the human plane as evil. Some Sufis, who have fixed their gaze upon the All-Good or the absolute goodness of God, have in fact denied the reality of evil. But, as already mentioned, on the plane of relativity in which we live, evil is real; it is as real as we are in our relative level of existence. It would in fact be a catastrophe for the soul on the road to the Garden of Truth to deny the evil forces within as well as without until it has transcended completely the realm of duality and opposition, until it has reached that absolute Goodness from whence one can deny the reality of evil because one has now gone beyond the domain of relativity, where evil exists.

As Rūmī, who composed so many verses concerning good and evil, said, "There is no absolute evil in the world; evil is relative. Recognize this fact."[2] We can have both a contemplative and an active life. We can contemplate the Supreme Good beyond all evil, but when we act in the world and confine ourselves to the external world of action, which in fact constitutes most of our ordinary life, we face the reality of good and evil, appearing to us as absolutes and irreducible opposites. For example, if we act to save a human life, that is considered an act of goodness, whereas if we act to kill or destroy human life, that is seen as evil, and the two types of action stand opposed to each other. It is this opposition between good and evil that is the basis of morality.

The soul has several faculties and dimensions. In the realms of knowledge and love the dichotomy of good and evil can be transcended. But in the part of our soul that is attached to and concerned with the world of action, good and evil remain as irreducible opposites and absolute on their own level. That is why religious scholars and even some of those opposed to religious ethics speak of moral absolutes. While the Sufis understand the claims of morality to absoluteness on this level, they seek to go beyond the realm of external action altogether and through love and knowledge of the Divine reach absolute Goodness, which transcends the opposition of good and evil and sees the relativity of what we call evil in relation to the absolutely Good and the absolutely Real. That is wherein Sufi ethics, which is a spiritualized ethics, differs from ordinary religious morality, while at the same time the Sufis attach great importance to morality on its own level.

Contemplatives in general, whether Sufi or otherwise, realize the relativity of all that is relative, including evil, and see evil as the absence of good. Without denying evil on its own level, they seek to transcend duality altogether through knowledge and love. Yet they remember that although they are transcending the duality of good and evil, they are not negating the significance of morality on its own level as they reach a reality even while they are in the relative domain that is in itself the All-Good. There is simply no ontological equivalence between good and evil. The latter is like a shadow of the former, which is a form of existence possessing reality. The problem is that for those caught in the shadows of earthly existence, the shadows are as real as themselves, and therefore they can hardly discern the shadow for what it is. The only hope of such people is to act according to the good, that is, to perform correct and virtuous actions in order to be able to leave the world of darkness for that of light and the relative for the Absolute. They can of course also turn to the paths of knowledge and love, but these paths also require good rather than evil action on the part of those who would aspire to follow them.

THE RELATION OF ACTION TO THE SOUL

God wants not our actions but our soul, but He judges our actions precisely because they affect our soul. There seems to be, from the external point of view, a vicious circle. The state of our soul determines what kind of action we perform, and our acts affect the state of our soul. Both of these assertions are true, but there is no vicious circle involved because we are beings with consciousness and the twin faculties of intelligence and will. Moreover, we possess a will that is free. Otherwise, the moral bearing of our actions would be meaningless. We must therefore begin where we are with our consciousness and then through discernment, which is a function of the intelligence, and the aid of revelation distinguish between good and evil and through our free will do that which is good, being always aware that how we act in turn affects the state of our soul.

As the Prophetic saying stated at the beginning of this chapter asserts, God judges our actions by our intentions. If the soul intends to do good but the action it undertakes results in what from the immediate human point of view appears as evil, then God judges the soul not according to the consequent evil but according to the original good intention. The judgment by God of human actions on the Day of Judgment, according to Islam, Christianity, and other religions, is therefore not opposed to the fact that our souls belong to God and it is our souls that He wants. Every evil act creates a blemish upon the soul, and every good act helps to purify and perfect the soul and is essential to the cultivation of the virtues, to which we shall turn in the next chapter.

We are beings who know, love, and act, and there is an interplay between our being and our knowing, loving, and acting. Ontologically our being comes before everything else, but existentially our knowing, loving, and acting are the realities that fill the moments of our lives and of which we are aware. Our soul knows, loves, and acts—the latter primarily through the body. Moreover, knowing and loving both affect our actions and are often expressed through them. Furthermore, all three affect our mode of being while our mode of being and level of consciousness determine what we know and can know, what we love and can love, and how we act.

Although there is no way to enter into intimacy with God save through knowledge and love—which also require faith—action remains, therefore, of the greatest importance on the path to the Garden, action not in itself but in how it affects the soul and how it reflects its intentions, both hidden and manifest. To know God is to love Him, and to love Him is to surrender our will to Him. Now, surrender is already a form of action. Furthermore, from the point of view of spiritual realization, one must begin with surrender to the Divine Will, or *islām,* which involves the plane of action and which also includes the fear of God, hence abstention from evil acts. This total surrender combined with abstention from that which separates us from God and is displeasing to Him leads to loving Him, and that love leads those with the necessary contemplative qualities to the knowledge of God.

Correct human action requires, furthermore, for fallen humanity, whose innate intelligence is no longer functioning as God created it, the presence of revelation and faith in that revelation. Human intelligence has become too deeply hidden in the hearts of almost all of us to be able to discern by itself between truth and falsehood, beauty and ugliness, and good and evil. It needs the help of the objective manifestation of the Divine Intellect or Logos/Word. This manifestation we call revelation, including its formal dimension concerned with religious rites and ethics. Furthermore, the will, which is free to accept or reject revelation, is called upon to attach itself to this theophany of the Sacred. That is what is called faith (*al-īmān*). It is faith that creates the dynamic within the soul to follow divine commands and to abstain from what the revealed sources consider to be evil. This *īmān* in turn leads to *iḥsān,* the virtue and beauty that must be attained in order to enter the Garden of Truth. That is why mystics in different religious climates have clung to the ethical teachings of their religion and its formal rites even while journeying in the illimitable sky of the Formless.

A great deal of debate has taken place in Christianity about whether it is faith or works that are the means of salvation. In Islam in general, and Sufism in particular, both have been emphasized. Faith is necessary for salvation, but faith must also lead to deeds acceptable in the eyes of God as determined by the Divine Law (*al-Sharī'ah*). All true Sufis begin with the *Sharī'ah,* which belongs primarily to the plane of action, and no matter how far they travel upon the path they remain faithful to its teachings. As long as we remain as human beings here on earth, we must perform acts of one kind or another. We can, therefore, never transcend the Divine Law. We can go beyond the legal teachings, which concern correct human action, only by transcending the level of action altogether through love and knowledge of the Divine.

Actions continue to have an effect upon the human soul as long as we are able to act according to our free will. At the moment of death our hands become cut off from acting in the world and our souls return to God, but they take with them the effects that our actions have made upon them. That is why human actions have a significance beyond this world. This includes both good and evil acts, for both leave an imprint upon our immortal souls. That is why also the road to the Garden is paved by our actions while the gates to the Garden are those of love and knowledge. Furthermore, those who, in contrast to the Sufis, remain bound to the realm of action in this world without reaching the realities of Divine Love and Knowledge but who have lived in goodness and performed virtuous acts will follow the path to the Garden of Truth in the next life, as Sufis seek to do here and now.

THE FRUITS OF ACTION AND DETACHMENT: SINCERITY IN ACTION AND CHIVALRY

All actions bear fruit of one kind or another whether we are aware of those fruits or not. To every action there is a reaction, and this principle is not only a law of classical physics but also holds true morally and cosmically. That is what the traditions that came from India call the law of karma. Our good acts bear positive fruit even if not immediately, and our evil acts have negative consequences that boomerang upon us sooner or later. The great moralist Persian poet who lived in the thirteenth century, after whom Ralph Waldo Emerson named one of his most famous poems, that is, Sa'dī, said:

> Do a goodly act and cast it into the Tigris River,
> For God will recompense thee in the desert.

The spiritual person who seeks the Garden, however, performs an act of goodness not for the sake of recompense but because of goodness itself, leaving the rest in the Hands of God. To be able to have the correct spiritual attitude toward action, one must become detached from the fruits of action. Detachment is a cardinal virtue required before one advances on the path. One must act for the sake of the Truth and in total detachment from the fruits of the act. This is of course much more easily said than done. There is a famous story in the *Mathnawī* of Rūmī that epitomizes the correct spiritual attitude toward selfless and detached action. It begins with the verse:

> Learn from 'Alī sincerity in action,
> Know that the Lion of God is untainted by blemish.[3]

In a battle 'Alī confronted a powerful enemy and after a fierce fight was able to throw the enemy to the ground and sit on his chest with his sword drawn. At this moment the enemy warrior spat in 'Alī's face, whereupon 'Alī immediately disengaged himself and abstained from delivering a blow with his sword. The enemy warrior, who was an idol worshipper, had never seen such an event. He became agitated and asked 'Alī why he had not killed him. The response of 'Alī, which in the verses of the *Mathnawī* constitutes one of the masterpieces of Sufi poetry, was that 'Alī was fighting at first for the preservation of the Truth, but once the enemy warrior spat in his face 'Alī became angry, and he would never react on the basis of anger and certainly not get into a battle or slay someone for personal or selfish reasons. In Rūmī's words, 'Alī responded:

> Said he, "I wield the sword for the sake of the Truth,
> I am the servant of the Truth not the functionary of the body.
> I am the lion of the Truth, not the lion of passions,
> My action does witness bear to my religion."

'Alī is said to have been the founder of spiritual chivalry (*futuwwah* in Arabic and *jawānmardī* in Persian), and this story bears witness to what constitutes the very essence of chivalry, namely, sincere and detached action devoted to a noble cause. Chivalry combines action with selflessness, actions devoid of worldly motifs or tainted by vices such as anger, covetousness, lust for power, or thirst for revenge. It is far from accidental that in Islam orders of chivalry became integrated into certain schools of Sufism and that within the Sufi tradition it is expected that those who aspire to march upon the path to the Garden of Truth possess the virtue of chivalry.

There is much talk of *jihād* today, both in the West and among certain Muslim extremists, most of whom are unaware of their own tradition. The word *jihād* means not war but exertion in the path of God. And then there is, according to a well-known saying of the Prophet, the inner or greater *jihād,* which is the constant battle of the followers of the spiritual path to correct the imperfections of their soul and make it worthy of inhabiting the Garden. This is the highest form of inner action. There is also the lesser *jihād,* which can include war to defend oneself, one's family, one's nation, and one's religion. From the spiritual point of view, however, even this kind of *jihād* must be selfless, detached, and not caused by anger or hatred. The fact that this story about 'Alī takes place on a battlefield, as does the great Hindu classic the Bhagavad Gita, demonstrates that selfless and detached action must extend to even that most trying and violent form of human action that is war.

Detachment from the fruits of one's actions is not unrelated to the Chinese doctrine of *wu-wei,* that is, to act without acting. Our ordinary actions plunge our souls into the cosmic chain of actions and reactions, or the chain of karma, as the Hindus would say. But that is because of our attachment to the fruits of our actions and the loss of the contemplative spirit, which reduces the soul to a substance that identifies itself solely with acts rather than with being, with preference for action over contemplation. But to act without acting requires also that one die before dying, as asserted in the famous Prophetic tradition, "Die before you die." It means to detach our will from our passions and impetus toward external actions and surrender it to God. The sage acts without acting like a lamp that illuminates its surroundings by simply existing. The sage contemplates and lives in the dimension of inwardness and by virtue of that interiority has a *sympatheia* with the inner reality of other beings and then acts upon them in the deepest sense without external action. The sage demonstrates in his or her reality the precedence of being over all external accidents and the priority of contemplation over action. But the sage nevertheless does act, and his or her acts are selfless, detached, and based upon sincerity, goodness, compassion, and truthfulness.

THE SPIRITUAL SIGNIFICANCE OF TRADITIONAL COURTESY *(ADAB)*

A term often used by Sufis is found also in most of the major languages of the Islamic peoples. It is *adab,* which means at once comportment, courtesy, culture, refined speech, literature, correct ethical attitudes, and many other concepts. It is really untranslatable and perhaps should be used in English in its Arabic form like terms such as *karma* and *guru,* which have entered English recently from Sanskrit, or *jihād* from Arabic. All traditional societies have tried to inculcate their own forms of *adab* within members of society from childhood, and Islamic civilization is no exception. For traditional Muslims, *adab* encompasses nearly all aspects of life from greeting people to eating to sitting in a gathering to entering a place of worship. As for quintessential *adab,* it has always been associated by Sufis with the actions and words of the Prophet himself. *Adab* is the means of controlling the passions, which affect and often originate human actions. It is also a way of formalizing human actions in such a way that they display harmony and beauty rather than disorderliness and ugliness. *Adab* even disciplines the body and brings out its innate dignity and its theomorphic nature and teaches us how to carry ourselves in a manner that is worthy of the human state. Its goal is to control the ego and the passions and to inculcate the virtues of humility and charity within the human soul as well as bring out the majestic aspect of our existence. It is therefore closely related to spiritual discipline and is of great value in performing acts of goodness. It teaches us to discipline ourselves and to prepare the soul for that supreme sacrifice of its will and being before the altar of the Absolute, which is also Truth, Beauty, Love, and Goodness, qualities that are reflected in one way or another in the quintessential *adab* of traditional Islam beyond all cultural and ethnic idiosyncrasies. No one on the path to the Garden can be devoid of inward *adab*.

TO ACT WITH TRUTH— TO ACT WITH LOVE AND COMPASSION: THE SPIRITUAL EFFICACY OF ACTION

Of course not all actions possess spiritual efficacy although every action leaves its effect upon the soul in one way or another. The most efficacious of all actions from the spiritual point of view is of course prayer, to which we shall turn shortly. But first of all we must deal with the relation between action and truth as well as action and love combined with compassion. Action does not produce truth; that is the function of knowledge. But action based on truth can lead to the concrete realization of the truth. In this sense should the famous Arabic proverb, "Knowledge without action is like a tree without fruit," quoted in so many Sufi texts, be understood. First of all, correct action, if it is to be spiritually efficacious, has to be based on truth and not falsehood. Many a person has performed actions that have resulted in catastrophic results even if the actor did not have such consequences in mind. The reason is that such actions have been based on falsehood and ignorance. Most of the tragedies of the modern world are based on some level not on the truth but on falsehood and belong to this category. They are actions based on ignorance of the real nature of humanity, the world, and the Divine Principle.

Knowledge of the truth is in turn related to action, albeit in an indirect manner. The veils covering the soul prevent it from seeing the truth, and these veils act as obstacles for our intelligence and prevent it from reaching the truth. Correct action, rooted in the good and the true, has the effect of removing these veils and allowing us to know the truth in more than an abstract manner. In this way knowledge is related to action in the process of realizing the truth as, conversely, correct action must be based on the truth. Action does not in itself produce knowledge, but within human beings and on the path to the Garden they are in a sense inseparable until one reaches the Abode of the One beyond the realm of all action and discursive thought based on the duality of subject and object. Furthermore, it is our actions that prove whether our knowledge of the Truth has been only theoretical or has become deeply rooted in our soul. Action based on truthfulness, especially such actions as prayer, charity, sacrifice, and truthful speech, help the knowledge of the Truth to become actualized in the soul. At all moments of human life a person who knows the truth must act according to the truth. In any case, no one can enter the Garden of Truth whose actions in this world have not been based on truth. Furthermore, no action here below is of any spiritual value if not based on truth.

The famous saying that the road to hell is paved with good intentions must not be interpreted as negating the primacy of our intentions over our actions. Rather, this saying refers indirectly to the necessity of basing actions on the truth. Action based on falsehood or ignorance rather than the truth can lead to the most negative consequences even if one holds good intentions. The Sufis would confirm this saying attributed by many to St. Augustine while insisting that God judges our actions according to our intentions. They add, furthermore, that our intentions must be pure and that knowledge of the truth (*al-'ilm*) always precedes action (*al-'amal*). Surely God does not judge us negatively for what we do not know if there is no means at our disposal to overcome our ignorance. But that does not alter the reality that in order to be spiritually efficacious, action must be based upon the truth, especially for those who want to set out upon the path to the Garden of Truth. To be based upon the truth means of course to be in accord with the profound reality and nature of things and also according to God's Will to the extent that we are able to know that Will. It must be in accordance with justice and characterized by compassion and goodness, which are inseparable from the very substance of things not in their outward appearance but as they are in their inner reality and at the root of their existence.

To act with truth is also to act with love and compassion because truth is ultimately reality and love flows through all levels of cosmic reality, in the arteries of the universe. Action carried out on the basis of passions and selfish desires can lead to gain or loss in the short run according to circumstance but will always bring about negative consequences in the long run. But love is like knowledge. The more one gives, the more one gains. To act with love means to always give without expectation of receiving in return. But because action with love breaks the walls of the ego and makes us realize that deep down the other is also our self, one receives the greatest recompense in return. As we saw earlier, it is God's command for us to love the neighbor and treat him or her as ourselves, as asserted by Christ as well as the Prophet. But in order for these acts of love to be spiritually efficacious, they must be based on our love for God. As for knowledge, the more one teaches to a student, the more one becomes a master of the knowledge that one transmits; in the same way that the more one gives of one's love, the more one experiences love. To act with love toward the other, however, without love for God is to act against the truth, for in truth the other, like us, comes from God, and it is His love for His creation that makes possible our love for the other.

Of course, no action with truth or love is possible without what the Abrahamic religions call the fear of God. There is an element in the soul that must be controlled through the fear of God in order for the flowers of illuminative knowledge and spiritual love to grow in the soil of the soul. We have already stated that Muslims do not believe in original sin, but they do believe in the fall (*al-hubūṭ*) of men and women from their state of primordial perfection. As the Quran asserts, "We created man in the best of stature; then reduced him to the state of the lowest of the low" (Quran 95:4–5). The Quran also refers to the soul of fallen humanity as possessing an element that commands and incites the soul to evil (*al-nafs al-ammārah bi'l-sū'*). This element did not exist in actuality in the Edenic state before the fall, but after the fall it became a part of the human soul. Hence the necessity of the fear of God, which serves to control this powerful element that exists within fallen humanity and that has become practically second nature to us.

Sufism, which contains the science and the art of curing the ailments of the soul, speaks often of this passionate and evil-inciting *nafs.* In fact, the word *nafs,* which means soul or psyche, is often used in Sufi texts to signify this lower element of the soul and not the higher elements, which participate in the final wedding between the soul and the Spirit. Even the most exalted Sufi texts on love and knowledge remind us of the necessity of fearing God before being able to love and know Him; they emphasize that action cannot be performed with truth and love unless it is based on reverential fear of the One who in contrast to His creatures draws us toward Himself even through fear of Him.

Coming back to action with love, a word must also be said about the role of compassion in Islam in general and Sufism in particular. Although God is just and majestic and also the Supreme Judge who judges our actions and can become wrathful if human beings do not act according to His Will and in goodness, according to the already stated sacred *ḥadīth* it is written on the Divine Throne, "Verily, my Mercy (compassion) precedeth my Wrath." The Arabic word used in this saying is *raḥmah,* which means at once goodness, mercy, and compassion. This word is related etymologically to the two Divine Names, *al-Raḥmān* and *al-Raḥīm,* which can be translated as the Infinitely Good and All-Merciful or All-Compassionate. These two Names along with the supreme Name of God in Islam, *Allāh,* constitute the formula called *basmalah* (*Bismi'Llāh al-Raḥmān al-Raḥīm*), with which Muslims begin all human actions worthy before the eyes of God, including such daily acts as starting the day, having a meal, going to sleep, or embarking upon a journey. It is in fact with this formula that this book begins. All the chapters of the Quran except one, moreover, start with this formula.

As mentioned earlier, the whole of the cosmos is understood by Sufis to have become existentiated through *nafas al-Raḥmān,* usually translated as the "Breath of the Compassionate." The Islamic universe is therefore plunged in the ocean of compassion. If we were only to understand the nature of things, we would realize that being compassionate is the most natural thing, in total accord with the deeper nature of all beings, including ourselves. Unfortunately, the imprisoning walls of the ego prevent this compassion from manifesting itself in most cases. The soul needs to be treated of its illness in order to be compassionate.

The Sufis, who aspire to enter the Garden of Truth, emphasize the Divine Mercy and Compassion, which precedes God's Wrath without in any way forgetting the significance of inner discipline and the necessity of living according to God's laws, thus abstaining from actions that can incur His Wrath. Nor do they forget the positive nature of holy anger when one is faced with falsehood and injustice. In Christianity holy anger is even associated with some of the saints and also certain episodes of the life of Christ—in a religion that is predominantly a religion of love. The same is seen in another form in Mahāyāna Buddhism, which emphasizes compassion as the central virtue.

Sufism asks its followers to ponder the meaning of compassion. The English word often used to translate *raḥmah,* that is, *compassion,* reveals through its etymology some of the profoundest meanings of this concept. The term implies coming together and sharing of passion in the sense of ardent love. It also implies sharing the suffering and pain of others as our own. A famous poem of Sa'dī states:

> The children of Adam are members of a single body,
> For from the moment of creation they were made of one substance.
> When fate causes pain in any member,
> The other members cannot remain still.
> O thou who hath no sorrow in seeing the sorrow of others,
> Thou art not worthy of being called a human being.[4]

Although Sa'dī speaks only of the human family in this poem, the virtue of compassion is not to be limited to humanity. Since *all* of the cosmos was existentiated by the "Breath of the Compassionate," our compassion must also extend to all beings, to animals and plants as well as to air and water and also to mountains, deserts, streams, and oceans, all of which have their own mode of life. We need not be compassionate toward the stars because fortunately our actions cannot reach them, at least for now, to pollute and disfigure the heavens as we have done the earth. A partial compassion, which would limit itself to the human species with total disregard for other creatures, is not real compassion, based as it is on the ignorance rather than knowledge of the interconnection of all beings. This partial compassion can in fact lead in the long run to much greater suffering, as the environmental crisis demonstrates so amply. In the same way, a sentimental charity devoid of the truth has led to some of the most ruthless social and political upheavals of the past century, as one sees in Communism, which is based on charity toward the poor and compassion for the working class while denying the reality of God, whose love and compassion for His creatures make possible our compassion toward others. On the level of action there must be both knowledge and love combined with compassion in order for the action to be efficacious, while conversely righteous action itself prepares the soul for ascent to the realms of love and knowledge and access to the Garden of Truth by freeing its wings from the fetters of this world and selfish actions.

DETACHMENT AND SURRENDER: TO DO GOD'S WILL

The first steps on the path to the Garden of Truth consist of detachment from the world and surrender to God, which means attachment to Him. By *world* we mean here not theophanies and signs of God that surround us even in this terrestrial abode, but the world as the veil that covers the truth and disperses our soul. The roots of our fallen human soul are sunk deeply in the soil of this world. The first action to take is to pluck these roots out of that which is transient and evanescent and sink them into the Divine Reality. At first this Divine Reality appears as unreal since our soul has become externalized and scattered, depending only on the outer senses for its awareness of what is real and what is illusory. Awakening from the sleep of forgetfulness, which is the necessary condition for following the path, brings about the realization that the world that we usually take as being the sole reality is itself a dream. The Prophet once said, "Man is asleep and when he dies he awakens." Spiritual discipline in Sufism commences with what is called "initiatic death" followed by awakening. Through the rite of initiation into a Sufi order, the disciple is supposed to die to his or her old self to be born anew. It is this transformation that is called initiatic death, and it is also found in the esoteric dimension of other traditions, including the Greek mystery religions.

The uprooting of the soul from this world requires the action of detachment and living in such a way as to be pure. It is to wear already inwardly the white shroud in which Muslims are wrapped when they are buried. The virtue connected with this detachment, combined with purity, has been often associated in Sufism with *taqwā,* or reverential fear of God combined with purity of action and mindfulness. This word is one of the most often used terms in the Quran and is hardly translatable into a single English term. In order to follow the path of Sufism one must possess *taqwā,* and the inhabitants of the Garden are all possessors of this virtue in addition to the perfections they have gained through love and knowledge of God. There is nothing more dangerous for the soul, spiritually speaking, than seeking to be drowned in the ocean of Divine Love and becoming illuminated by the Divine Light without *taqwā*. The practice of *taqwā* is at first difficult precisely because it requires detachment from the world and control of our passions, which are like a dragon within. *Taqwā* is like the lance of St. Michael, which is able to slay this dragon before the dragon consumes us with its fire—the fire of hell. The history of Sufism, especially its earliest period, is witness to many Sufi saints who attained supreme gnosis but kept emphasizing the necessity of *taqwā* and the reverential fear of God that it implies.

Detachment from the world must be accompanied by attachment to God through surrender to Him. It might be said that all beings are in surrender (*taslīm*) to God by virtue of existing within the confines of their particular nature as created by God. This is one of the meanings of *muslim,* that is, being in surrender to God. But we differ from other creatures in having free will. We therefore are free to surrender our will to God or rebel against the Will of Heaven. God has given this free will precisely because in humanity He created a being worthy of being His interlocutor, a being reflecting all the Divine Names and Qualities, a being whom He loves and who can and should love God. As mentioned before, on the human plane love cannot be based on coercion if it is to be real love. The lover values the love of his or her beloved precisely because this love is given in freedom and is based on free will. In any case, basing ourselves on our consciousness and immediate experience, we have the certitude of having free will. It must be remembered, however, that we have relative free will on the level of our own reality, which is itself relative, and that we cannot possess absolute freedom while bound to this relative state of existence. We can gain absolute freedom only by transcending our relative mode of existence and becoming immersed in the illimitable ocean of divine and absolute Reality.

To gain that absolute freedom we must exercise our relative freedom in giving up this freedom and surrendering our will to God, thereby becoming attached to Him. This action, which complements detachment from the world, must begin with surrender, *islām,* which in Arabic means both surrender and gaining of peace. This surrender must also be combined with confidence in God (*tawakkul*). In human life we often surrender our will to the will of someone we love, but even this kind of surrender becomes sometimes difficult. How much more difficult it is to surrender our will to God, whom most of us have not as yet experienced! Nevertheless, since God resides at the center of our being, with faith in Him those who aspire to reach Him surrender their will to Him as we see in the case of Bāyazīd Basṭāmī discussed previously. This great Sufi did not will this or that but his only wish was not to will so that he would not desire anything independent of what God willed for him. He also said the prince of this world is one who cannot choose anything because God has already chosen for him.

The Lord's Prayer, uttered by Christ himself, states, "Thy Will be done on earth." For Muslims the doing of God's Will on earth begins with the practice of the *Sharī'ah* or Divine Law, which Islam considers as the concrete embodiment of the Divine Will for its followers. Not only are we free, however, to follow or not follow the injunctions of the *Sharī'ah,* but the teachings of the *Sharī'ah* still leave many domains and arenas of life to our discernment and free will. That is why it is not easy to be certain that we are doing God's Will in so many of our activities.

Throughout history there have been figures in Islam, Christianity, and other religions who wreaked havoc upon society and committed the worst kinds of injustice and iniquitous acts by claiming to be doing the Will of God. That is why Sufism emphasizes the necessity of *taqwā,* or reverential fear of God, before claiming to do God's Will in this world, for the gaining of *taqwā* is itself the first act that God wishes us to perform. Surrendering one's will to Him necessitates having the free will to surrender. But how can we surrender our free will to God if our will is still a slave of our passions and in surrender to the world? There can be no true *taslīm* and *tawakkul* without *taqwā.*

The complete surrender of one's will to God is a high spiritual station transcending the realm of action for it involves the attachment of our whole being to Him and the sacrifice of our passionate ego before the altar of the One. It requires a most difficult form of *jihād* within our souls. The verse of the Quran quoted at the beginning of this chapter addresses the Prophet in these terms: "Thou didst not throw when thou threwest; rather it was God who threw" (Quran 8:17). The spiritual station of "thou didst not throw when thou threwest" (*mā ramayta idh ramayt*[a]) is considered by Sufis to be an extremely exalted spiritual station. For ordinary men and women who believe, there is only one act wherein one can be certain of doing God's Will and that is death. Pious men and women also try to do His Will in their lives by performing righteous actions, such as charitable works, according to the teachings of their religion. Those who aspire to reach the Garden also perform good works, but in addition they seek to be attached to God in such a way that everything they do reflects the Divine Reality within and beyond them rather than the whims and fancies of their passionate souls.

In any case, detachment and attachment on the plane of action involve the various faculties of the soul in countless ways and prepare the soul for the love and knowledge of God. That is why it was mentioned at the beginning of this chapter that the roads to the Garden are paved with correct action. The cycle of fear, love, and knowledge of God, the *makhāfah, maḥabbah,* and *ma'rifah* of Sufism, must be experienced by all souls journeying toward the goal of perfection. The history of Sufism itself is also characterized by these three dimensions of spirituality following one upon the other, from the asceticism of the early Mesopotamian Sufis to the flowering of love especially in the School of Khurasan to the gnostic teachings of a figure such as Junayd and the School of Baghdad and associated especially with the School of Ibn 'Arabī. But in the historical unfolding of Sufism, the later developments contain the earlier ones, and this development in Sufism as a whole must not be considered as progress in the ordinary sense of the term so that one would place later Sufi saints above earlier ones. As for the soul, these stages mark its journey toward its ultimate goal, and the soul contains permanently within itself the spiritual effects of the earlier stages of its journey.

OUR SPIRITS ARE OUR BODIES AND OUR BODIES ARE OUR SPIRITS

An esoteric saying attributed to the Shi'ite Imams says, "Our spirits are our bodies and our bodies are our spirits" (*arwāḥunā ajsādunā wa ajsādunā arwāḥunā*). This saying has many meanings, one of which is that in the other world the effect of our actions on the soul become corporealized. Here, we are not concerned with the eschatological significance of this saying but with its establishing of a direct rapport between the soul and the body. As already mentioned, on the one hand our souls affect our actions, and on the other hand our actions affect our souls, this effect being related especially to the intention behind an act. We are responsible for our actions because we have free will, and this will resides in the soul. I am responsible for what my pen held in my hand is writing right now because I have the free will to not write what you are reading but something else. I am not responsible for the flow of blood in the vessels of my hand at this moment because that is beyond the control of my mind and will. No action, even within our own bodies, can affect our souls spiritually if the soul has no control over that action even if there be physiological and psychological effects. Certain illnesses can bring about depression, and from the other side controlling our anger can reduce our blood pressure.

Spiritually speaking, however, the body as the instrument of our actions interacts with the soul in numerous ways based on our voluntary actions and conscious and free choice. There is also the obvious fact that while we live in this world we are given control over much of our bodies through which we act physically upon the world and receive the effects of the world upon us. While we make the spiritual and moral choice to do or not to do this or that, we use our hands and feet, tongues and eyes, to actualize what the soul has willed according to our intention. Therefore, although from one point of view the body is a prison in this world from which we must try to escape, from another point of view it is our companion on the journey to God. The subtle bodies within us survive physical death, and Muslims, like traditional Christians, believe in corporeal and not only spiritual resurrection. That is why a Sufi philosopher such as Suhrawardī, who lived in the twelfth century, speaks of the body as the "Temple of Light" and other Sufis have spoken of the luminous bodies of saints, as we also see in Orthodox and Catholic Christianity and elsewhere. In a sense, in the posthumous states, we have bodies woven of our actions in this world and the nexus between the soul and body continues beyond the grave. In the spiritual journey we must transcend the plane of action associated with the body for the exalted horizons of Divine Love and Knowledge, but the physical body remains a part of our total reality to be integrated at the end in our full and complete being.

PRAYER: THE INTEGRATING OF BODY, SOUL, AND SPIRIT

In various religions there are three modes of prayer, and Islam is no exception: individual supplications, canonical prayers, and what Sufism, like Christianity, calls the prayer of the heart. Not all the three modes are performed by everyone belonging to an integral religious tradition, but they are certainly all used in Sufism. In Christianity all the three modes can be found in Hesychasm, the mystical dimension of Orthodox Christianity, not to mention the mysticism of the Latin Church. In fact, prayer like metaphysics is universal and found across religious borders. If prayer is discussed in this chapter devoted to action, it is because in most of its forms it is an act but an act that, while often associated with the body including the tongue, transcends the corporeal and unites body, soul, and spirit.

Sufism, as the rest of Islam and also other religions, includes in its practices individual prayers and supplications in which the faithful speak to God in either silence or vocally in their own language and open their hearts to Him. Muslims also perform canonical prayers (*al-ṣalāh*), whose form has descended from Heaven, and through their performance the individual worshipper conforms his or her particular soul to a form and reality that transcends the individual. The movements of the body and what the tongue recites (always in Arabic) were revealed to the Prophet by God, according to Islamic belief; they are not man-made. Through these prayers, the individual grows into a form that transcends him or her. If performed with perfect intention, total concentration, and in-depth understanding, these prayers reintegrate the human being into his or her archetypal reality. In the case of these canonical prayers, the body plays a very important role. Its various postures, all impregnated with profound symbolic significance, help to integrate the soul while also serving as the vehicle for the integration of the body, soul, and spirit. In these conditions the body is seen no longer as a prison of the soul but as its complement, a steed that the soul rides on its way to the Garden. While performing these ritual acts associated with the body as perfectly as possible, the person utters the various verses of the Quran and formulae that together constitute the canonical prayers. If the inner meaning of this mode of prayer is understood, one sees that it contains all the stages for our journey to God. That is why the *ṣalāh* is called the spiritual ascent (*al-mi'rāj*) of the faithful, in allusion to the nocturnal ascent of the Prophet bodily to Heaven from the Dome of the Rock in Jerusalem, the ascent that serves as the prototype for all Sufi journeying to the One.

As for the prayer of the heart, it is associated in Sufism with *dhikr,* or invocation of God's Names. This quintessential form of prayer begins with invocation with the tongue, then with the mind and with our imaginal faculty, and finally with and in the heart, where the Divine Spark has always resided. Inasmuch as the body is the extension and projection of the heart, this prayer can also be associated with prayer by the body, but a body in which the Spirit resides in an active way. Some Hesychast masters considered the saint as a person whose spirit resides completely in his or her body while a Sufi such as Rūmī said that one should invoke until one's toe says, *"Allāh, Allāh."* In this highest form of prayer there is a complete integration of body, soul, and spirit in a consciousness that transcends the individual level.

The *dhikr* is in the final analysis the act of God Himself within us. In reality only God can utter His Name, and in the *dhikr* we become simply the instrument through which God utters His own sacred Name. In the *dhikr* the prayer of Christ, "Thy Will be done," is realized in the most essential way, for in order to invoke with concentration, the one who invokes must surrender all of the will and mind to God and place the whole of his or her being in God's Hands. In this process, the invocation of the Name, whose abode is the heart, transforms not only one's soul, psyche, imagination, and mind, but also the body. We see similar uses of the body in Yoga, certain schools of Buddhism, and many other spiritual disciplines. This quintessential mode of prayer, or the prayer of the heart, also brings about the wedding between action, love, and knowledge as it integrates body, soul, and spirit.

Those who follow the path of action and good works seek to live a righteous life and to enter Paradise when they die. Those who follow the path of love and knowledge seek God here and now and aim at this very moment at the highest Paradise, which is the Garden of Truth, what the Quran calls *Riḍwān,* where the Gardener is to be found, the Paradise that is also here and now in the center of our being. In ordinary prayer men and women address God in an I-Thou relationship. In the prayer that is intertwined with love, the I and the Thou melt into each other. In contemplative prayer, the inner intellect or spirit, which is itself a Divine Spark to which Meister Eckhart refers when he says that there is in the soul something uncreated and uncreatable and that something is the Intellect (*alquid est in anima quod increatus et increabile et hoc est intellectus*), is able to transcend the I-Thou dichotomy altogether. This faculty is able to plunge into the Supreme Reality and, in drowning in the Ocean of Divinity, to know it. It is to these realities that Plotinus was referring when he spoke of the flight of the alone to the Alone. In the *dhikr* all of the elements of our being are integrated, and prayer in its quintessential form becomes the means par excellence for unifying body, soul, and spirit and integrating in our being the paths of action, love, and knowledge.

So far we have traveled a long way by posing the universal questions concerning our identity, origin, and end. We have spoken of the Garden of Truth and the significance of the ways of knowledge, love, and action in our spiritual lives. It is now time to answer concretely the question of how we can reach the Garden of Truth and what are the different components of the path leading to that Garden. In a sense we have completed the description of the *theoria* or vision of what we could also call the mountain of Truth. Let us now turn to the nature of the path leading to its summit and see how we can ascend this path or, in other words, how to reach the gate of the Garden of Truth and gain entry therein.

Five

HOW DO WE REACH THE GARDEN OF TRUTH?

The Path to the One

Guide us upon the straight path.
Quran 1:6

There are as many paths to God as the children of Adam.
Ḥadīth

The spiritual master of the person who has no spiritual master is Satan.
Bāyazīd Basṭāmī

THE STRAIGHT PATH

Five times each day, Muslim men and women all over the world stand before God in prayer and recite the opening chapter of the Quran, which, as already mentioned, includes the verse "Guide us upon the straight path" (Quran 1:6). The straight path concerns our basic relation as human beings to God. To be guided upon the straight path is not only to follow God's Will and His laws here on earth, but in the highest sense it is to ascend to the Divine Reality. To reach the Garden requires following this path of ascent, which, moreover, can be seen as both a journey beyond ourselves to the Reality that is transcendent and a penetration within to that same Reality in its aspect of immanence residing in our heart center. The idea of the Straight Path (*al-ṣirāṭ al-mustaqīm*) is so central to Muslims that they identify Islam as the religion of the straight path. For Sufis it means above all the path of ascent to God. When Sufis recite this verse, they concentrate on the vertical and atemporal rather than the temporal and horizontal trajectory of the path and pray to God to be guided now on the path of ascent and therefore to transcendence of ordinary human consciousness and life, a path that is also one of inwardness, until they reach "there," which is also "here" at the center of our being. According to the *Ḥadīth*, "the heart of the person of faith is the Throne of the All-Good (and Compassionate)," that is, God.

This path leading one from the periphery of the circle of existence to its Center is called in Arabic *al-ṭarīq* or *al-ṭarīqah*, and this is also the term used for a particular Sufi order. As long as we are in the human state, there exists a link that binds us directly to God and a path that we can follow to reach Him whether we accept or reject the Divine and the path leading to Him. As Rūmī said:

> There is a link, without asking how, without analogy,
> Between the Lord of man and the soul of man.[1]

THE PATH

In Islam the path of ascent to God in this life goes back to the origin of the tradition, to the inner dimension of the Quran and the inner reality of the Prophet as the Universal Man. Any integral religion must offer its followers not only guidance for a righteous life in this world and the hope of the beatific vision in the next, but also the means of attaining that vision in this life for those who aspire to intimacy with God while still in this world. Those two dimensions of religion have been often called the exoteric and the esoteric, or inward and outward. It must not be forgotten that in the Quran God Himself is called both the Outward (*al-Ẓāhir*) and the Inward (*al-Bāṭin*). In the same way that the Gospel of John or the Song of Solomon in the Bible are esoteric, certain verses of the Quran have clearly an esoteric meaning, such as "Whithersoever ye turn, there is the Face of God" (Quran 2:115). The *Ṭarīqah* is the way that, if followed, allows us to realize this truth. That is why the full name of the *ṭarīqah* is *al-ṭarīqah ila'Llāh,* the path to God.

Not only certain verses of the Quran but also many of the sayings of the Prophet constitute the revealed and canonical basis for the *Ṭarīqah,* especially those sayings that are called *sacred* sayings, or *al-aḥādīth al-qudsiyyah*. The *ḥadīth* of "I was a Hidden Treasure" mentioned earlier belongs to this category. Among those who were privileged to be companions of the Prophet, many possessed saintly qualities, as we see also in the apostolic period of other religions such as Christianity. But a small number are especially known as those to whom the esoteric teachings of Islam were transmitted, such as Abū Bakr, Abū Dharr al-Ghifārī, and Salmān al-Fārsī. But the main figure in the transmission of the inner teachings of Islam was 'Alī ibn Abī Ṭālib, the first cousin and son-in-law of the Prophet. 'Alī appears at the beginning of the spiritual chain (*al-silsilah*) of almost all *ṭuruq* (plural of *ṭarīqah*) in both the Sunni and the Shi'ite worlds whatever their differences might be on the external role of 'Alī after the death of the Prophet. The famous saying of the Prophet, "I am the city of knowledge and 'Alī is its gate," has been interpreted by followers of the path, who in the eighth century came to be known as Sufis, to mean not just any form of knowledge but knowledge of the Garden of Truth as well as the knowledge that leads to that Garden.

Sufism interacted later with other forms of spirituality and intellectuality, including Christian, Hindu, Buddhist, and Zoroastrian and metaphysical expositions such as Neoplatonism and Hermeticism. These interactions, however, concerned only external forms and symbols or intellectual aids for the expression of the truth. The Sufis sometimes made use of propitious and efficacious symbols and intellectual formulations from other traditions appropriate for pointing to a spiritual reality that is purely Islamic. The essence of Sufism is rooted in the Quranic revelation and the inner reality of the Prophet, and its practice is made possible solely through the transmission of initiatic power (*walāyah/wilāyah*) going back to the Prophet. Gradually, on the basis of these earliest teachings, a number of disciples assembled around spiritual guides, and these assemblies became in turn foundations for the major Sufi orders that appeared later.

WHAT IS *WALĀYAH/WILĀYAH?*

The Arabic root of the terms *walāyah/wilāyah* is *wly.* This root has numerous meanings, including having domination over something, lordship, sanctity, being a master, ruler, friend, and intimate. In Arabic orthography one can read the term in question as both *walāyah* and *wilāyah,* and over the centuries authorities have debated how it should be pronounced since this affects the meaning of the term. That is why I have written it in both forms. To indicate the breadth of meaning of this key concept, it is sufficient to mention that first of all it is related to a Name of God (*al-Walī*). In addition, *wālī* means ruler or governor in the political realm, but also *walī Allāh* means saint (literally, "friend of God") in the intellectual and spiritual sphere. *Mawlā* (from which most likely the Persian term *mullā* derives) had a social meaning in early Islamic history and signified non-Arabs attached to a particular Arab tribe, but it is also an honorific title meaning master as, for example, when reference is made to Rūmī by most of his disciples as Mawlānā, that is, our Master. Furthermore, one of the names of the Mahdī or Twelfth Imam in Shi'ism is Walī al-'aṣr, the Ruler of the Epoch.

Fallen human beings are cut off from the higher or more inward dimensions of their own being and confined to the prison of the ego. Furthermore, the gates to the higher states are locked for the ordinary person. The Sufis believe that in addition to the function of prophecy (*al-nubuwwah*), bestowed upon the Prophet by God, he was also given the initiatic power of *walāyah/wilāyah.* His prophetic function brought about the establishment of the Divine Law or *Sharī'ah,* and his power of *walāyah/wilāyah* the *Ṭarīqah* or the Way through which the doors of this prison are unlocked and the journey beyond the individual self is made possible. Furthermore, he was the "seal of prophecy," and with his death the prophetic cycle came to an end. But the function of *walāyah/wilāyah* continued and has been transmitted from generation to generation until our own day and will continue until the end of time. No Muslim has ever accepted that prophecy continued after the death of the Prophet, while Sufis as well as mainstream Shi'ites believe that we are still living in the cycle of *walāyah/wilāyah* and that the "Muḥammadan Light" and the Muḥammadan grace (*barakah*) continue to be transmitted through initiation and spiritual practice from generation to generation.

In any case, when a person wishes to embark upon the path to the Garden, he or she must find an authentic spiritual master in whom this power is present and receive through a rite that goes back to the Prophet the initiation transmitting the power of *walāyah/wilāyah* to him or her. Through this rite the locks on the door that opens to the path of ascent or inwardness are removed. It is now for the disciple to open the door and to march upon the path to God through spiritual practice and by God's Grace. To become a friend of God or saint, one must be able to fly in the heavenly empyrean lifted by the power of the current of *walāyah/wilāyah* but also to exert effort by using the wings of the soul. There are of course those who are drawn to Heaven through the power of spiritual attraction alone and beyond their will. But they are the exceptions who prove the rule. They are often called *majdhūb,* that is, totally attracted to God and by God, but they cannot guide others because they have not traversed the steps of the path. As for those who have, they are called travelers (singular, *al-sālik*), and they constitute most of those who reach the exalted station of knocking on the door of the gate to the Garden of Truth. They are those who have undergone spiritual training under the direction of an authentic master and have journeyed through all the stages of the path.

THE SPIRITUAL MASTER AND THE DISCIPLE

The Master

In the Quran in chapter 18 (*al-Kahf* verses 65ff.) there is a famous story of Moses, representing here the bringer of Law and hence the exoteric aspect of religion, and Khaḍir (more commonly known as Khiḍr), the mysterious prophet who is associated in Judaism with Elias and the Eliatic function of initiation and spiritual guidance, hence also for Islam the esoteric dimension of religion. Moses asks to accompany him on the journey, but he first refuses until Moses promises not to be critical of any of his actions.

They set out on a boat, and in the middle of the sea Khiḍr begins to drill a hole in the bottom of the boat. Moses protests, and Khiḍr reminds him of his promise. Then they meet a young man whom Khiḍr slays. Again Moses protests, and again Khiḍr reminds him of his promise. Finally they come to a town, where the people refuse them hospitality. Khiḍr and Moses find a wall in ruin whereupon Khiḍr rebuilds the wall. Moses asks him why he did this free of charge in such an inhospitable town whereas he could have been paid for his labor. Khiḍr declares that since Moses keeps criticizing his actions he can no longer travel with Khiḍr, but before departing from Moses he reveals to him the inner meaning of the acts he performed, pointing out through his explanations the truth that every outward form has an inner meaning. Khiḍr tells Moses that he drilled a hole in the boat to prevent it from going farther to a place where a king was confiscating all the ships; since this boat belonged to poor people, Khiḍr wanted to prevent its confiscation. As for the young man, his parents were believers and he was a disbeliever who was oppressing them and going to kill them. God would replace him with pious and merciful progeny. Finally, as for the wall in that town, there was hidden underneath it a treasure belonging to two orphans and left there by a righteous father. He rebuilt the wall so that the treasure would not be unearthed and taken by others but would be preserved until the orphans came of age. Moses and Khiḍr leave the town, but through these new experiences Moses is made aware of the inner reality of things hidden from him before undertaking the journey.

This story is the prototype of the function of the spiritual master to instruct disciples and to reveal to them when they are ripe for the understanding of the inner significance of things. In Sufi literature, in fact, the spiritual master, who is usually called *shaykh, pīr* (both meaning elder), *murshid* (the guide), and *murād* (the person sought by the will of the disciple), is also called the Khiḍr of the spiritual path (*khiḍr-i rāh* in Persian). As Ḥāfiẓ says in one of his famous poems:

> We are traversing darkness, where is the Khiḍr of the Path?
> If he not be here, the fire of deprivation will our worth destroy.[2]

The spiritual wine, the pure wine mentioned in the Quran and cited so often in Sufi works, is at once the fire of Divine Love and the light of illuminative knowledge and gnosis. It is also the invocation of God's Names. The disciple is the vessel, into which this wine is poured once the vessel is emptied of its pungent liquid of selfish passions. The spiritual master is therefore the *saki* who pours the celestial wine into the being of the disciple. The serious seeker is in quest of the authentic *saki* and does not cease his or her quest until the *saki* is found.

> Where art thou O Saki, where art thou?
> Come forth for my soul yearns for that wine,
> That ruby wine tasted by the pure in paradise.
> Come O Saki pour thy wine into the vessel of my soul,
> Wherever thou art, I shall search and find thee,
> And having found thee shall never let thee go,
> Until my thirst is quenched and my being drenched
> In that wine which we drank in the pre-eternal dawn,
> And shall drink again in the beatific eve of our earthly life.[3]

A *shaykh* or spiritual master may be appointed by his or her own master, or the function may descend from Heaven upon the person. In both cases there is need of divine investiture. Throughout history many people have pretended to be masters and at no time as much as now, especially in the West. During the past century there have appeared a number of so-called Sufi circles in both America and Europe that disassociate Sufism from Islam and that claim as so-called masters some whose attachment to the traditional chain of transmission of esoteric power and authority (*silsilah*) is either absent, suspect, or mysteriously hidden. A case in point is Gurdjieff, who claimed in the early twentieth century in France to be disseminating Sufi teachings without ever demonstrating his attachment to an authentic Sufi chain. Or one could mention Idris Shah, who sought to teach Sufism independent of Islam in America and Europe. The authenticity of a master is judged by the quality of his or her disciples for as the proverb states, a tree is judged by its fruit. But there are also some external criteria for determining who is a real master, such as orthodoxy in the deepest sense and not only on the formal plane, familiarity with the doctrine, mastery in being able to cure the ailments of the soul, spiritual authority, and an element of sanctity. The master may be old or young, male or female, Arab, Persian, Turk, or from any other ethnicity but in all cases must exude something of the Muḥammadan grace, or *barakah,* and display knowledge of the path for which he or she is the guide. One of the greatest Sufi masters of the past century writes in a poem that pertains to himself:

> Friends, if the truth of my state ye have understood,
> Here lies your path before you: follow in my footsteps,
> For by Heaven, here are no doubts, no vague imaginings;
> I know God, with a knowledge part secret, part proclaimed.
> I drank the cup of love, and then possessed it,
> And it hath become my possession for all time.
> God reward him who lavished his Secret upon me,
> For bounty, true bounty, is to bestow the Secret.
> I hid the Truth on a time, and screened It well;
> And whoso keepeth God's Secret shall have his reward.
> Then when the Giver vouchsafed that I might proclaim It,
> He fitted me—how I know not—to purify souls,
> And girded upon me the sword of steadfastness,
> And truth and piety, and a Wine He gave me,
> Which all who drink must needs be always drinking,
> Even as a drunk man seeketh to be more drunk.
> Thus came I to pour It—nay, it is I that press It.
> Doth any other pour It in this age?[4]

This poem contains the basic features of being a true Sufi master, including the ability to guard the secrets of God as well as to divulge what needs to be divulged to those ready to receive it. Sufism is sometimes called the School of Secrets (*asrār*), the latter term referring to the Divine Mysteries. The function of the master is to receive those Mysteries, realize that Divine Knowledge, attain the wine, and pour it into each cup, that is, the being of each disciple according to his or her capacity. The master represents the authority of the Prophet in the domain of *walāyah/wilāyah* and reflects within his or her own being the Divine Names of Mercy as well as Rigor. But above all the master is a reflection on the human plane of the Divine Name, the Guide (*al-Hādī*), by virtue of which he or she is able to pour the wine into the cups of the being of the disciples.

Not everyone, even if initiatically qualified, is meant to be the disciple of every master he or she encounters, even if that disciple be qualified, nor is every master appropriate for every disciple even if he or she be spiritually authentic. There are different human types and various dimensions to the vast spiritual reality that Sufism embraces. In the same way that through His Mercy God has revealed different religions to correspond to the needs of different human collectivities and within Islam has made possible the development of many Sufi orders, within each of which He has brought forth *shaykhs* with various characteristics. It is natural that members of a particular order will aggrandize and in some cases even absolutize the stature of their own master, as many followers of a religion absolutize their own religion and the message of its founder. In both cases there is an element of absoluteness present. The "sense of the absolute" in a religion or in an authentic spiritual path does not, however, negate other authentic paths or other religious traditions since they also come from the Absolute.

Today there are not as many great Sufi masters as in days of old. And yet one can find authentic masters in both East and West even amid so much pseudo-Sufism. This type of phenomenon—claiming Sufi origins but being usually cut off from Islam—flourishes, unfortunately, so easily in the West today, whereas the authentic Sufi master and his or her teachings that are deeply rooted in the Islamic tradition and always begin with the foundations of the Divine Law or *Sharī'ah* has greater difficulty functioning appropriately. The role of the disciple is to seek an authentic master, one to whom he or she can submit completely. The person seeking guidance must always remember the initiatic saying of Christ, "Many are called but few are chosen."

The Disciple

Many have asked, if there is revelation and the Divine Law, why does one need a master? It needs to be made clear first of all that the Sufi master does not correspond to a priest, who acts as an intermediary between the laity and God in high-church Christianity. In Islam the priestly function is divided among the faithful and all Muslims face God directly in the canonical prayers, which correspond in many ways to the Christian Eucharist. The difference between the two is that (in high liturgical traditions) the latter needs the presence of a priest or ordained minister, while in the Muslim canonical prayers each Muslim, man or woman, performs the priestly function himself or herself. The role of the Sufi master is something else. It involves guidance in climbing the cosmic mountain and even flying beyond it, transcending the ordinary human state. The practice of religion, which is meant for everyone, is like walking on level ground or this "horizontal straight path." The Sufi path, however, is like mountain climbing or the "vertical straight path." Anyone who is able to walk can do so on this "horizontal path" by himself or herself, and of course with Divine confirmation, for even on the horizontal plane one can become lost. Mountain climbing is, however, something else. Especially in high mountains one cannot do it without an experienced guide as well as, of course, Divine aid. Now, the cosmic mountain is vastly higher than the peaks of the Himalayas, and one needs a guide to reach its peak and to ascend ever further to the Infinite Reality beyond the cosmos. Yes, some have achieved the climb successfully without a human guide, through the agencies of what Sufism calls "absent" or invisible guides (*rijāl al-ghayb*), such as Khiḍr, or the Hidden Imam. But they represent the exception and not the rule. In Sufism the duties laid upon the shoulders of the disciples require their being active and not only in a passive state of waiting for graces to descend from Heaven, although he or she must posess both active and passive perfection. That is why the disciple is called *murīd,* that is, the person who exercises his or her will, or *sālik,* which means traveler. It is as a traveler seeking to reach the peaks that the disciple has need of a guide, who is none other than the spiritual master.

The very term *disciple* implies discipline. The potential disciple (*murīd,* also called *faqīr* or *darwīsh*) must have several basic qualities in order to be a viable candidate for the Sufi path. That person must first of all become dissatisfied with his or her present state and realize the need for perfection. One cannot pour anything into a cup that is already full. The candidate must therefore have a yearning (*ṭalab*) for God and for his or her own perfection. That person must also possess enough intelligence to realize that this world is transient and ultimately unreal while God is permanent and the Real and that we must attach ourselves to what is Real. He or she must also possess ardor (*himmah*) and a strong will (*irādah*) to actually march upon the path. Above all, the potential disciple must have faith, love God, and have the yearning to know and encounter Him to such an extent that he or she is willing to sacrifice and undergo the necessary discipline to accomplish this task here and now rather than waiting for the afterlife.

Some think that entering Sufism will correct psychological imbalances. Of course, Sufism possesses a science of the cure of the soul, with which we shall deal soon. Spiritual cure, however, is one thing and clinical treatment of psychological illnesses another. Usually the adept must be psychologically wholesome and balanced, which does not mean spiritually perfect. In fact, if a soul were perfect, of what use would the path be? The *Ṭarīqah* is the school wherein the soul gains perfection, but this school is not for everyone. Initiatic requirements include a psyche healthy enough to be able to bear the weight of the spiritual practices and disciplines of the way.

THE DISCIPLINES OF THE WAY: THE PRACTICES OF THE SUFIS

The first practical question that arises for an aspirant of the path as well as those seeking general knowledge of Sufism in its operative aspect is "what do Sufis do?" And the simple answer is that they undergo a set of physical, psychological, and spiritual disciplines and perform certain practices that make progress upon the path to the Garden of Truth possible. These disciplines begin with the practices of the rites of the *Sharī'ah,* such as the daily canonical prayers, fasting, pilgrimage, and obeying the general moral injunctions of Islam, which bear many similarities to those of Judaism and Christianity. In contrast to what many have written, the vast majority of Sufis are among the most observant of all Muslims in the performance of the *Sharī'ite* rites, and if this or that Sufi wrote verses pointing to the meaning behind the rites at the expense of outer forms, the aim was to bring out the spiritual dimension of religious practice, not to flout it. Rūmī, who sang,

> O people who have gone to the *ḥajj,* where are you, where
> are you;
> The Beloved is here come, come

and who called the heart the real Ka'bah (the cubic temple in Mecca built according to Muslims by Abraham and considered to be the house of God), performed the rites of the *ḥajj* himself. And Ibn 'Arabī, who wrote of theophanic prayer, never missed the daily canonical prayers. A very small number of Sufis in each epoch, who were in a state of spiritual attraction so intense it might be called spiritual drunkenness, did not perform the rites, but even for them there is a *Sharī'ite* reason, which is that a drunken person should not perform the sacred rites. For the vast majority of Sufis, the basis of discipline and practice is the prescribed rites of Islam, which they share with other Muslims while seeking to be aware of their inner meaning in performing them.

Sufis also try to follow the actions or wont (*Sunnah*) of the Prophet to the extent possible and are known as close followers of Prophetic *Sunnah* within the traditional Islamic community. We shall discuss the imitation of the Prophet below, but here suffice it to say again that the Sufis seek to be aware of the inner significance of their acts while imitating consciously the quintessential *Sunnah* of the Prophet, and this includes constantly reciting the Quran, which punctuates their lives as it did the life of the person to whom it was revealed. Of course he was the Prophet and the Quran is the Word of God revealed through him so that something of his soul is to be found in the Quran while a Sufi, no matter how exalted his or her spiritual station, cannot gain such an intimacy with the Sacred Text. Nevertheless, frequent recitation of the Quran in emulation of the Prophet brings nearness to God and constitutes an essential Sufi practice. Ibn 'Arabī once said that one should continue to recite Quranic verses until one reaches a state in which one feels as if the Quran were being revealed to the reciter at the moment of the recitation.

It is on the firm basis of these acts and the corresponding states of the soul of the person performing them that the practices specific to Sufism take place. I mentioned in the last chapter quintessential prayer, which in Islam is called *dhikr,* that means invocation, remembrance, and mention. This practice constitutes the central reality of the life of the Sufis. God has revealed certain of His Names in the Quran and thereby sanctified them. In a mysterious way He is present in His Names. To reach the Named, one must invoke the Name (*Ism*) after receiving initiation and under the guidance of a qualified master. One must be present with all of one's being in the invocation until the invoker, the invocation, and the Invoked (*dhākir, dhikr,* and *madhkūr*) become one beyond all limitations of individual existence.

Human beings, moreover, possess mental activity, an activity that is, however, usually dispersed. For most men and women, especially in this age, no mental activity is more difficult than concentration and meditation. As Rūmī says, we are not masters of our thoughts; our thoughts are our masters. Therefore, we need to make use of various forms of meditation, which aid the soul in remaining in the *dhikr* and being able to concentrate on the Reality whose Sacred Name is being invoked. According to Sufism, it is easy to become a saint because all we have to do is to put ourselves through invocation in the Divine Name and put the Divine Name in our heart. But at the same time it is very difficult because we lack the concentration to remain in the Name and do not even know where our spiritual heart, this center of our being, is since it has become covered by a hard crust as a result of our fall and forgetfulness of our true identity. Every Sufi order therefore teaches certain methods of meditation to enable those who embark upon the path to be able to concentrate upon and remain in the *dhikr,* with their minds and imaginal faculties and, in a more advanced stage, with their hearts and even bodies, as well as with their tongues. While forms of *dhikr* are similar in most Sufi orders, forms of meditation differ from one order to another, as do litanies (*awrād,* plural of *wird*), which are usually recited between the canonical prayers and the *dhikr.*

The basic Sufi practice of *dhikr* is therefore combined with *fikr* or meditation and is primarily carried out alone either in spiritual retreat (*khalwah*) or in daily practices at certain moments put aside for this central practice. The *dhikr* involves repetition of a Divine Name or formula sanctified by the revelation, while *fikr* is meditation upon some aspect of the Divine Reality and/or Its manifestations. *Fikr* allows the invoker to concentrate upon the *dhikr* and prevents the mind from wandering. The *dhikr* can also be performed in a gathering of Sufis (*jalwah*) usually in an audible manner and in unison, but sometimes silently. This gathering or assembly is called a *majlis.* It is a sacred gathering that fortifies one's inner life and brings great grace or *barakah* to those fortunate enough to participate in it. It is led by the spiritual master or one of his or her representatives.

THE SPIRITUAL CONCERT *(SAMĀ')*

The *majlis* is usually combined with the performance of Sufi songs and a sacred dance that brings the Divine Presence right into the body. In many orders only a drum is used, while in others different traditional instruments such as the reed flute and stringed instruments are employed in addition to percussion. In the old days such gatherings were open only to the members of the order, and this remains true in many cases even today. But some orders now allow outside observers, chief among them the Khalwatī-Jarrāhī and Mawlawī of Turkey. The Mawlawī Order, founded by Jalāl al-Dīn Rūmī, has developed the most elaborate spiritual concert associated with a whirling that symbolizes the movements of the heavens. This beautiful spiritual concert has attracted the attention of many Westerners, including European travelers to the East in the nineteenth century, and as a result some have associated Sufism with the whirling dervishes.

Most of the classical music of the Islamic peoples has been deeply influenced by Sufism and is meant to be interiorizing, as one sees in the major classical traditions of western Arabic (including Andalusian), eastern Arabic, Persian, Turkish, and north Indian music. Many of the greatest performers of these traditions belonged and still belong to Sufi orders while many orders such as the Mawlawiyyah in the Ottoman world and now Turkey and the Chishtiyyah in the Indian subcontinent have had their own elaborate orchestras. Certain forms of music, such as *qawwālī,* which one hears often in India and Pakistan, were developed exclusively by Sufis. Furthermore, Sufi music is usually closely associated with Sufi poetry.

Sufi music is like a ladder that connects the soul to God. There is a fire in the human soul. If the fire is that of love for God, Sufi music intensifies it, and if it is only the fire of passion, that too is intensified by music. That is why there are conditions set in Sufi orders for participating in the spiritual concert or *samā',* and disciples are required to curb their passions before being able to benefit spiritually from the *samā'.* What the *samā'* does is to intensify love and longing for God while carrying the soul forward in its journey to the Spirit. The Sufi whose soul is attuned to the celestial harmonies hears the voice of the Friend in that miraculous event, which is the hearing of spiritual music. A poem attributed to Rūmī, who was especially sensitive to the emancipating beauty of traditional music, refers to this miracle in this verse:

> Dry wood, dry string, dry skin,
> From whence therefore cometh the song of the Friend?

And again it was Rūmī who spoke of the musician beginning to speak of the mysteries of the covenant made in pre-eternity between God and humanity behind the veil of melody. The *samā'* carried out traditionally in Sufi centers (*zāwiyah* in Arabic, *khānqāh* in Persian, Urdu, and most other Indian languages, and *tekke* in Turkish) is traditionally experienced only by members of a particular order, and it is this already spiritually disciplined group that the music addresses, although others can of course benefit from this remarkable art.

THE GOAL OF SUFI PRACTICES

The goal of all Sufi practices is the remembrance of God, but since God is the One and the Absolute, to remember Him in a manner worthy of His Reality, human beings must become integrated and whole. Since He is the Sacred as such, He demands of us all that we are. *Tawḥīd* or Divine Oneness, which is the central reality of Islam and Sufism, corresponds in the human state to totality and integration. And so Sufi practices seek to integrate the totality of the subject who is to remember God. In fact, without integration of one's being it is not possible to remember God fully and constantly as the Quran directs the believers to do when it asserts that one should remember God whether one is standing up, sitting down, or on one's side. And the Quran adds, "O ye who have faith, let not your wealth nor your children divert you from the remembrance of God (*dhikr Allāh*). Those who do so, they are the ones who are losers" (Quran 63:9).

There is no monasticism in Islam, and to follow this supreme command of the Quran to remember and invoke God throughout life does not require formal and organized withdrawal from the world, as we find in some forms of Christianity, Buddhism, and Hinduism. But it does require inner withdrawal and detachment from the world considered in its aspect as veil and not as theophany. A dervish once said, "It is not I who have left the world. It is the world that has left me." Modes of leading the life of a follower of Sufism, or being a *mutaṣawwif,* to use the classical Arabic term, can differ greatly outwardly. One could be a scholar or a butcher, a housewife or a general, a king or a beggar and still practice Sufism, as the history of Sufism reveals clearly. But whatever the outward mode of life, the *mutaṣawwif* or dervish must be detached inwardly from the world and attached to God through the invocation of His Sacred Names, an act that must be performed inwardly whatever one might be doing outwardly.

Sufism also usually includes the integration of the contemplative and the active modes of life although one might take more precedence over the other in different cases. The model of the life of the Prophet, 'Alī, and many of the great saints who came later, such as 'Abd al-Qādir al-Jīlānī and Abū'l-Ḥasan al-Shādhilī, all display this integration of the contemplative and active lives, which is a hallmark of Sufi spirituality. This fact does not, however, in any way compromise the reality of the superiority of contemplation or knowledge over action and has not prevented a number of Sufis from spending their whole lives on top of mountains or in holy sanctuaries invoking and remembering God. Their effect upon their environment has been, as already mentioned, like that of a lamp, which illuminates the space around it without acting and moving. But for most followers of Sufism the mode of life has been to be in the world but not of the world, as Christ said.

THE SCIENCE OF THE CURE OF SOULS

No one can enter the Garden of Truth whose soul has not been cured of the deviations, dislocations, and dispersions caused by the fall, and especially the consequences of the modernism and secularism of the past few centuries, as a result of which most people live in a world without center. Like other spiritual methods, for example, Yoga, Sufism possesses a science of the soul and the real Sufi master is also a physician who can cure the ailments of the soul of his or her disciples. There is a sacred psychology as well as sacred psychotherapy in Sufism not to be confused in any way with modern secular theories and practices with the same names. Modern psychology speaks of the freedom *of* the self while Sufi psychology has for its goal freedom *from* the self or the ego. Sufi psychology is concerned with the integration of the elements of the soul and its subsequent wedding to the Spirit. This traditional psychology, also amply treated in Hinduism and Buddhism, should in fact be called pneumatology as well as psychology inasmuch as it deals with the spirit or *pneuma* as well as the psyche.

All the elements of our soul were created by God and are precious if they play the role for which they were created. But the souls of most human beings have become chaotic and the various elements of the soul are no longer where they should be or functioning as they should. Fallen man usually loves what he should disdain and disdains what he should love. For example, fallen humanity loves dispersing activity, which should be disdained, and has disdain for contemplative quiet and calm, which it should love, there being of course exceptions. The fallen human soul is full of knots, which result in all the negative feelings and emotions that the soul experiences, such as anxiety, aggression, egocentrism, depression, and so forth, and these forces lead to the committing of what theologically and morally is called sin or vice. Moreover, the dispersion of the soul, so common today, is related to excessive externalization and loss of the sense of the sacred. Modern society has developed a culture that emphasizes activity over contemplation through the creation of urban spaces full of noise and distraction and of an atmosphere filled with information and advertising, which bombard us all the time. This prevailing atmosphere serves to turn the soul evermore outward and away from its center. Inner peace has become more difficult to attain because of the hectic life that characterizes the human condition in much of the world today. One must remember that there is a correspondence between the ephemeral and transient phenomena in the world and phenomena within the soul. And as like attracts like, the soul that is chaotic within becomes even more mesmerized by the chaotic world that surrounds us today, forgetting its own center and God, who resides at the heart/center of all human beings whether they are aware of this Reality or not.

Yet the soul yearns for wholeness and is never completely satisfied with transient multiplicity even if it derives momentary gratification from the fulfillment of this or that passionate desire. Were there to be no yearning for one's primordial nature, which is always centered and in communion with the Spirit, no one would seek to follow the Sufi path. But some do realize their spiritual illness and search for the physician of the soul who would cure their illness, who would untie the knots of the soul and put its various elements in their proper places, with each faculty in the soul functioning as it was meant to according to the spiritual teachings of various traditions. The medicine given for this process of curing the malady of the soul is spiritual practice and the acquiring of virtues. In one of the most famous *ghazals* in his grand *Dīwān-i Shams,* Rūmī sings:

> The proclamation of Heaven hath come, the physician of lovers
> hath come,
> If thou wishest that he cometh to thee, become ill, become ill.[5]

The first step toward perfection is awareness of our imperfection. Those in need of a physician will not go to one unless they realize they are ill and in need of medical help. This is as true for our souls as it is for our bodies. Those who come to the Sufi master with serious intention are those who realize the imperfections of their inner state and the need to be cured of the illnesses from which their souls suffer before the journey of their life comes to an end.

THE RELATION BETWEEN THE MASTER AND THE DISCIPLE

In order to be cured, the disciple has to have complete trust in the physician of the soul to whom he or she has come for help, and there must exist a personal relationship between the disciple and the master. That means not only listening to the master's advice as to what to do but also acting upon it. A prescription from the best of physicians is useless if we simply put it in our pocket. We have to take the medicine that is prescribed even if it be bitter. So it is with the medicine that cures our souls. Sometimes it is bitter and very difficult to take, but we must persevere if we are going to get well. For example, the disciple may be given certain forms of invocation and meditation that are difficult to perform. Or a person with pride may be made to perform such apparently humbling acts as sweeping the floor and cleaning the toilets in order to break the stranglehold of pride upon his or her soul. In any case, there is great significance in having trust in the spiritual master in order to follow fully his or her instructions, and there is also much danger if the person claiming to be a master is not a real physician of the soul.

As already mentioned, one of the names of the disciple in Sufism is *murīd,* that is, one who wills. The master is also called *murād,* that is, the person who is the object of that will or *irādah*. The relation between the *murīd* and *murād* must be based on the complete surrender of the will of the *murīd* to the master, not as just another human being but as the representative of the Prophet and transmitter of the power of *walāyah/wilāyah*. Sufi authorities of old said that a disciple in the hands of the master should be like a cadaver in the hands of the washer of the dead. They also spoke of three stages of annihilation or extinction (*al-fanā'*), to which we shall turn shortly: *fanā'* in the *shaykh, fanā'* in the Prophet, *fanā'* in God. Without the surrender of one's will, trust, and love for the master, spiritual guidance is not possible.

The relation between a master and disciples concerns not only advice on technical spiritual matters dealing with practice of the methods of the path, given individually, but also discourse on the doctrine and general problems of the spiritual life, given often in the gathering of the disciples in a *majlis* and also more informal discourse (*suhbah*), through which disciples learn many concrete truths that concern both their inner and outer lives. There is also a relation between the master and the disciple in higher levels of reality manifested sometimes in veridical dreams, which provide important keys for the life of the soul on the subtle plane.

IMITATION OF THE PROPHET

The relation of the master to the disciple is modeled upon that of the Prophet to those companions who were close to him and to whom he imparted esoteric knowledge. This is one of the instances that reveals the importance for Sufism of the imitation of the Prophet and his *Sunnah,* which has been transmitted from generation to generation to us. For nearly two millennia Christians have spoken of *imitatio Christi,* and one of the great classics of Christian mysticism is *The Imitation of Christ* by Thomas à Kempis. The same is true for Islam in general and Sufism in particular. For Christians, Christ is considered to be divine, and certainly they do not claim to imitate his divinity or seek the power to raise the dead to life or walk on water. What they seek to emulate are his spiritual virtues, which stand out clearly since he did not participate in the ordinary affairs of human life and did not have to deal with certain human imperfections. In Islam the spiritual virtues of the Prophet are less evident from the outside since his role was to enter into the arena of ordinary life and sanctify it. Many Christians have in fact asked how one could emulate the Prophet spiritually since his life seems to have been so much mixed with being ruler of a human community, engaged in political and military activity, being concerned with family affairs, and so forth. For Muslims these activities serve as the model for the outer life while the Prophet's inner life, demonstrated in his frequent prayers and fasting and constant remembrance of God, serves as the model for the spiritual life.

The Prophet said, "Poverty is my pride," a saying that is similar to the words of Christ, who spoke of the blessedness of the poor. The Prophet realized poverty (*faqr*) in its deepest metaphysical sense, which, as mentioned earlier, means to realize that all reality and all positive qualities belong to God and that in our basic nature we are the poor whereas He is the Rich, as a Quranic verse states explicitly. This spiritual poverty is so central to Sufism that Sufism is often called Muḥammadan poverty (*al-faqr al-muḥammadī*) and those who practice Sufism, *faqīr,* that is, possessors of *faqr.* In seeking to realize this fundamental and primordial state of *faqr,* all Sufis seek to emulate the Prophet.

In the same way that no Christian can possess a virtue not possessed on the highest level by Christ, no Muslim, even the greatest saints and sages, can possess any virtue not possessed in its perfection by the Prophet, who for Muslims is the Perfect or Universal Man (*al-insān al-kāmil*), in whom all possibilities of cosmic existence are realized. For Muslims he is the perfect mirror reflecting all of God's Names and Qualities, and his inner reality, called the Muḥammadan Reality (*al-ḥaqīqat al-muḥammadiyyah*), is identified with the Logos. He is the most perfect of human beings and hence the most perfect human model to be imitated. When Sufis think of the spiritual reality of the Prophet, they think of the sacred saying in which God addresses the Prophet in the following words: "If thou wert not, I would not have created the heavens." They also remember always the name of the Prophet, *ḥabīb,* which means both he who loves God and he who is the beloved of God. The Prophet is the supreme guide to the love and knowledge of God and to the realization of the ever-present link between human beings and Him. As already mentioned, no one can love God who does not love His Prophet. That is why among prayers and supplications performed by Sufis, much is devoted to the praise of the Prophet, as are many of the masterpieces of Sufi poetry.

The emulation of the spiritual reality of the Prophet is also closely related to his Nocturnal Ascent (*al-mi'rāj*), which took place shortly before his migration to Medina. According to tradition, this spiritual journey started in Mecca, proceeded to Jerusalem, and then continued vertically from Jerusalem through the heavens and higher levels of existence to the Divine Presence; the Prophet then returned to Jerusalem and finally to Mecca. Many Sufis have correlated the stations of the path with stages of the *mi'rāj,* and some, like Bāyazīd Basṭāmī, have described their own *mi'rāj* to the Divine in their sayings and writings. The description of Bāyazīd's *mi'rāj* based on his words has been recorded in many standard hagiographic Sufi works. In a sense the spiritual imitation of the Prophet in Sufism can be summarized in the attempt of Sufis to go on *mi'rāj,* also following in his footsteps but realizing that their *mi'rāj* is only spiritual while that of the Prophet was also bodily.

Of course, all the great prophets and other manifestations of the Logos are pinnacles of perfection of the human state and possess all the basic spiritual virtues. The emphasis, however, differs from one prophet to another. As far as Islam is concerned, the virtues are associated with the very substance of the being of the Prophet, and it is the content of this substance that is crystallized into the various virtues described in classical Sufi texts. This spiritual substance is impregnated by spiritual power and esoteric knowledge stretching to the highest level of Reality and is determined by the two poles of truth and heart, which are therefore so central to Sufism, these two poles being also openness to transcendence and immanence. The path consists ultimately of putting the Truth in one's heart and knowing the Truth through the heart/intellect or what the Sufis call the "eye of the heart."

The Muḥammadan Reality is also, esoterically speaking, a model of the cosmos, and as Frithjof Schuon has said, the Muḥammadan Substance possesses a quaternary cluster of virtues corresponding to the four cardinal points of space. These clusters of qualities or virtues are purity, which is related to serenity and resignation; strength, related to fervor and vigilance; beauty, related to recollection and gratitude; and goodness and love, related to certitude and generosity.[6] The Prophet had a purity of soul that enabled him to be serene, standing above the din of the world and resigned to the Will of God even during the many excruciating trials that he faced in his life. He had inner strength, which was related to the great fervor of his faith in God combined with being awake, free from the daydreaming of ordinary men and women, and always vigilant. The Prophet was beautiful both outwardly and inwardly, and even his simple life, combined with relative poverty even when he was the ruler of a whole cosmic sector, was combined with beauty. And this love of beauty brought with it remembrance of God, one of whose Names as mentioned already is the Beautiful, and gratitude for all the beauty and goodness that surrounded him and that was given by God. Finally the Prophet was full of goodness and love for both God and His creatures, and these virtues were closely tied to certitude in the nature of Truth as summarized in the first testimony of faith, "There is no god but God," with all its metaphysical and cosmological meanings. These virtues were also closely related to the generosity and nobility that characterized the Prophet's life, for he was always strict with himself and generous and noble toward others. That is why in the Quran God addresses the Prophet, "And verily thou art of a super eminent character" (Quran 68:4), meaning that the Prophet had the deepest receptivity for the highest truths.

The Quran also states, "Verily in the Messenger of God you have a good model" (Quran 33:21), adding that he is the example and model for those who look to God and accept the Day of Judgment and remember and invoke God (*dhikr Allāh*) often. Although all pious Muslims seek to follow the *Sunnah* of the Prophet, it is especially the Sufis who have taken the lesson of this verse to heart. Since they are those who remember or invoke often, they believe that this verse is especially addressed to them. They seek to follow, however, not only the outer *Sunnah* but also the inner *Sunnah* related to the spiritual substance of the Prophet. They therefore seek to cultivate within their souls the Prophetic virtues. In fact, the famous Sufi classical treatments of the virtues are no more than expansions and elucidations of the basic virtues mentioned above. They are descriptions of states and stations traversed by the Prophet but systematized for those who aspire to march upon the path to the Garden of Truth.

STATES AND STATIONS

Classical texts of Sufism distinguish between a state (*ḥāl*) and a station (*maqām*) in the spiritual journey, and before turning to the main steps of the ladder to the Garden, it is important to understand this distinction. A state is a spiritual condition that is transient, descends suddenly upon a *faqīr,* and leaves him or her with the same suddenness. While practicing the disciplines of the path, one may suddenly experience an expansion (*basṭ*), which brings with it indescribable elation or joy, or one may experience a contraction (*qabḍ*), as if God had forsaken that person. A disciple may experience fear or hope, the joy of union or the sorrow of separation, a desert or a garden. His or her duty is to continue the spiritual practice through all these states, including ones in which he or she has a powerful experience of overwhelming love or inebriating beauty.

Even ordinary people have once in a while an inner experience that is like the *ḥāl* of the Sufis. In the face of great tragedy or a great work of art including music, for a moment the walls of the ego seem to crumble and one can experience a spiritual state associated with awe or sorrow, joy or expansion. Usually such rare experiences in the life of ordinary people remain only as a memory, but for some it is the occasion for turning the direction of the movement of their life toward God rather than away from Him. For the practitioner of Sufism such experiences usually occur more often and affect the spiritual life more directly. For example, for those who have an ear for sacred and traditional music but who do not practice the disciplines of the path, hearing such music can put them in a *ḥāl,* which terminates, however, when the music comes to an end. For the *faqīr,* such music associated with *samāʿ* is like a wind current that helps the wings of the soul to fly higher toward the Empyrean, and its effect on the soul persists after the music itself is terminated. In any case, spiritual states are an important element of spiritual wayfaring and aid the soul on its journey, provided a person does not become fixated by a *ḥāl* and continues to remember that the goal of the path is not the experience of this or that phenomenon, even if it be of a spiritual nature, but of God. Many who have experienced a transient or even permanent spiritual state and have ceased to continue on the path have gained various psychic powers and even visions of the intermediate world but have failed to reach the One who is the goal of the path.

In contrast to states, stations (*maqāmāt,* plural of *maqām*) are permanent. They are like various plateaus that one reaches during mountain climbing, where one can rest on the way to the summit, but of course one should continue to struggle to reach the top. The reaching of a station implies a high degree of spiritual attainment. It is the fruit of a great exertion (*jihād*) within the soul to overcome its infirmities combined with grace. When someone in a Sufi order is called "the possessor of a station," it means that he or she has reached a high level of spiritual realization. The stations, sometimes also called by certain Sufis places of descent (*manāzil*) and halting places or spiritual stayings (*mawāqif,* which concern especially the end of various stations), are usually identified with spiritual virtues, the attainment of each of which marks a station on the path.

THE VIRTUES

Sufi doctrine, like all truth, comes from God. What we bring to the path is our soul, which must become embellished with the virtues in order to be worthy of entering the Garden of Truth. But even the virtues belong ultimately to God, who has made them available to us through the Prophet. Also from the practical and operative point of view the duty of the *faqīr* is to remove the vices that prevent the virtues from manifesting themselves in the soul. In order to gain the virtue of humility we must overcome the vice of pride, and in order to be embellished with the virtue of truthfulness we must stop being hypocrites and remove from ourselves the vice of deceitfulness. For the vast majority of members of Sufi orders, the spiritual life consists of the battle to become virtuous. Only a few are able to devote themselves to Sufi metaphysics, but from a more profound point of view each virtue *is* an aspect of the truth as reflected in the soul. Virtue as understood in Sufism is not simply moral virtue but rather spiritual virtue with a noetic and existential dimension. For example, humility is not simply the sentimental attitude of humbling our egos before God and the neighbor. It is the metaphysical awareness that before the Absolute we are nothing and that the neighbor is not incomplete in the same way as we are and that even in his or her incompleteness possesses existence, which comes from God and before which we must have an attitude of humility.

Classical Sufi texts are replete with the description of the virtues. I shall mention later some of the early Sufis, who wrote on this subject and whose writings culminate in al-Ghazzālī's *Iḥyā' 'ulūm al-dīn* (*Revivification of the Sciences of Religion*), the most important work of spiritual ethics in the history of Islam. Since the steps to God or the stations can be enumerated in different ways and seen from different perspectives, the number of stations and their ordering is not the same everywhere. Some speak of three main stations, some of seven, some of forty, and some of even higher numbers. In what follows I shall mention some of the main stations, whose understanding opens the door for the comprehension of this subject in general.

The three cardinal virtues of the Universal Man, or for Muslims the Muḥammadan Reality, which encompass the others and which are found in one way or another in every integral and authentic spiritual tradition, are humility, charity and nobility, and sincerity and truthfulness. From the Sufi perspective, each of these virtues is illuminated by the light of the intellect and is not only sentimental. Many people put on an air of humility to hide the pride of the ego; this is not humility but hypocrisy. It is also against intelligence and knowledge of the truth not to admit one's superiority in a particular matter pertaining to the truth while remaining humble. If a person knows that the square root of nine is three and someone comes along and insists that it is two, it is not spiritual humility not to insist upon the truth that it is three because one fears being seen as proud. Much of theological truth has been destroyed in the modern world through the practice of sacrificing the truth at the altar of a sentimental and opaque humility. For example, many Christian theologians have refused to criticize what is theologically an error because of false humility often combined with a sense of compassion that remains impervious to the truth, with the result that it is no longer fashionable today to speak of theological heresy or for that matter truth as such. In all authentic spirituality, however, the demand of the truth is the highest demand upon us.

Likewise, charity is not simply a sentimental giving on the basis of wanting to feel good. In order for charity to be spiritually efficacious, it must be based on the metaphysical awareness that the other is in the deepest sense ourselves and that in giving we also overcome the walls of our own ego, which separates us from others, and consequently we also receive. This virtue is of course related to love and compassion, which, as mentioned earlier, run through the arteries of the universe. We must first love God, who is the source of all compassion, in order for our acts of charity to have a positive spiritual effect upon us. As for nobility, it is closely related to the virtue of charity. To be noble is to give of oneself, and it places great responsibilities on our shoulders. As the French proverb asserts, "*noblesse oblige,*" that is, nobility places obligations upon us. We have an obligation to be charitable and compassionate in order to realize our own nobility, which might be hidden under a heavy crust of selfishness.

The virtue of truth is, in this scheme, the crowning virtue. It is like the apex of a triangle whose other angles are humility and charity; the attainment of truth in fact requires both of these other virtues. Furthermore, truthfulness is inseparable from sincerity. Truthfulness means first of all halting in complete surrender before the Truth. It means also to see the truth of things, to be honest in thought and deed, to be sincere, and to remain always on the side of the truth no matter what consequences it might have for us. There is no higher virtue for in being truthful we confirm most clearly our theomorphic nature since God is the Truth. In attaining fully this virtue we become ready to enter the Garden of Truth.

These three sets of cardinal virtues of humility, charity and nobility, and sincerity and truthfulness are the ornaments of the soul of the Prophet, as are the quaternary sets of virtues discussed above. Moreover, inasmuch as he is the supreme exemplar of the Perfect or Universal Man, he is the perfect mirror reflecting the virtues, which, as mentioned, belong on their highest level to God. These three sets of virtues correspond to the phases of contraction, expansion, and union, which are to be found universally in all integral mystical traditions, including the Christian. Within the soul of the person in quest of reaching God, something must shrivel and die. In the next phase what remains in the soul must expand to fit the mold of the Universal Man or, more specifically for Muslims, the Prophet in his inner reality.

Only then can one speak of the possibility of union, which in Sufism does not mean the union of the creature and the Creator or the servant and the Lord. As a Sufi poem states, "How can this dust be united with the world of purity?" Union means our becoming aware of our nothingness before God, becoming a perfectly polished mirror that has nothing of its own but reflects what is put before it. In the case of human beings, it is the totality of Divine Names and Qualities that are reflected in the mirror of our inner being. It is not our individual ego but the divine spark within that unites with the Divinity. Henceforth, as already stated, God becomes the eye with which we see, and we become the eye with which God sees. Nay, we realize that God is the Light with which we see all things. That is why it is not possible to see God simply as object in the ordinary sense although He is both the Supreme Object and the Supreme Subject. To use classical Sufi terminology, in the state of union the servant remains the servant and the Lord the Lord, while the divine spark within, the immanent intellect, achieves union with the Divine Self, from which it issues directly. Furthermore, union does not mean the destruction of the positive aspects of the self but its absorption into the highest Reality. We are able to swim in the ocean of Divinity, to quote Meister Eckhart, in a state of fusion without confusion.

Some Sufi metaphysicians and Shi'ite gnostics such as Mullā Ṣadrā have spoken of four stages in the journey of the soul. It is of interest to mention them here in conjunction with the discussion of union. There is first of all the basic distinction between the Truth (*al-ḥaqq*) and creation (*al-khalq*), of which we are a part. The first stage of the spiritual journey is from *al-khalq* to *al-Ḥaqq,* and the stations corresponding to the cardinal spiritual virtues crowned by annihilation or extinction (*al-*

fanā') in God deal with this part of the journey. The second journey involves traveling in *al-Ḥaqq*. Subsistence in God (*al-baqā'*) concerns this phase. Certain Sufis such as Bāyazīd Basṭāmī spoke openly of journeying in God. The third stage is a return from *al-Ḥaqq* to *al-khalq,* but with *al-Ḥaqq*. The fourth stage is the journey in *al-khalq* with *al-Ḥaqq*. The supreme example of the last two in Islam is the return to earth of the Prophet from his Nocturnal Ascent to the Divine Presence and his subsequent carrying out of the Prophetic mission. Or in a somewhat different context it is the Buddha delaying entry into nirvana in order to guide and save other beings. The last two stages of this journey are meant for prophets and great saints given the mission to establish or renew sacred institutions and structures for the guidance of human beings. Very few Sufis throughout Islamic history have claimed to have completed the third and fourth stages. As for those who claimed to have done so without actually journeying through the third and fourth stages, they have often performed the most dangerous acts and caused the destruction rather than establishment of sacred institutions for they have thought that their will was the Will of God without it being so. How many ravages have been brought upon human societies by those convinced that their will is God's Will? We have all seen examples of it in history, from those who burned Joan of Arc or so-called witches at the stake to Oliver Cromwell to some present-day Muslim extremists.

Technically speaking, Sufism is concerned on the practical level with only the first two stages because once a person reaches God, He will decide what the person is to do the rest of his or her life. If the four stages of the journey are mentioned in certain later works of Sufi metaphysics, it is in order to complete the description of all possibilities open to human beings including prophets. They want to provide an intellectual vision that embraces not only the stages of the perfection of the disciple in traveling from *al-khalq* to *al-Ḥaqq,* but also the descending of Moses from Mt. Sinai to accomplish the Will of God for his people as well as the prophetic missions of Christ and the Prophet.

As already mentioned, classical Sufi texts elaborated and systematized the discussion of the virtues in such a way as to be a practical guide for the followers of the path. One can see such treatments in the famous Sufi manuals of Abū Ṭālib al-Makkī, Abū Naṣr al-Sarrāj, Abū'l-Qāsim al-Qushayrī, 'Alī ibn 'Uthmān Hujwīrī, 'Abd Allāh Anṣārī, Ibn al-'Arīf, of course al-Ghazzālī, and many others. Each of them treated the stations and the virtues in a somewhat different manner in light of his vision of what was needed by disciples, for surely the goal of these masters was not to simply describe the nature of the wine of gnosis but to make it possible to actually taste that pure wine. What follows is a synthesis of the teachings of these classical texts.

Many classical sources speak of seven virtues related to seven stations of the path. A great many Sufis have sung over the centuries the poem attributed to Rūmī:

> 'Aṭṭār [the great Persian Sufi poet and saint] has traversed the
> seven cities of Love,
> We are still stuck at the turn of one street!

The cities of love are none other than the stations associated with virtues, to which we now turn.

All spiritual journeys for fallen humanity must begin with contrition (*inābah*) and repentance (*tawbah*) because the soul in its ordinary state is exteriorized with its back to the world of the Spirit and its face toward the external material world characterized by multiplicity, dispersion, ephemerality, corruption, and death. *Tawbah* is Arabic meaning literally "turning around." We must change the direction of our souls, turn around and face the Divine Reality with our backs to the world. There are men and women who repent and then go back to their old ways and repent again. Although God does not like such a pattern in the life of a person determined to follow the path leading to Him, He is also aware of human weaknesses and is forgiving. The great master Rūmī had the following poem engraved on his mausoleum:

> Come back, come back,
> even if you have broken your repentance a thousand times.[7]

But those who wish to progress upon the path must make this turnabout permanent. They must continue to move toward the spiritual world with their faces turned to that world and their backs to this world. Turning one's back to this world means overcoming the vice of the soul's attachment to the multiplicity that surrounds it externally, and therefore the practice of the virtues of detachment, mindfulness, piety, chasteness, and scrupulousness in matters of religion. It means asceticism in the inward and spiritual sense. That is why this station is called *zuhd* or *wara'*, the first referring to asceticism and the second to detachment and piety. Many of the early Sufis were ascetics, and some have therefore identified Sufism with asceticism, but the later masters made sure to preserve the distinction between the two. As Ḥāfiẓ says in one of his celebrated *ghazals:*

> Criticize not the sagacious Sufis, O ascetic of pure nature,
> For the sins of others will not be accounted against thee.[8]

But in order to advance to higher stations it is necessary to possess the ascetic virtues. It was from the ground of asceticism and fear of God prepared by the early Mesopotamian Sufis that the trees of Sufi love and gnosis grew in later centuries. Likewise, in the case of individuals it is necessary to gain the virtues associated with the station of *zuhd* and *wara'* in order to be able to drink the wine of Divine Love and to bathe in the light of illuminative knowledge.

The mastery of the state of asceticism and God-fearing piety leads to absolute surrender to God and reliance upon and trust in Him (*tawakkul*). A real traveler upon the path relies upon God under all conditions in both joy and sorrow, ease and difficulty. This is a station hard to reach for it is the habit of the soul to rely on itself or external forces and causes as if they were independent realities. There is also the danger that travelers will mistake this utter dependence upon God for lack of need of effort on their own part. Once a Bedouin came to see the Prophet and left his camel untethered outside. When the Prophet asked him why he did so, he answered that he relied upon God. The Prophet told him to first tether his camel and then have trust and reliance in God. Rūmī recounts this *ḥadīth* in the verse, "Tie the knee of the camel with *tawakkul.*" Many Sufi masters were careful in making this point clear when they spoke of this station, as we see in the writings of Abū Ṭālib al-Makkī and al-Ghazzālī. Sufis identified *tawakkul* with faith and in the case of Dhū'l-Nūn al-Miṣrī with certitude, and they emphasized the importance of human efforts in the attainment of this state.

Furthermore, *tawakkul* must be combined with the virtue of patience (*al-ṣabr*), for how can we rely on God with all our being without patience in confronting the tribulations and obstacles of life and even in attaining our basic physical needs? This station is reached by one who is both patient and trustful, realizing that while we must exert our efforts to the best of our abilities, everything occurs in its due time according to God's Will and also according to a wisdom that is often beyond our ken. The Gospels say that with God all things are possible, but they do not say when.

To have complete trust in God is to live in peace and be happy, content, and satisfied (*al-riḍā*). Everyone wants to be content, to be satisfied with life, but the very flow of earthly life and the fluid nature of the soul make remaining in this state well nigh impossible as long as we base our contentment on external factors in a transient and uncertain world. Contentment is a high spiritual station attainable only if one is able to repose in the Divine Reality and be satisfied with such a condition. Such a person is also one with whom God is satisfied, and this person is ready to enter Paradise. As the Quranic verse states, "O thou soul which art at peace, return unto thy Lord with gladness that is thine in Him and His in thee. Enter thou among My Slaves; enter thou My Paradise" (Quran 89:27–30).[9] This gladness is precisely *al-riḍā*. It is only in this station that the soul experiences the joy of contentment and the peace that, as Christ says, "passeth all understanding." This contentment also brings with it gratitude (*al-shukr*), for having been given such a condition of the soul that one is totally content with what God has given requires being thankful. In this state of contentment the soul can ask for nothing more.

We have already discussed spiritual poverty (*al-faqr*), which characterizes all of Sufism. But some masters have considered it as a station, sometimes mentioned before contentment and sometimes after. One has to realize fully the truth of the Quranic verse that God is the Rich and we are the poor, that ontologically He is Absolute Being while we are nothing in ourselves, having received our existence from Him. From one point of view one has to have achieved the station of *faqr* in order to reach the station of contentment. From another one must travel through all the aforementioned stations to realize the deepest meaning of *faqr*. In any case, *faqr* is the gate to both Divine Love and Divine Knowledge.

In order to be able to attain the highest stations one has to have sincerity (*al-ikhlāṣ*), avoiding all hypocrisy and impurity of character. One can reach the Truth only by being completely sincere and of pure intention. There are some hidden corners of the soul that are not easy to reach and only under certain circumstance reveal their distorted nature and bring out a person's hypocrisy. This trait is considered one of the great dangers of the path. To confront this hidden hypocrisy certain Sufis went in the other direction of hiding their virtues and performed acts that were considered externally as blameworthy. Hence they were called the People of Blame (*al-malāmatiyyah* or *malāmiyyah*).

There are many stories about the People of Blame in Sufi literature. For example, it is recounted that one of the *malāmatī* Sufis decided to lie down in front of a mosque with his eyes closed at the time of the Friday congregational prayers when everyone was going into the mosque. A self-righteous merchant kicked the apparently sleeping Sufi as he entered and severely scolded him for not getting up and going to the prayers. The Sufi opened his eyes but said nothing and seemed to go back to sleep. An hour later when the prayers were finished, the merchant came out, whereupon the Sufi opened his eyes and said to him, "While you were outwardly standing in the line of worshippers and making the various movements of the prayers, inwardly your thoughts were completely engrossed in your business affairs and not concerned with God at all, whereas although I was lying down here with my eyes closed, I was thinking only of God." The merchant, having his thoughts during the prayers thus recounted to him by the apparently lowly dervish sleeping at the gate of the mosque, was filled with remorse and was cured of his self-righteous hypocrisy. The People of Blame were indeed an antidote to hypocrisy and the tendency of some people in a strongly religious ambience to falsely display great piety and even assume the traits of certain exalted stations, including reception of theophanies of Divine Names, without in reality possessing these traits. Ibn 'Arabī calls the People of Blame perfect gnostics. The relation between the virtue of sincerity and gaining access to the Truth is brought out in the Quran, where *Sūrah* 112, which deals with Pure Truth and summarizes the Islamic doctrine of Divine Unity (*al-tawḥīd*), is known as both "Sincerity" and "Unity."

The stations described thus far lead finally to the highest stations, which are those of love (*al-maḥabbah*) and unitive knowledge or gnosis (*al-ma'rifah*). We have dealt with both of these subjects already and need not return to them here except to mention that classical Sufi texts deal with levels of both love and knowledge when they are considered as stations of the path. And needless to say, these are crowning virtues and the highest stations because they concern the love and knowledge of God as well as knowledge by God of us and His love for his servants.

The virtues and stations have also been envisaged in other ways. What I have presented here is a synthesis of many classical works and, even more important, the actual stations that the soul must experience in order to become worthy of the supreme goal of the path of ascent, considered by the Sufis to be extinction or annihilation (*al-fanā'*) and subsistence (*al-baqā'*). These stations also pertain to levels of existence beyond the ordinary and are concerned with stages of our ultimate return to our Divine Origin.

Paradoxically, the greatest gift that has been given to us is the possibility of realizing our own nothingness. The process of cosmogenesis has brought forth and bestowed existence upon all things from the Origin, which is Absolute Being. In the cosmos there is generation and corruption, but only God can bring being out of nonbeing and turn being into nonbeing. Usually when we say that this or that object has become extinct or annihilated we are using these terms only metaphorically, if we consider the existence as well as the form of things. Annihilation comes from the root *nihil,* or nothingness, and we cannot turn any existing thing outside ourselves into literally nothing as far as the existence (and not only form) of that thing is concerned. We can "annihilate" a building but are not able to turn its material into nothingness. Even in contemporary physics, matter can be turned into energy and vice versa but not turned into nothing. Physicists do speak of black holes or antimatter, but the understanding of such objects is based on their accidents and mathematical characteristics, not on their existence and ontological reality in the philosophical sense, for in most of modern physics there is no interest in ontology. The handful of physicists who have a metaphysical perspective do, however, speak of a subtle "field" that fills the whole universe, even where there seems to be emptiness. Some have called this the *Akashic* field, using a term drawn from Hindu cosmology. The transformations associated with annihilation that occur in the material world are really integration and absorption into this subtle field and not annihilation in the ontological sense. Only God can reverse the effect of His Command, "Be!"

And yet in a universe in which each existent, from the dust to the archangel, occupies its own distinct state of being, from which it cannot transgress, God Himself has allowed human beings to undo the cosmogonic process and realize their own nonexistence before the Truth, which alone is, giving their existence back to its Origin. Through the threshold of what the Sufis call annihilation or extinction (*al-fanā'*), humanity is able to enter the Garden of Truth and to subsist in God (*baqā'*). The absolutely necessary condition for entering remains the realization that in ourselves we are nonexistent and that all being belongs to God. The Khurāsānī Sufi Kharaqānī said, "A true Sufi is he who is not." It was in this state that Rūmī sang:

> We are non-existence appearing as existence,
> Thou art Absolute Being appearing as the perishable.[10]

As human beings, we have the ability to reach the state of extinction and annihilation and yet have the consciousness that we are nothing in ourselves and that all being belongs to God. We can reach a state of unitive consciousness prior to bifurcation into object and subject. To reach such a state involves, according to certain Sufis, the three stages mentioned already: annihilation in the spiritual master, who represents the Prophet; annihilation in the Prophet, whom God has addressed directly; and finally annihilation in God. Also in the Divine Order there are again three stages, that is, annihilation in God's Acts, in His Names and Qualities, and finally in His Essence.

That supreme level implies the annihilation of annihilation (*fanā' al-fanā'*), which is also called subsistence (*al-baqā'*) in God. That is the state that would be called in English spiritual union, although Sufism usually uses other terms. This state also corresponds to what certain Oriental religious doctrines call the Supreme Identity. In this state one swims in the ocean of Divinity and Unity and could assert with Ḥallāj:

> He am I whom I love, He whom I love is I,
> Two Spirits in one single body dwelling.
> So seest thou me, then seest thou Him.
> And seest thou Him, then seest thou Us.[11]

No one reaches God without going through the gate of *al-fanā'* and realizing the truth that in ourselves we are nothing, ontologically speaking, and that God alone is Reality as such. It is through *al-fanā'* that human beings gain the "Truth of Certainty" (*ḥaqq al-yaqīn*). The person in whom such a truth has become all-pervasive is called *muḥaqqiq* literally, the person in whom Truth has become realized; this person has become embellished with the Qualities of God, realizing fully the order of the Prophet given in the *ḥadīth,* "Qualify yourself with the Qualities of God" (*takhallaqū bi-akhlāqⁱ'Llāh*). Such masters as Ibn 'Arabī consider the *muḥaqqiq* to possess the highest rank among Sufis. A person who has realized subsistence in God is worthy of becoming an inhabitant of the Garden of Essence, or *Riḍwān,* which stands at the center of the Garden of Truth and which is identified with the Gardener, the Supreme Reality, that is also the Self of ourselves, residing at the center of our being.

"There" is also "here" because Reality is at once transcendent and immanent. The practices of Sufism that have been outlined in this chapter take us from the ordinary consciousness and level of being through the cosmic mountain and the heavens to the very Divine Presence, but this process also is an even deeper penetration into the center of our own being, into the heart, where the Divine Reality also resides. The spiritually realized person is aware that to be really "here" is also to be "there" and to be "there" is to be really "here." The Garden is at once beyond us and within us. Furthermore, when the heart of a traveler upon the path has been opened to God through moral and spiritual discipline, spiritual practice, the acquisition of virtues, and the grace of Heaven, or what the Sufis call Divine Confirmation (*ta'yīd*), that heart *is* in its inner reality the Garden. As a contemporary sage and Sufi master has said:

Das Herz will heilig werden
Und steht vor Gottes Tür.
Ist Paradies auf Erden
Dann ist hier, ja hier.

The heart wants to be holy
And stands before God's gate.
If there is a Paradise on earth
It is here, yea, here.[12]

Part Three

Six

ACCESS TO THE CENTER

Sufism Here and Now

If My servant asks thee about Me, truly I am near.
I answer the call of the caller if he calls upon Me.
Quran 2:186

Say: "To God belongs the East and the West;
He guideth whom He willeth upon the
straight path."
Quran 2:142

From coast to coast there is the army of oppression,
  and yet,
From pre-eternity to post-eternity is the
  opportunity of the dervishes.[1]
Ḥāfiẓ

All is assembled in the present moment,
The descent of Jesus and the creation of Adam.[2]
Maḥmūd Shabistarī

As long as we are in the human state, we remain inseparable from here and now no matter where we are and when we live. Here and now are connected to human consciousness by an unbreakable bond. Wherever we are we can be here, and whenever we come to our senses we find ourselves in the present moment, or now. God is always near to us, the here and the now being the ever-present gateway to Him. And yet fallen humanity, whose soul is dispersed and attention turned to the world of multiplicity, does everything possible to escape from here and now. Most of our lives are constituted of daydreaming, whereby we seek not to be here but somewhere else and not to be in the present but either in the past or the future. The goal of the spiritual path is to bring us to the here and now, to the Center, which is also the eternal present moment.

In relation to this world, which determines the contents of the consciousness of most human beings, especially believers, the spiritual world and ultimately the Garden of Truth is There, in the beyond, and reaching it lies in an eschatological future, past the days and years of our terrestrial life. Esoterically, however, it can be said that the There is Here and the eschatological future Now. This inner doctrine espoused by Sufism, like other esoteric teachings, does not in any way diminish the sacred character of the Beyond or the Tomorrow, which comes after the days of our earthly existence. Rather, it makes possible the realization of the truth that There *is* Here and the eschatological future, of which most religions speak so often, *is* Now. Of course the Here, when seen as the locus of There, is no longer here as usually understood; nor is Now, as the eternal moment, the same as now as fallen humanity usually perceives it.

The Garden of Truth is utterly beyond all limitative existence; it is the Beyond in the ultimate sense of the term. Yet, as already stated, it resides also in the very center of our being, Here, in the deepest sense of the word. Although reaching it is associated with our eschatological future, it can be realized right Now at the present moment. As mentioned before, this truth does not, however, diminish the reality of the Garden beyond all spatial and temporal confines so that we can continue to think of it as beyond, transcendent, and eternal. Sufism is an Islamic spiritual path that makes possible for us to reach the Here and the Now, which are so close to us and yet so unattainable. It possesses a key that can open the door to our inner levels of existence and allows us to know who we are, what we are doing here, and where we should be going. It also makes possible knowledge and love of God at the highest level. It is not the only path that provides such possibilities in this day and age, but it is, relatively speaking, one of the most complete, well preserved, and accessible of spiritual paths in our world.

WHAT DOES SUFISM HAVE TO OFFER?

In order to find a path to the Garden of Truth and follow it to its conclusion, one does not have to master the knowledge of various Sufi orders and gnostic writings summarized in the appendixes that follow. One can become a Sufi saint in the Pamir Mountains without ever having heard of the Tijāniyyah Order in Senegal. But considering the present-day situation of most readers of this book, who are used to the historical setting of ideas, I felt it necessary to present in the appendixes something of the vast Sufi tradition so that they can better judge the nature of the teachings and guidance upon the path provided by Sufism. Otherwise, what has been said in this book thus far suffices for those who are not interested in information about the paths to the Garden but want to actually reach the Garden themselves. The historical and literary accounts that follow this chapter can have a spiritual significance to the degree that they make clear the traditional roots and foundations as well as historical manifestations of Sufism that have made possible the continuous emanation of the light of this torch of wisdom down to this day.

In light of the long Sufi tradition, one can ask what legacy Sufism has left for those who are attracted to it. Perhaps *legacy* is not the proper term, however, because it usually refers to someone who has died, while Sufism is very much a living tradition. Perhaps we should ask what present-day Sufism has inherited from its long past that it can offer to those in quest of the spiritual life.

METAPHYSICAL KNOWLEDGE

Since Sufism is a path of liberating knowledge, it is natural that it would leave for posterity a complete doctrine of the nature of the Principle and Its manifestations, both macrocosmic and microcosmic, that is, metaphysics along with cosmology and traditional psychology, including pneumatology. Sufism has provided for us simple utterances on gnosis as well as elaborate treatises, symbolic tales as well as esoteric commentaries upon the Quran and *Ḥadīth,* prose letters as well as mystical poems, all of which offer teachings about metaphysics and gnosis as well as love and correct action.

These writings include systematizations that are more philosophical and that combine metaphysical unveiling (*kashf*) with intellection (*ta'aqqul*). Such treatises deal with the nature of Reality, the inner meaning of creation, levels of being both macrocosmic and microcosmic, grades of knowledge, the esoteric significance of the Quran and of Islamic sacred rites, ontology as the science of Being as well as a metaphysics dealing ultimately with the Beyond-Being, and many other subjects. There is hardly any legitimate philosophical or rational question arising in the mind that cannot be answered through recourse to the knowledge provided by Sufism and applications of the principles of this knowledge to the matter at hand. Sufi writings include furthermore the most profound exposition of love, divine and human, and the relation between the two.

LITERATURE

Sufism has also provided for us a vast literary treasure in many languages, especially in the form of poetry, some of which has been translated in earlier chapters of this work. In this book I could not address in detail Sufi literature in the sense of the art of writing rather than simply written works, although I have mentioned some literary figures here and there. I have dealt more fully in the appendixes that follow with some foundational Sufi writings that are also important from the literary point of view. Suffice it to say here that there are a large number of prose masterpieces in Arabic dealing with Sufism, while the most universal poets of that language who can still speak to us across the barrier of time and culture are Sufi poets, such as Ḥallāj, Ibn 'Arabī, Ibn al-Fāriḍ, and in the recent period Shaykh al-'Alawī, Shaykh Ḥabīb, and Asad 'Alī.

The second major Islamic language, Persian, is even richer than Arabic in terms of Sufi poetry. Such poets as Bābā Ṭāhir, Sanā'ī, 'Aṭṭār, Rūmī, Ḥāfiẓ, Shabistarī, Jāmī, and many others have made Persian perhaps the richest language in the world in mystical poetry. For those who are Persian speakers this body of poetry is like a vast garden of spiritual reality in which they can become absorbed, reposing and taking refuge in it from the vicissitudes of the world. Such poets provide not only knowledge of the path, in both its theoretical and practical aspects, but also an "alchemy" that has the power to cure the ailments of the soul. Since most people are not given to the reading of metaphysical texts, Sufi poetry is also the means for the dissemination of the teachings of Sufism to the larger public. The Sufis have used beauty to adorn the expressions of the Truth, and they attract souls to the Truth through the beauty of the literary form in which it is dressed.

Sufi poetry also has the power to induce a spiritual state (*ḥāl*) even in the souls of those who are not following formally the path to the Garden but who possess spiritual taste (*dhawq*). Very few people in my country of origin, Persia, can read a metaphysical and gnostic treatise by a figure such as Jāmī, even if this work be in Persian. But I know of very few Persians who do not know some poems of Rūmī and Ḥāfiẓ, which they recite on various occasions in their lives. After the Quran, perhaps no book is found more frequently in the homes of Persian speakers than the *Dīwān* of Ḥāfiẓ. I can hardly overemphasize the importance of Sufi poetry for the followers of the path as well as the larger public. Such poetry is the gift of Sufism to Islamic culture in general as well as the means of attracting those with the necessary capabilities to the path itself.

What is said of Arabic and Persian Sufi poetry also holds true for other Islamic languages. In Turkish, the poetry of Aḥmad Yasawī, Fuḍūlī, and Yūnus Emre are still read by many even in modern Turkey, which sought to ban Ottoman Sufi literature. One still hears the verses of the greatest popular Sufi poet of Turkey, Yūnus Emre, who lived in the fourteenth century, on the radio and in concerts as well as in the everyday speech of many Turks. Likewise, the most outstanding poets of the Urdu language, such as Bīdil and Ghālib, were rooted in the Sufi tradition. Moreover, in Bengal, Persian Sufi poetry served as the model for Bengali poetry that appeared after the Islamization of the land, as we see in the poetry of Muḥammad Ṣaghīr. Many other Indian languages such as Sindhi and Punjābī have as their greatest literary figure a Sufi poet, for example, the famous Sufi saint and poet of Sindh, Shāh 'Abd al-Laṭīf, whose poems are widely sung to this day.

A similar situation prevails in Africa among Berbers as well as in sub-Saharan Africa. The literature of this region, much of which remains oral, is usually crowned by works on Sufism and poems in praise of God and the Prophet with Sufi color. Some of the best-known poems are translations from Arabic, such as the famous *Burdah* (*The Mantle*) of Sharaf al-Dīn Būṣīrī (d. between 1294 and 1297), whose translation into Berber, Fulfunde, and other African languages remains popular to this day. In any case, in sub-Saharan Africa from Senegal to Somalia one can find Sufi poetry of great power that continues to move the souls of men and women and that remains an integral part of the culture of the people.

In the Malay world, with the most homogeneous Islamic population, linguistically and ethnically speaking, the Malay language has been the most important Islamic language during the past five centuries and remains so today despite the presence of other languages such as Javanese. In this ambience, as mentioned earlier, Sufi literature played a definitive role in molding Malay into an Islamic language. I have already alluded to the role of Ḥamzah Fanṣūrī in connection with this question but must add here that he also wrote Sufi poetry and that such poetry continues to be read widely in Indonesia, Malaysia, Singapore, Brunei, and southern Thailand.

Some of this vast body of Sufi literature in various Islamic tongues has been translated into English, German, French, and other European languages, especially from Persian. In fact, it was mostly through such translations that the modern West first became acquainted with Sufism. During the last few decades some European languages such as English are themselves becoming primary vehicles of Sufi literature and especially poetry, and it becomes difficult to draw a line between translation of poetry and original poetic composition, as we see in the poems translated by Martin Lings, several of which I have quoted in this book. When the supreme Sufi poet of the Persian language, Rūmī, becomes the most widely sold poet in America, it is time to realize that Sufi poetry in English has become a part of the contemporary American literary landscape rather than a literature that is of interest only to scholars of Islamic culture and history.

In any case, Sufi literature, and especially poetry, is among the most important legacies of the Sufi tradition. It provides for the contemporary world an exposition of both the doctrine and practice of Sufism and the spiritual universe in which it breathes, in language more accessible than that found in abstract treatises on doctrine or long expositions on spiritual practices, the virtues, and so forth, such as those mentioned in the appendixes. This legacy is of central significance for the Islamic world and is also growing in importance in the West as the number of translations, many carried out in a highly poetic form, increases in various European languages.

MUSIC

Harmony is the result of the manifestation of the One in the many, and since the manifold is created by the One, harmony pervades creation. The cosmos and its functioning are based on a harmony whose origin is beyond the cosmos. We human beings are given eyes to see and ears to hear this harmony if only we become cured of the habitual blindness and deafness that now are second nature to us as fallen beings. One of the miraculous manifestations of this harmony is music, whose melodies, rhythms, and harmonies in the technical musical sense *can* reflect the cosmic harmony and lead us back to the Origin if music remains faithful to its traditional nature and cacophony is not mistaken for music. Of course, not all that is called music today falls under the category of the traditional and particularly sacred music that we have in mind.

The power of sacred music is, needless to say, universal, hence its importance in sacred rites and spiritual practices of nearly all religions, from the chanting of the Vedas to the sacred songs of Native Americans and including, of course, the great Christian tradition of sacred music going back to Gregorian chants.

From the beginning, Sufism was fully aware of this power of sacred music. It interiorized the musical traditions in the Islamic world and made them vehicles for the flight of the soul to God. I recall several decades ago when the great European violinist, Yehudi Menuhin, visited Tehran after spending some time in India studying and hearing classical Indian music. Until that time he had had no experience of classical Persian music, which is deeply impregnated by the spirituality of Sufism. A number of friends and I arranged for him an intimate concert of this music with only a few people present so that he could listen to this music in a private ambience. Listening intently, he was deeply moved and when asked his evaluation of what he had heard, he said, "This music is a ladder of the soul to God." Being a great musician with spiritual sensibility, he found immediately in this music what the Sufis have claimed throughout the Islamic world for all forms of sacred music that have in fact been cultivated and performed to a large extent by the Sufis themselves over the ages. A Sufi master once said that the effect on the soul upon hearing one hour of a spiritual concert (*samā'*), when the soul is ready to hear its message, is equivalent to a thousand days of spiritual practice. Rūmī, who was a great lover of music and very sensitive to its beauty, spoke of music as the vehicle for the expression of the deepest spiritual realities and would fall into an exalted spiritual state (*ḥāl*) upon hearing just a few rhythms or melodies of music.

Sufism was the main force in the creation of several major musical traditions in the Islamic world, from what in Arabic is called *musīqā'l-andalus* (Andalusian music) to Sundanese music in Java. In India and Pakistan, Sufis and even non-Sufis with some spiritual proclivity listen to *qawwālī* and *khayāl* singing, as well as *rāgs,* which were taken from Hindu music and Islamicized. In Persia and Afghanistan they listen to *ghazals* of Ḥāfiẓ and other Sufi poets accompanied by the classical modes as well as *mathnawīkhānī,* which means chanting of the *Mathnawī* of Jalāl al-Dīn Rūmī set to a special genre of music. In the eastern Arab world the classical modes continue to convey the ethos of Sufism while many poems, including those in praise of the Prophet, are sung (this and the chanting of Sufi songs in general being called *nashīd*) and sometimes accompanied by instruments. In the western part of the Arab world in addition to Andalusian music there is also the specifically Sufi chanting to be found in many Sufi centers. In Turkey the tradition of classical music is closely associated with the Mawlawiyyah Order of Rūmī, and most of the orders also have regular sessions in which *ilāhīs,* meaning Sufi songs, consisting of Sufi poems of such masters as Yūnus Emre, are sung accompanied by musical instruments. The same holds true for sub-Saharan Africa, the Malay world, among Kurdish, Baluchi, Berber, and other local ethnic groups, and even among Chinese Muslims, especially those of Xinjiang, who have preserved a rich musical tradition. Each of these musical traditions has a distinct language, as do Sufi poems in diverse Islamic languages, but they all speak of our separation from our Beloved and provide wind currents for the wings of the soul to fly and return to Her abode.

The musical heritage provided for us by Sufism is of great contemporary importance. Besides its spiritual and even therapeutic value for Muslims, the heritage is one of the most accessible means for Westerners to approach the realities of Sufism and Islam itself. With the eclipse of sacrality in much of Western music after Bach, and especially in recent times, many Western lovers of music have turned during the last few decades to non-Western musical traditions. It is remarkable how in this ambience Sufi music is playing such a central role. This fact is notable particularly because there is such aversion to matters Islamic in many circles in the West and especially in Europe today. And it is precisely in Europe, in such countries as France and Spain, that there is such a powerful attraction to the various traditions of Sufi music. The Fez Festival of Sacred Music, held annually in the city of Fez in Morocco, draws not only performers but also many listeners from Europe. Furthermore, whenever there is a good concert of Arabic, Persian, Turkish, and other forms of music of the Islamic peoples in Europe, the concert is usually sold out long in advance. Sufism has of course left its imprint upon many other arts, such as calligraphy and architecture, but its musical heritage is of particular significance today for the world at large. On the wing of melodies, rhythms, and harmonies, beyond the concepts of theology and the dicta of the legal aspects of religion, these musical traditions are playing a vital role in bridging the divide between the West and the Islamic world at a time when there is so much need of bridge building. But above all, the sacred music of the Sufis has the power to awaken in the soul its need to travel to the Garden of Truth and also to help it along on the journey.

A SPIRITUAL ETHICS

A morality that is intellectually and spiritually opaque and is purely sentimental can drive many an intelligent person away from religion or reduce religion to only externals and lead to what is called fundamentalism. The first possibility has been realized extensively in the West since the Renaissance, while the second is to be found worldwide today in Christianity as well as in Islam, Judaism, and Hinduism. Sufism, while always emphasizing ethical behavior and the necessity of morality for those who wish to follow the path, has also sought to spiritualize ethics, to cast the light of intelligence upon the virtues. The works of Imam Qushayrī, Ibn al-ʻArīf, Imam Ghazzālī, and many others, some already cited in earlier chapters and some not, bear testimony to this fact. But more important than writings has been the manner of living of Sufis, who have demonstrated in a concrete fashion what it means to live ethically in a spiritual manner and in opposition to hypocrisy, false humility, ostentatious charity, and the like. As mentioned, some Sufis, like the *Malāmatiyyah* or the People of Blame, went so far as to perform acts that appeared outwardly as blameworthy, thereby inviting blame by self-righteous hypocrites upon themselves, while in reality their actions were virtuous and not against legal injunctions of the religion. Such people provided an antidote to religious hypocrisy, which can and usually does manifest itself in societies where religion is as strong as secularism and secular hypocrisy are in the secular societies of today.

The spiritual ethics of Sufism, based on the spiritual and intellectual significance of such virtues as humility, charity and compassion, and sincerity and truthfulness, is a great treasure for the contemporary Islamic world and the antidote to self-righteousness and fanaticism. But it can also be of great value to those Westerners who seek to be ethical in a religious manner but find ordinary morality as taught in many churches or synagogues to be unintelligible and opaque. They do not have to be Muslims to appreciate the easily accessible Sufi ethics, which has its equivalents in the writings of many great Western mystics.

TECHNIQUES OF SPIRITUAL REALIZATION

To walk upon the path to the Garden, to get from Here to There and then realize that the There is Here, requires certain specific spiritual techniques beyond simply thinking about the spiritual world and having faith, although both of these are indispensable prerequisites for the journey. There is the need to learn how to control the mind through meditation; how to control the body through correct breathing and right postures; how to place the Divine Reality through the Names revealed by that Reality at the center of our being; how to escape from the labyrinth of the psyche and to transmute the psyche in an alchemical manner so that it can become wed to the Spirit; how to become aware of our subtle bodies, deeper levels of being, and higher orders of consciousness; and many other matters. One can simply wait upon God and expect Him to lift us to His Presence. That is certainly a possibility, one followed by many Christian and some Muslim mystics. But walking upon the path to the Garden is an active matter requiring the necessary spiritual techniques, and Sufism is a tradition that, while allowing for the possibility of a passive form of mysticism, emphasizes the active role of the adept and therefore seeks to teach the adept how to walk, how to become a wayfarer (*sālik*), and finally how to fly.

Like all integral spiritual traditions such as Zen and Shin Buddhism and Hindu Yoga, Sufism is still in full possession of its techniques of spiritual realization. This living treasure is of course of the greatest importance for Muslims who wish to begin the journey back to God while they are alive here and now, but it is also precious for Westerners. After the Second World War, a number of people from the West realized how important it was to master the techniques of spiritual realization, and they turned first to Zen and Yoga before becoming interested in Sufism. What Sufism offers that is especially significant for the West is that it is a living esoteric path within the Abrahamic family of religions, to which Judaism and Christianity, the main Western religions, also belong. Some Catholic and Protestant theologians and spiritual practitioners have tried to incorporate certain spiritual techniques from East and South Asia into Christianity and have spoken of Zen Catholicism or Christian Yoga, as also have some Jewish seekers for Judaism. In this domain, however, the most accessible and easily applicable techniques to a Jewish and Christian setting are perhaps those of Sufism, which belongs to the world of Abrahamic monotheism and shares many basic tenets with Judaism and Christianity. In the Middle Ages there developed in fact a Jewish school of mysticism called Jewish Sufism associated with such figures as the grandson of the great Maimonides. Such a possibility certainly exists today.

METAPHYSICAL AND COSMOLOGICAL DOCTRINES

Pure metaphysics, which is also the theoretical dimension of salvific knowledge, is the science of the Real and is therefore most essential for human beings, since they have ultimately no possibility of escaping from reality. In the modern West, metaphysics and gnosis soon became a branch of philosophy, understood in the modern sense, and this subordination was followed by the complete rejection of metaphysics by many schools of Western thought, especially from the nineteenth century onward, as we see in Marxism, Comptianism, logical positivism, Anglo-Saxon analytical philosophy, and the like. Soon real metaphysics was forgotten, not to mention the means of realizing its truths. But the thirst for real knowledge continued to manifest itself in certain Western souls, who again turned to the Orient and, with its help, to the forgotten metaphysical tradition of the West. In this quest for metaphysical knowledge Hinduism, especially the school of Advaita Vedanta, attracted many people. It is only during the past few decades that the metaphysics of Sufism, as elucidated primarily in the works of Ibn 'Arabī and his school (to which I shall turn more fully in appendix 2), has become available to the larger Western public.

This vast body of metaphysical knowledge, along with traditional cosmology, which results from applying metaphysical principles to both the macrocosmic and microcosmic domains (not what is understood by cosmology and psychology today), is one of the great legacies of Sufism. This body of knowledge provides a key to understanding the nature of the Real, the reality of the cosmos, and our own being. It contains a map for getting from Here to There as well as the means of realizing that There is Here and Now, at the center of our being and in the present moment.

In the traditional Islamic world this knowledge was known to only a few, but now with the spread of all kinds of modern secular philosophies and problems created by ill-posed questions that threaten the very citadel of faith, this metaphysical and cosmological knowledge bequeathed by over a millennium of Sufism to the present-day generation is of the utmost importance for the Islamic tradition as a whole. It also provides the necessary preliminary map for those, including non-Muslims, who want to know who they are, where they are, and where they should be going.

INITIATIC CURRENT

Above and beyond all that we have mentioned, Sufism offers here and now what is perhaps the rarest and most precious gift in today's conditions, and that is an authentic initiatic current (*walāyah/wilāyah*), discussed earlier in this book. This current has been transmitted over the centuries in an unbroken chain going back to the Prophet. Sufism is not the only esoteric tradition today in which is found authentic initiation and the power and grace that are its concomitants. One can find this possibility in certain forms of Hinduism and esoteric Buddhism, as seen in such schools as Vajrayāna or Tibetan Buddhism, and even in Christianity, where this aspect of the tradition has been eclipsed to a large extent for a long time except in Orthodoxy. The availability of the initiatic current in Sufism to those qualified to receive it is of the utmost importance in present-day conditions, not only for Muslims but within the whole Abrahamic world and even for those who have left Western exoteric religion altogether in quest of other paths of spiritual realization and genuine esoteric teachings. This aspect of the Sufi heritage is also particularly significant in a world in which there is so much pseudoesoterism and so-called teachers with extravagant claims, some of whom unfortunately also wear the garb of Sufism. There is therefore the need for discernment and the presence of an orthodox framework to be able to distinguish the wheat from the chaff and to be able to benefit in an authentic manner from the initiatic current present within Sufism.

SUFI SHRINES

While the Sufi saint is still alive, the saint's *barakah,* or grace, is mostly confined to his or her companions and followers. But after death this *barakah* becomes more public, and members of the Islamic community at large are drawn to the shrines of these saints through a profound intuition. Putting aside those affected by either modernism or fundamentalist puritanism, the vast majority of Muslims, who still follow traditional Islam, visit such shrines in great numbers and draw spiritual sustenance from such pilgrimages. These shrines are in a sense the extension of the tomb of the Prophet in Medina and connect the pious to the foundational figure of their religion and through him to God.

Sufi shrines are found everywhere in the Islamic world from Malaysia to Morocco. They are located on the tops of mountains and in the middle of the desert, in small villages as well as in urban centers. Many Islamic cities, such as Cairo and Fez, came into being as a result of the tomb of saints who were descendants of the Prophet but who were also considered pivotal figures of Sufism. Furthermore, after the pilgrimage to Mecca and Medina (and until a few decades ago Jerusalem), the most extensive pilgrimage by hundreds of thousands if not millions of pious Muslims is to such shrines, as one sees in the annual pilgrimage to Ajmer and the tomb of Mu'īn al-Dīn Chishtī in India or Tanta in Egypt, where the tomb of Aḥmad al-Badawī is to be found.

It might be thought that such shrines belong to popular piety and have little to do with those who walk on the path to the Garden of Truth. This claim is, however, false. First of all, many Sufi including even advanced ones, often visit such sites and derive special inspiration from them. Second, in many places in the Islamic world Sufi gatherings are held in or adjacent to these shrines, whose *barakah* plays an important role in the spiritual practices of members of various Sufi orders. Some Sufis even call such shrines a reflection of the paradisal Garden. Of course, of all the legacies Sufism has left for us today, this one is of consequence almost completely only for Muslims while the others are also of great value for all men and women who are attracted to the spiritual life whether they are Muslim or non-Muslim. And yet even this legacy can be like a magnet for certain non-Muslims, drawing them to the transcendent and immanent Reality that they seek.

CAN CONTEMPORARY PEOPLE BENEFIT FROM THE HERITAGE OF SUFISM?

We live in a world, especially in the West, that emphasizes change and worships the deity of newness, a world in which practically everything around us is considered outmoded faster than at any time in human history. The thought, art, culture, and even religion of an earlier generation are made to appear old and not pertinent to us except in fits of nostalgia, which themselves change rapidly. In such a world, how can one benefit from the heritage of Sufism, which over a millennium of history has addressed men and women very different from us? The answer to this question is that in the deeper sense we carry within ourselves the same reality as did our ancestors in the past. Our deepest needs, such as having hope, finding meaning in life, discovering happiness, learning to face tribulations, pain, sorrow, and misery, and being able to confront the reality of death, are the same for us as for men and women who lived in the past and whom the teachings of Sufism addressed over the ages.

Human beings are still born, live, and die. Our consciousness and our intelligence still seek meaning in our lives and in the world about us. We still face inner and outer obstacles in our earthly life. We still become despondent and need hope. We still seek a haven in the storm of life. And in the deepest sense we are still beings created for immortality and in need of the Infinite Reality, which is beyond our mental, psychological, and physical limitations and constraints. Some still crave the love that "moves the heavens and the stars"; they are thirsty for the wine of gnosis, for that light of liberating knowledge that alone can illuminate our whole being. Amid the fanfare about all the ways modern science and technology transform modern life, the inner person, who stands beyond all the din of the world and who does not surrender to external forces, is still alive within us.

It is this inner person, whom some Sufis have called "the man of light" within us, who is attracted to the heritage of Sufism, not as a heritage of only historical and archaeological interest, but as a living reality of significance for us here and now. For the spiritual person not mesmerized by the glitter of a world that has lost its spiritual mooring and is spinning out of control, the message of Sufism—its literature and music, its ethics, its spiritual methods, and its *barakah*—are of interest not simply because they were addressed to men and women of this or that culture in days of old. They are of interest because they address us here and now, because they deal with matters that are terribly real and have the deepest existential consequences for us. For example, Sufism teaches us how to be alone with God and be happy in this solitude. How many people today suffer from loneliness and become thereby depressed? The Sufi message can turn this state from one of misery to one of joy. What greater need is there today than being able to see the other as ourselves and not as the enemy? Sufism teaches us the means of breaking the walls of the ego and realizing directly that the other *is* us in the deepest sense. How many of us yearn for love? Sufism enables the spring of love for both God and His creatures to gush forth within our souls. And how many yearn for intellectual clarity and unity of modes of knowing in a world in which knowledge has become so compartmentalized? Again Sufism in its doctrinal aspect can provide the solution.

The journey to the Garden of Truth is not something that interested only men and women of old. It remains the supreme journey for us as human beings today even if so many of the external conditions of our lives are different from the patterns of that traditional world in which such teachings were first cultivated. Nothing is more timely than the timeless: surely this dictum applies to the message of Sufism, which being timeless is of pertinence to all instances of time and all loci of space wherein human beings have lived, live today, and shall live in the future, a message that relates to our ultimate future in the Beyond as the Now, and our final destination There as the Here.

SUFISM IN THE ISLAMIC WORLD TODAY

In dealing with Sufism today, it is important to say something about the state of this spiritual tradition in the Islamic world at the present moment. One has to avoid two extremes, both of which are erroneous:

first, that Sufism was a medieval phenomenon like medieval Christian mysticism and that even if Sufism survived beyond what the West calls the medieval period, classical Sufism died out, being replaced by so-called popular Sufism; and second, that the Sufi tradition has continued with the same strength as in centuries past. Actually, Sufism did not die in the Middle Ages, and even what is called classical Sufism in the West has continued to this day. Many great saints have continued to appear. Many important intellectual expositions have been written right up to today. Sufi poetry continues to appear in most Islamic languages, and Sufi music continues to be performed on the highest level. There is of course a popular dimension to Sufism, but it does not define the whole of Sufism today any more than it did hundreds of years ago. One can observe altogether a remarkable continuity in the Sufi tradition, which remains a living spiritual reality and which continues to be practiced by numerous people.

And yet Sufism has been weakened to some extent by attacks against it within the Islamic world since the nineteenth century. During that century one can observe the revival and even founding of certain Sufi orders, such as the Sanūsiyyah. Yet at the same time Sufism was opposed by two forces that were themselves totally opposed to each other but in the deeper sense were two sides of the same coin. These two forces, which are still present, were modernism and puritanical reformism, now called by many fundamentalism. The modernists were completely infatuated with everything modern and Western, and of course for them *Western* did not mean St. Francis of Assisi or St. Teresa of Ávila, but worldliness, power, and material gain. Reacting against the domination of much of the Islamic world by the West, the modernists tried to find a scapegoat for the defeat of Muslims, and many turned their wrath against Sufism, accusing it of preaching passivity and otherworldliness and therefore causing the weakness of Islamic society. Nowhere is this modernist opposition to Sufism more evident than in Turkey, where, after rising to power, the very modernistic Ataturk banned the Sufi orders and many Sufi masters were imprisoned and some killed. This negative attitude toward Sufism can be seen even in a figure such as Muḥammad Iqbal, the ideological father of Pakistan, who was a gifted poet and an admirer of Rūmī and yet who strongly opposed much of Sufi literature, doctrine, and practices.

The second force that began to oppose Sufism in the nineteenth century, an opposition that continues to this day, was that of the puritanical reformism associated most of all with Wahhābism, which arose in what is today Saudi Arabia, and more generally with what is called the Salafiyyah movement, that is, a movement that claims to return to the pure Islam of the ancestors (*salaf*). This movement was not confined to one country but spread in different forms to many Muslim lands, being more successful in some areas than others. Those who followed these ideas sought to overcome the weakness of the Islamic world by brushing aside thirteen or fourteen centuries of Islamic history, opposing traditional Islamic art, philosophy, and theology and cultural habits of Muslims that they considered the consequence of decadence resulting from luxury and wayward living in Islamic cities. But most of all they were opposed to Sufism. This is especially true of Wahhābism, which opposed both Sufism and Shi'ism virulently, considering the visitation to the tomb of saints as "saint worship" and idolatry. For a long time Sufism was completely banned in Saudi Arabia, whose religious orientation has been Wahhābī since the founding of the state. Only recently has there been a change of attitude on behalf of the government with some freedom given to Sufi orders to function in the kingdom.

These two forces were able to weaken Sufism to some degree but not by any means to destroy it. The Sufi orders remained strong and open into the twentieth century in such countries as the Sudan, Egypt, Syria, Algeria, Morocco, Senegal, Caucasia, Persia, Central Asia (before Lenin), and Muslim India. If anything, after the Second World War Sufism made a comeback, especially among well-educated classes, who were becoming aware of the spiritual crisis in the modern West and sought to return to their spiritual roots. Of course, the situation is not like the thirteenth century, when, in one lifetime, you could have met Abū'l-Ḥasan al-Shādhilī in Egypt, Ibn 'Arabī in Syria, and Jalāl al-Dīn Rūmī in Anatolia, as you could sit at the feet of St. Francis or St. Clare, Meister Eckhart, and St. Thomas during the same century in Europe. But the situation of Islam is not that of the West today as far as mystical and esoteric teachings are concerned. Probably there is no church in Germany today where one can hear an Eckhartian sermon any more than there is a university in France where one could study with someone like Hugh of St. Victor or St. Bonaventure. In the Islamic world, however, the mystical tradition continues to subsist, and there are still saintly figures, initiatic practices, and mystical teachings, as one sees in the vitality of such Sufi orders as the Qādirriyyah, Khalwatiyyah, Shādhiliyyah, and Naqshbandiyyah. (I shall deal with these and other orders and some of the contemporary saintly figures of Sufism in the appendixes that follow.) Despite being weakened to some extent by the onslaught of modernism and fundamentalism, Sufism, which is the antidote to both, is still very much alive and accessible for those who seek. The saying of Christ, "Seek and ye shall find," still holds true in its esoteric sense for the world dominated by the Quranic revelation.

SUFISM IN THE WEST YESTERDAY AND TODAY

It is strange that during the European Middle Ages, when so many Islamic works in the sciences, philosophy, and even theology were translated into Latin, no Sufi texts were rendered into this language; at least none has been discovered so far. The case is different for several vernacular languages such as Provençal and Catalan, in which local versions of Sufi narratives can be found. Moreover, certain initiatic organizations in the West had contact with currents of Islamic esoterism, for example, the Order of the Temple and even the *Fedeli d'amore,* to which Dante, who used the architecture of the Nocturnal Ascent (*al-mi'rāj*) of the Prophet in his *Divine Comedy,* belonged. In Spain, contact with Sufism carried into the fifteenth and sixteenth centuries, as one sees in the works of both St. John of the Cross and St. Teresa of Ávila.

All such contacts came to an end in Europe from the late Renaissance to the nineteenth century despite the presence of many Sufi orders in areas at the heart of Europe such as Bosnia and Albania. Interest in Sufism in the West in modern times had to wait for the translation of Sufi classics from Persian and Arabic into German, English, French, and some other European languages beginning at the end of the eighteenth century. With access to translations, some major figures of the Romantic period became attracted to Sufism. One needs only recall Goethe, who was so devoted to Ḥāfiẓ, Rückert, both poet and translator of Sufi literature, and many others. The translations of Sufi texts into German were also of special significance for the first contact of the United States with Sufism, for the school of New England Transcendentalism where this contact took place became interested in Persian Sufi literature mostly through German rather than English translations. New England Transcendentalists, such as Emerson, who were intensely interested in Sufism were called the "Persians of Concord," a remarkable phenomenon of American cultural history to which not enough attention has been paid. In any case, the influence of Sufism is quite evident in the work of Emerson, such as his long poem "Sa'dī," as well as in the thoughts and words of Thoreau and Hawthorne.

One had to wait until the twentieth century for the Sufi orders to sink their roots into the soil of the Occident, for it was at the beginning of that century that a small number of eminent Europeans entered the Shādhiliyyah Order. In the 1920s a teacher of the Chishtiyyah Order, Pir Inayat Khan, came to the West and settled in Europe, where a group assembled around him, although many of his entourage were interested in Sufism only culturally and not as a spiritual path and did not even embrace Islam, which, as mentioned, is absolutely necessary for the serious practice of Sufism. In addition to the Shādhiliyyah and Chishtiyyah, other Sufi orders gradually spread to the West, including the Qādiriyyah, the Naqshbandiyyah, the Ni'malullahiyyah, the Tijāniyyah, the Murīdiyyah, the Khalwatiyyah-Jarrāḥiyyah, and many others. The twentieth century marks the first time that the Sufi tradition became part and parcel of the spiritual landscape of the Occident. During that period there appeared in Europe and America authentic masters with serious followers as well as pseudomasters with pretensions that would never be accepted in the Islamic world. There has even appeared in the West a so-called Sufism outside the framework of Islam, which is totally unknown to the followers of that religion. As I mentioned already, Islamic history includes a few who, being "attracted to God" (*majdhūb*) and in an "intoxicated" state of consciousness, did not practice the *Sharī'ah* (although they were still Muslims), but these were rare exceptions. The wholesale marketing of Sufism divorced from the Islamic tradition is a modern, Western innovation having nothing to do with the authentic Sufi tradition.

Nevertheless, many traditional and orthodox Sufi orders have spread to the West and now have many followers, including those of Western origin, and an ever growing body of Sufi literature is being made available in European languages, especially English and French. How significant is this body of teachings and availability of methods of spiritual practice for the West? I believe that the impact of this major spiritual and intellectual tradition on the West can be seen on three levels. First, there are those who yearn for the knowledge of the Garden of Truth and the means with which to reach it and who, not having found such a possibility within their own tradition, turn to Islam and Sufism. They are those who enter Islam and the Sufi tradition and practice this spiritual path fully. Second, there are those who follow spiritual paths in their own religion, primarily Judaism and Christianity, but draw from Sufism certain ideas, symbols, methods of meditation, inspiration, and so forth, as some Christians and Jews have done from Yoga and Zen. Third, there are those for whom the Sufi tradition is the occasion for recollecting elements lost in their own religion, aiding in the rediscovery and recovery of the integral reality of their own tradition.

All of these possibilities have been realized to some extent in both Europe and America and are bound to be realized even more in the future. In any case, the Sufi tradition makes available in the Occident a metaphysical doctrine and means of its realization, which have become less and less available in the West since the Middle Ages. This tradition also provides the most important means for the creation of understanding between various religions in general and the members of the Abrahamic family in particular as well as mutual comprehension between the West and the Islamic world on the highest intellectual and spiritual level.

ENTRY INTO THE GARDEN OF TRUTH: THE GOAL OF HUMAN LIFE

We were created to transcend the finitude and limitations of the human state. The mystery of our life on earth is not only that we are born, live, and die in a journey whose beginning and end we know not; it is also that within this horizontal journey we are given the possibility of wayfaring vertically beyond all the temporal and spatial accidents of our terrestrial existence. And it is essentially for the sake of making this second journey that we were put here on earth. This journey, which takes us to the abode of the One and the Garden of Truth, is the primary raison d'être of our existence in this world and the end of the journey, the ultimate goal of human life.

From one point of view, the journey considered horizontally seems to be long, but from the metaphysical point of view, which is based on the vertical dimension, it is nothing other than that single instant when we surrender ourselves to God and begin the path of ascent toward Him. We were created to know the Garden of Truth and ultimately the Gardener Himself, and to reach it through the full realization of this knowledge. Sufism is one of the major paths that the Gardener has created, within the framework of Islam, to the Garden. Surely there are other paths and Sufism would be the first to attest to the universality of revelation. But we are concerned in this book with this particular path and have sought to say something on the basis of this particular path about the nature of the Garden and the Gardener, the nature of the path to the Garden, and the long and rich tradition that over the centuries has made possible journeying upon this path and still does today.

Let us then take advantage of the here and now to travel beyond all times and places, before the hand of destiny removes from us the possibility of that vertical journey, which begins here and now and finally returns to Here and Now. We travel to the There only to discover that it is Here, and to the future that is beyond earthly time only to see that it is Now. To make the journey to the Garden means to go from here to There, and the fruit of the journey is the realization that There is Here. That is why in the Quran, God addresses the Prophet, "If my servant asks thee about Me, truly I am Near." That Divine Reality, the Gardener, is Near; we have only to realize His Nearness. As for the Garden of Truth, like the Gardener, it resides at the center of our being. Happy are those who are able to reach this Garden while they are still in the human state and have the possibility of doing so.

O Saki, with the light of wine kindle our cup,
O musician, play, for the world has to our wish surrendered.
We have seen in the cup, the image of the Face of the Friend,
Oh how ignorant thou art of the delight of our constant drinking.[3]

Ḥāfiẓ

wa'Llāh^u a'lam
And God knoweth best

Part Four

Appendix One

THE SUFI TRADITION AND THE SUFI ORDERS

Reflections on the Manifestation of Sufism in Time and Space

The earth shall never be empty of the "proof of God."
Ḥadīth

On this path the saints stand behind and before,
Providing a sign of their spiritual station.
When they became aware of the boundaries of their state,
They spoke of what is known and the person who knows.[1]
Maḥmūd Shabistarī

They extinguished a thousand candles,
Yet the gathering remains.
Popular Sufi saying

THE MEANING OF THE HISTORY OF SUFISM

With respect to the Garden of Truth and the means of reaching it within the Sufi tradition, the text of this book is now finished. But lest one think that what has been said thus far is contrived by me or someone else and has no roots in a tradition extending over centuries, it is necessary to say a few words about the historical unfolding of Sufism. This exposition can also be helpful to the many who are accustomed to learning about a subject through its history, although it is necessary to recall how important it is to escape the entrapment of historicism in order to understand a reality that transcends time and history.

The reality of Sufism, like all spiritual reality, is in its essence metahistorical, beyond the accidents of time and space, and what we have discussed in the earlier chapters of this book pertains to a tradition whose message transcends history and geography and at the same time extends over fourteen centuries and across lands as separated as Iberia and Java, Tataristan and Senegal. The metahistorical reality of Sufism has been manifested in many times and climes, among diverse ethnic groups and in numerous languages, without its essential reality ever becoming simply an accident of particular social and historical circumstances.

We live in a world in which the transcendent dimension of reality is negated by many prevalent philosophies, and therefore reality is identified with becoming and the domain of the temporal and the transient. Even religion, which is based on the reality of the Transcendent as well as the Immanent, is often reduced to its history, and this has been especially true since the nineteenth century. At that time historicism became dominant in Western philosophy, and later reactions to this historicism, such as the phenomenology of Edmund Husserl, were not able to obliterate from the minds of most educated Westerners the habit of reducing any claim of truth to its history and making historical evidence the sole criterion for judging the validity of that truth claim.

This is the philosophical background most Western scholars of Sufism have brought to their study of it, reducing the reality of Sufism to its history—a history, moreover, that, as seen by them, is limited in scope, being based solely on written documents and impervious to the all-important oral transmission. They have for the most part neglected the famous Sufi poem:

The Book of Sufi is not black ink and words,
It is none other than a pure heart white like snow.

Consequently, since the nineteenth century, when Sufism began to be studied seriously in the West, all kinds of theories of its origin were posited. Some wrote that it came into being as a result of the influence of Christian monasticism, others as a result of Neoplatonism, and yet others of Zoroastrianism and Manichaeism, while another group sought its origin in India. No one at that time, of course, bothered to ask the Sufis themselves. Such views of Western orientalists are just as absurd as claiming a non-Christian origin for Christian spirituality or a non-Jewish origin for the schools of Jewish spirituality and mysticism. It remains to the great credit of the foremost academic European authority on Sufism in the twentieth century, the French scholar Louis Massignon, and the British Islamicist David Margoliouth to assert that the roots of Sufism must be sought in the Islamic revelation itself. Yet this fundamental truth does not negate the possibility of one spiritual tradition borrowing symbols, metaphysical language for the formulation of inner spiritual experiences, and other manners of expression from another tradition. The fact that St. Teresa of Ávila based her idea of the seven castles of contemplation upon a work of the Baghdadī Sufi Abū'l-Ḥusayn al-Nūrī does not make her any less of a Christian saint, just as the love of Ḥallāj for Christ does not make him a secret Christian.

In any case, the historicism that provides the framework of most Western studies of Sufism must be thoroughly rejected in order to understand the reality of Sufism as understood by the Sufis themselves. This does not mean, however, if a Western scholar has discovered a manuscript that shows that a particular work was not written by such and such an author but rather by another that this discovery must be rejected. Far from it! What it means is that the reality of Sufism cannot be reduced to its external history. This metahistorical reality has manifested itself in the lives of numerous saints and followers of various Sufi orders, in a vast literary corpus including some of the greatest mystical poetry ever written, in metaphysical and philosophical writings of premier importance, in music and other arts, as well as in social, economic, and political aspects of Islamic civilization. And it is this manifestation that constitutes the legitimate history of Sufism if viewed from its own perspective. In the pages that follow I shall turn to at least some of the most significant figures, movements, and works of that history.

Before embarking on this task, however, it is important to recall that we are dealing with a tradition that has been followed over a vast area of the globe from major cities such as Fez, Cairo, Damascus, Baghdad, Istanbul, Isfahan, Tus, Lahore, and Delhi to small villages in the Hindu Kush as well as in the forests of Senegal, from ports by seas and rivers in Sumatra to oases in the middle of the African desert. Also, there are many important Sufi figures who never wrote a word but left an indelible mark upon the hearts of their followers and are known and still venerated locally.

Another Sufi poem asserts:

> After our death seek not our remains in the earth,
> For our tomb is in the breast of the gnostics.

In light of this incredibly vast spiritual tradition it is not difficult to understand why there does not exist a thorough history of Sufism on a global scale even at the level of the study of only names, works, places of pilgrimage, and so forth associated with Sufism. This is true not only for European languages, but for Islamic languages as well. Some areas such as the Maghrib, Egypt, Turkey, Iran, and Muslim India have been better studied than other places such as West and South Africa, but even areas that are better known still carry many unstudied treasures that continue to be discovered.

THE ORIGIN OF SUFISM

Metaphysically speaking, the origin of Sufism is none other than God Himself. The earlier chapters of this book should have made this truth clear, for how can a path lead to God if it does not come from Him? To summarize what we have already discussed, this origin must be sought in the Word of God, that is, the Quran, and in the inner reality of the Prophet, who received this Word and transmitted it to the world. Certain verses of the Quran have a direct spiritual and inward meaning, as already mentioned, while the Quran as a whole is considered to have inner or esoteric levels of meaning, as mentioned in a *ḥadīth* of the Prophet. Moreover, many of the *ḥadīths* themselves, especially the sacred *ḥadīths,* some of which have been already cited, contain the basic teachings of Sufism. To these texts must be added the actual initiatic power (*walāyah/wilāyah*) that God bestowed upon the Prophet and that he disseminated among certain of the companions. The initiatic chain (*al-silsilah*) of every Sufi order goes back to the Prophet and through him and the archangel Gabriel to God. The reality of Sufism on the historical plane therefore starts with the Prophet, even if the name of this inner reality as *taṣawwuf,* or Sufism, was to come a century later.

THE EARLIEST SUFIS

After the Prophet, the most important figure in Sufism is ʻAlī (d. 661), who was the main inheritor of the esoteric teachings that emanated from the founder of Islam as well as of the power of *walāyah/wilāyah.* That is why he is as revered among Sunni Sufis as he is among Shiʻites, for whom he is the First Imam. There are many stories in traditional sources about ʻAlī's leading a simple ascetic life, being the great champion of justice, having unbounded love for God and the Prophet, considering the primacy of truth in all aspects of his life, and other spiritual matters associated with his remarkable life. These stories in themselves demonstrate why he was and is so revered by Sufis. For example, there is the story that just before a battle that was to determine the whole future of the young Islamic community, when ʻAlī was already on his horse and ready to march, one of his companions came toward him and asked, "ʻAlī, what is the truth?" One of ʻAlī's lieutenants told the person who had posed such a question that this was not the time for it, whereupon ʻAlī said that he would answer this question immediately because it was precisely the matter of truth for which they were going to battle. ʻAlī then made one of the most profound discourses on the metaphysical meaning of truth to be found in the Islamic tradition. One cannot but be reminded of the responses of Krishna to Arjuna on the field of battle as recorded in the Bhagavad Gita.

ʻAlī's discourses, sermons, and letters were later collected in a book called *Nahj al-balāghah* (*Path of Eloquence*), which remains widely read to this day. His words and his life based on virtue and marked by sanctity have continued to inspire Sufis over the ages. Some Sufi orders such as the Baktāshī have gone in fact to the extreme of practically divinizing 'Alī. Abū Bakr, the first caliph (d. 634), is also considered by certain Sufi orders to be in the chain linking them to the Prophet, but his role in Sufism is not nearly as central as that of 'Alī.

Contemporary with the Prophet are a few other figures whom Sufis consider their spiritual ancestors. One of these is Abū Dharr al-Ghifārī (d. 652–53), who lived a very ascetic and simple life combined with great humility. An important transmitter of *Ḥadīth,* he was compared in his spiritual and external poverty to Jesus. His contemporary Salmān al-Fārsī (d. circa 656) was a Persian who represents the prototype of a Persian Muslim. Having dreamed of meeting the veritable Prophet, he left his hometown of Isfahan and set out for Syria. He was sold into slavery and brought to Arabia, where the Prophet saw him. He was made free and became a member of the household of the Prophet. He later joined 'Alī in Iraq, where he died and where his tomb near Baghdad is to this day a famous site of pilgrimage, although other sites have also been mentioned as his tomb. Salmān is one of the founders of Sufism and spiritual chivalry (*futuwwah*), and he even plays a role in the esoteric hierarchy of certain sects in the Islamic world.

Another contemporary, Uways al-Qaranī from Yemen, who also joined 'Alī in Iraq and died in the battle of Ṣiffīn in 657, never met the Prophet but became a Muslim from afar. He is the most famous of all Sufis of Yemen and the founder of a special spiritual strand in Sufism called Uwaysī. This strand is associated with men and women who are Sufis but do not have a human master. They are led by members of the invisible hierarchy of the Sufi cosmos or by the prophet Khiḍr. Many major figures in the history of Sufism, such as Abū'l-Ḥasan Kharaqānī in Khurasan and Aḥmad Sirhindī, have been Uwaysīs.

Of course, along with 'Alī, these figures are perhaps the most eminent of those around the Prophet who were associated with the reality that soon became known as Sufism. These men, and especially 'Alī, play an important role in the subsequent unfolding of the Sufi tradition over the centuries down to our own day.

The next generation of figures of early Sufism are called the "followers" (*tābi'ūn*), those who lived in the second half of the seventh century, and among them none is more important than Ḥasan al-Baṣrī (d. 728), who was endowed with a long life, during which he instructed several generations of students in both the religious sciences and what was soon to become known as Sufism. This great patriarch of *taṣawwuf,* who was born and brought up in Medina but later moved to Basra, gave moving sermons and uttered sayings in eloquent Arabic that have been quoted in many later works. Among his well-known sayings is, "Exist in this world as if you had never set foot here, and in the next world as if you had never left it." He also wrote a number of letters, including a particularly important one on spiritual chivalry. The message of Ḥasan was otherworldliness, abstinence, poverty, and reverential fear of God, although he also spoke of the knowledge and love of God, which he contrasted with love and knowledge of the world. He is at the beginning of the ascetic phase that characterizes the first epoch of Sufism associated with Mesopotamia.

During the late seventh and eighth centuries, as the Islamic community became wealthy and many turned to worldly pursuits, the early Sufis acted as the conscience of the community, calling the faithful back to the simple and pure life of early Islamic society. This period is marked by strong ascetic tendencies, as seen also in the life of Ḥasan's student, 'Abd al-Wāḥid ibn Zayd (d. 794). Among other leading figures of Sufism of this period in Iraq one can mention Ḥabīb al-'Ajamī (d. 737), who was a disciple of Ḥasan al-Baṣrī, and Dā'ūd al-Ṭā'ī (d. 777), who was Ḥabīb's disciple and who like Ḥasan left a deep impression on later Sufism.

It is not possible to discuss this period without mentioning the name of Ḥasan ibn 'Alī (d. 669–670), the older son of 'Alī, and the Second Shi'ite Imam. Unlike his younger brother, Ḥusayn, who chose the active life and who was martyred in Karbalā' in Iraq, Ḥasan soon retired from political life and led a quiet and contemplative life in Medina, where he died and is buried. In the oral tradition of Sufism, he is considered as the person who taught the esoteric interpretation of the Quran and sowed the seed of Sufism in the western lands of Islam.

Another descendant of 'Alī, Ja'far al-Ṣādiq (d. 765), played an even more evident role than Ḥasan in Sufism. Master of both the exoteric and the esoteric sciences, he trained many disciples in both domains. He also authored the first surviving esoteric commentary of the Quran, which served as prototype and model for the long tradition of Sufi commentaries upon the Sacred Text that have continued to appear in Arabic, Persian, and other Islamic languages over the centuries. It is interesting to note that while some of the sayings of Imam Ja'far are expressions of pure gnosis (*ma'rifah*), the law of the school of Twelve-Imam Shi'ism, which constitutes the great majority of Shi'ites, is also named after him and thus called Ja'farī Law. He was also a teacher of Abū Ḥanīfah, the founder of one of the Sunni schools of law. Ja'far al-Ṣādiq was the Sixth Shi'ite Imam, accepted as such not only by Twelve-Imam Shi'ites but also by Ismā'īlīs, the other important branch of Shi'ism, and he is highly revered in Sunnism. He represents the unity of the inward and outward dimensions of Islam and was a preeminent authority in both.

More generally speaking, it can be asserted that while Sufism represents the main crystallization of Islamic esoteric teachings, these teachings are also found in Shi'ism. The first eight imams of Shi'ism are in fact also Poles or Axes of Sufism and appear in the initiatic chains of many Sufi orders. The Eighth Imam, 'Alī al-Riḍā, is buried in Mashhad in Iran, and to this day pious Shi'ites who seek a spiritual master often go on pilgrimage to his tomb to ask his help in finding an authentic teacher. The common origin and various forms of interplay and interaction over the ages between Sufism and Shi'ism in its gnostic aspect, or what Persians called *'irfān-i shī'ī* (Shi'ite gnosis), constitute in fact one of the most fascinating aspects of the Islamic tradition. Suffice it to say that although the paths to the Garden of Truth are found in the Islamic universe mostly within the tradition of Sufism, it is necessary to remember that there are also authentic means of access to that Garden through the inner dimension of Shi'ism, which, although not outwardly called Sufism by many authorities during the past few centuries, is nevertheless concerned ultimately with the same reality as Sufism. This truth is seen fully in the writings of the Shi'ite gnostic Sayyid Ḥaydar Āmulī (d. after 1385), who spoke of Sufism and Shi'ism as constituting a single reality.

Coming back to the historical unfolding of the manifestations of the reality of Sufism, it can be said that in the eighth century, as other aspects of Islamic intellectual disciplines such as law, theology, and grammar became defined, codified, and delineated, the spiritual knowledge and means of access to it inherited from the Prophet also became clearly defined. It became known as *taṣawwuf* ("Sufism" in English), and it is said that the first person to be called a Sufi was an ascetic of Kufa by the name of Abū Hāshim (d. 767). Scholars, both Muslim and Western, have argued about the origin of this word. Some have said that it comes from *ahl-al-ṣuffah,* people of the bench, who were outstanding companions of the Prophet who often sat on a bench in front of the Prophet's mosque in Medina. Others claim that it comes from *ṣafā,* meaning purity, and some have even tried to derive it from the Greek *sophia.* The most widely accepted view is that the term is derived from *ṣūf,* which means wool, since the early Sufis usually wore a long woolen garb similar to the present-day Moroccan *jallabah* and what the prophets and patriarchs of Israel used to wear. This derivation also receives support from the fact that in early Persian the Sufis were called *pashmīnah-pūsh,* or "wearers of wool." Many Sufi masters have claimed, however, that like *Allāh,* the Name of God, *ṣūfī* and *taṣawwuf,* that is, the words "Sufi" and "Sufism", have no etymological root but that through the symbolic numerical value of the letters of *taṣawwuf,* similar to the Kabbalistic and Hassidic *gematria,* this term corresponds to *Divine Wisdom (al-ḥīkmat al-ilāhiyyah).*

In any case, Sufism began to grow in the cosmopolitan center of Basra, where Arabs and Persians met and intermingled, as well as in other Mesopotamian cities such as Kufa. Characterized at first by strong asceticism, based on the fear of God, it laid the solid ground for the flowering of love and knowledge of God, which were to follow. In the same way that on the path to the Garden of Truth our souls must experience the reverential fear of God and the grandeur of His Majesty before they can experience love and knowledge of Him, the external manifestation of Sufism in history likewise demonstrates clearly the three phases of fear (*makhāfah*), love (*maḥabbah*), and knowledge (*ma'rifah*).

Already in the latter part of the eighth century we see the beginning of the unfolding of the cycle of love with the appearance of the first great Arab woman Sufi, Rābi'ah al-'Adawiyyah (d. 801), along with Imam Ja'far al-Ṣādiq, who was her contemporary. Born in Basra where she also died, Rābi'ah has been considered by some as a disciple of Ḥasan al-Baṣrī, but this is most likely in reference to her following his spiritual teachings rather than being his direct disciple. The account of her life is mixed with many myths of spiritual significance but not based on historical verification. Over the centuries, in fact, she became the prototype of female sanctity in Sufism and was claimed by many groups. She even has several tombs purported to be authentic, all visited by pilgrims and all bearing the perfume of her sanctity. What is known about her historically is that she was sold into slavery but was freed because of her exalted spiritual state. She shunned public life and lived as a celibate. Her function was to state the primacy of God over everything else, including Paradise. She was also a gifted poet and left behind some of the most beautiful verses of Arabic poetry on selfless Divine Love. One of her most famous poems states:

> Two loves I give Thee, love that yearns,
> And love because Thy due is love.
> My yearning my remembrance turns
> To Thee, nor lets it from Thee rove.
> Thou hast Thy due whene'er it please Thee
> To lift the veils for me to see Thee.
> Praise is not mine in this, nor yet
> In that, but Thine is this and that.[2]

Although more or less a recluse, Rābi'ah did teach Sufism and had disciples, the most famous among them being Ṣufyān al-Thawrī (d. 778) and Shaqīq al-Balkhī (d. 809) from Khurasan, who spoke so profoundly about reliance upon God (*tawakkul*) and was also the first Sufi to discuss the spiritual states while emphasizing "the light of the pure love of God."

Before turning to the schools of Baghdad and Khurasan, it is important to mention a ninth-century figure who did not belong to either school, Thawbān ibn Ibrāhīm, known as Dhū'l-Nūn al-Miṣrī (d. circa 861). An Egyptian Sufi who traveled to Baghdad and was also known as an alchemist and philosopher, he not only spoke of the love of God and called Him the Beloved but was also the first Sufi to develop the theory of gnosis, or *ma'rifah*. He also developed the theory of annihilation (*al-fanā'*) and subsistence (*al-baqā'*), discussed above, on the basis of Quranic teachings. Like Rābi'ah, Dhū'l-Nūn was an accomplished poet who left behind many beautiful poems, usually with the theme of the love of God, and also prayers that have echoed over the ages. In one of the most famous of these prayers he says:

> O God, I never hearken to the voices of the beasts or the rustle of the trees, the splashing of the waters or the song

> of the birds, the whistling of the wind or the rumble of the thunder, but I sense in them a testimony to Thy Unity, and a proof of Thy Incomparability, that Thou art the All-Prevailing, the All-Knowing, the All-True.[3]

Some have considered Dhū'l-Nūn as the first expositor of the doctrinal formulation of Sufism usually associated with the name of Ibn 'Arabī, who often cites Dhū'l-Nūn in his works. Dhū'l-Nūn, this extraordinary figure of early Sufism, returned to Egypt, where he died. His tomb with its mysterious vertical black tombstone is still found in one of the old and less visited quarters of Cairo.

THE SCHOOL OF BAGHDAD

One does not know what has befallen the holy sites of Baghdad after the recent tragedies that have occurred in this historical city. Until a few years ago, however, the older quarters of the city were dotted with tombs of early Sufi saints, such as Abū'l-Qāsim al-Junayd (d. 910), along with many of his contemporaries and disciples and of course 'Abd al-Qādir al-Jīlānī (d. 1166), whose mausoleum dominates the city along with the shrine of the Seventh Shi'ite Imam, Mūsā al-Kāẓim, who was also a Pole of Sufism. (The Pole [*al-Quṭb*] in Sufism refers to the central figure of the esoteric spiritual hierarchy that rules over the spiritual domain during each generation.) This galaxy of tombs of some of the greatest Sufi saints points to the importance of Baghdad as a center of Sufism going back to the ninth century, when what later authorities called the School of Baghdad was established.

Many place the origin of this school in the teachings of Ma'rūf al-Karkhī (d. 815), who was himself a disciple of the Imam 'Alī al-Riḍā (d. 817). Ma'rūf had great influence not only in Baghdad but also in the later history of Sufism elsewhere. He spoke especially of the state of contentment (*riḍā*) and its importance in the spiritual life. His most famous disciple, Sarī al-Saqaṭī (d. circa 867), developed further the theory of states and stations, which we have already discussed, as well as the meaning of Unity (*al-tawḥīd*), the central doctrine of Islam, which was more fully developed by his nephew Junayd, the central figure of the School of Baghdad. Another student of Sarī al-Saqaṭī, Abū Bakr al-Kharrāz (d. 899), who dealt in depth with the meaning of *tawḥīd,* was also a master of Junayd. It was Kharrāz who asserted that only God as the Truth (*al-Ḥaqq*) could utter "I" in the deepest sense of the meaning of "I," and it was this doctrine that was celebrated by Junayd's student, Manṣūr al-Ḥallāj.

One cannot discuss this early period without mentioning another eminent Baghdādī figure, al-Ḥārith al-Muḥāsibī (d. 857), who was an authority in both theology and Sufism. Born in Basra, he was influenced by the teachings of Ḥāsan al-Baṣrī. Al-Muḥāsibī was instrumental in the development of the technical language of Sufism and is famous for his method of constantly examining one's conscience and psychological states. He is also particularly known for his profound discussions of hypocrisy and means of curing this subtle sickness, with which so many souls are afflicted, often without being aware of their condition.

Let us now turn to the central figure of the School of Baghdad, Abū'l-Qāsim al-Junayd. He was so honored by the other saints of Sufism that he was given such honorific titles as "Master of the Group (of Sufis)" and the *Shaykh,* or spiritual master, of *shaykhs.* A few of his treatises are extant, dealing mostly with gnosis, and many of his sayings were preserved in later compilations. But what is most important about Junayd is that he marks the synthesis of earlier Sufism and the beginning of a new phase in its history. With him, Sufism became more organized to the extent that some refer to the Junaydiyyah Order, although the organized Sufi orders, to which we shall turn soon, did not come into being until over two centuries later.

There was a remarkable cluster of eminent Sufi figures around Junayd, some his friends, companions, and contemporaries and some his disciples. In this circle one can mention Abū'l-Ḥusayn al-Nūrī (d. 907), a friend of Junayd and again a great poet. In his *Maqāmāt al-qulūb* (*Stations of Hearts*), Nūrī analyzed the psychological states of the soul in relation to the human heart. He described the various stations of the soul in its contemplation of God as seven citadels, and as current scholarship has shown, this symbolism served as inspiration for the seven castles of St. Teresa of Ávila's *Interior Castles.* Nūrī also spoke of the garden of the heart, and through him the image of the heart as the interior garden became prevalent in Sufism.

This great troubadour of the love of God is known for numerous ecstatic poems, such as:

I would, so overflowing is my love for Him,
Remember Him perpetually, yet my remembrance—
Wondrous to tell—is vanished into ecstasy,
And wonder upon wonder, even ecstasy,
With memory's self, in nearness-farness vanished is.[4]

Ḥallāj is perhaps the best-known Sufi figure associated with the School of Baghdad and one of the most famous of all Sufis. Furthermore, thanks to the Herculean efforts of Louis Massignon, who wrote a monumental work titled *The Passion of al-Ḥallāj,* in which he compares his death to that of Christ (hence the word *passion* in the title), Ḥallāj became the best-known Sufi in Western academic circles. This is somewhat unfortunate because the life and destiny of this great master were truly exceptional and must not be taken as the norm for the life of Sufi saints and sages in general.

Like many other Mesopotamian Sufis and members of the School of Baghdad who were of Persian origin, including Ḥabīb al-'Ajamī, Junayd, and Nūrī, Ḥallāj hailed from Persia and was in fact born in the province of Fars in present-day southern Iran. It is therefore even more remarkable that he should be such a great master of Arabic poetry to the extent that many have considered him, along with 'Umar ibn al-Fāriḍ and Ibn 'Arabī, as the most outstanding Sufi poet of the Arabic language. In any case, Ḥallāj grew up in Wasit and Tustar and attached himself early in life to Sahl al-Tustarī (d. 896), with whom he journeyed to Basra. Later he went to Baghdad, where he became a disciple of Junayd, but because of Ḥallāj's audacious theophanic sayings (*shaṭḥiyyāt*), of which the most famous is *anā'l-Ḥaqq* ("I am the Truth"), many other Sufis opposed him for not being careful enough in divulging the divine secrets to the public at large. And so Ḥallāj set out for Khurasan, where he stayed for some five years. He also made the pilgrimage to Mecca (*ḥajj*) twice and traveled to India and Central Asia. Through these long journeys he gained many disciples and was known as a man with miraculous powers, such as healing the seriously ill.

Upon completing a third pilgrimage to Mecca, Ḥallāj returned to Baghdad, where he bought a house and decided to settle. He was, however, arrested and imprisoned in 912 on the charge of propagating heretical ideas. He became victim to political machinations at the

Abbasid court and was finally put to death in 922 on the gibbet. He faced his death cheerfully as the means of realization of Divine Love, and it was then that he composed one of his most famous Sufi poems, which begins with the line:

> Kill me o my trustworthy friends,
> For in my being killed is my life.[5]

It was the destiny of Ḥallāj to divulge esoteric teachings in order to restore a balance between the esoteric and the exoteric, and he paid for this act with his life, something very rare in the history of Sufism. Later generations recognized his greatness and echoed his assertion "I am the Truth" in a thousand and one ways. In fact no phrase outside of the text of the Quran has had such a profound impact and continuous usage among Sufis as the Ḥallājian *anā'l-Ḥaqq,* which expresses the highest doctrine of Unity by pointing out that only God can say "I" and that this Divine Reality resides at the center of our being and is none other than the Truth. Just to give an example of Ḥallāj's influence, in one of his most beautiful poems Rūmī says:

> Before there was in this world the cup, wine and grape,
> Our soul was drunk from the everlasting wine,
> From the days of the pre-eternal covenant we were beating the
> drum of "I am the Truth,"
> Before there was this commotion and calamity of Manṣūr.

The Divine "I" resides at our center now as it did at the time of Ḥallāj and will do so as long as human beings continue to walk on the earth. That is why the cry of Ḥallāj, *anā'l-Ḥaqq,* continues and will continue to reverberate in the souls of those on the Sufi path, men and women who seek the Truth, as it has done during the past millennium.

Other important Sufis, such as Abū Bakr al-Shiblī (d. 945), continued to appear in Baghdad, but in a sense the death of Ḥallāj marks the end of a period that witnessed some of the greatest saints of early Islam, those who laid the foundation, along with masters of the School of Khurasan, of later Sufism.

THE SCHOOL OF KHURASAN

Baghdad was an important but not the only center of Sufism in the eighth and ninth centuries. Khurasan, which at that time embraced a large area including the present-day province of Khurasan in Iran, northern Afghanistan, and parts of Central Asia, also became a center of Sufism and vied in importance with Baghdad and other areas in Iraq. Khurasan produced so many Sufi saints that there developed a saying among later Sufis that while in other areas if one plants a seed it grows into a tree, in Khurasan it grows into a saint. Also it was here that Persian Sufi literature developed, a literature that transformed the religious and cultural map of much of Asia from western China to Bengal and indirectly Southeast Asia.

One of the first notable members of the School of Khurasan was Ibrāhīm ibn Adham (d. circa 790), who was originally a prince, like Gautama the Buddha, and like him abandoned the life of the court to devote himself fully to the spiritual life. Similar to the early Sufis of Mesopotamia, Ibrāhīm was an ascetic devoted to the life of poverty and renunciation of the world based on reliance upon God. In fact, he became the proverbial prototype of the Sufi ascetic. And yet Junayd called him "the key to the esoteric sciences." Ibrāhīm spoke not only of the renunciation (*tark*) of the world, but also the renunciation of this renunciation (*tark-i tark*), and finally indifference to the world. His contemporary, Fuḍayl ibn 'Iyāḍ (d. 803), was also an eminent Khurāsānī saint known for his asceticism, as was another contemporary, Shaqīq al-Balkhī, whom I mentioned earlier.

The School of Khurasan was known, however, primarily for its emphasis upon intoxication through Divine Love. This is seen in the greatest early figure of this school, Bāyazīd al-Basṭāmī (d. 874), one of the supreme saints of Islam, who became the symbol of Sufism all over the Islamic world. Although he lived in Khurasan and died in Bastam in that province, where his tomb in that small town is still visited by pilgrims and the room in which he made his spiritual retreats (*khalwah*) is still preserved, there are places dedicated to his memory from the Maghrib to Bengal. This incredible figure, who left such an indelible mark upon the whole of the Sufi tradition, was the first to speak of his own spiritual ascent (*al-mi'rāj*), based on the model of the Nocturnal Ascent of the Prophet.

Bāyazīd left behind many audacious sayings, for example:

> As soon as I attained to His Unity I became a bird with a body of Oneness and wings of Everlastingness, and I continued flying in the air of Quality for ten years, until I reached an atmosphere a million times as large, and flew on, until I found myself in the field of Eternity and I saw there the Tree of Oneness.[6]

He was known especially for his theophanic sayings (which are also translated as words of ecstasy), such as "Glory be unto me" in place of "Glory be to God," or "There is no one in my garment except God." These sayings along with similar sayings of other Sufis were compiled and commented upon later by a number of authors including the Sufi master from Shiraz, Rūzbahān Baqlī (d. 1209). In contrast to Ḥallāj, however, Bāyazīd was not oppressed by exoteric authorities and was in fact recognized as an exalted saint by those who had the privilege of being in his presence.

In discussing the School of Khurasan, one cannot neglect the master Sahl-al-Tustarī and his circle, although he did not hail from that province. Tustarī was concerned with the significance of *walāyah/wilāyah* and the inner meaning of the Quran. His writings on this subject are important in the long tradition of Quranic hermeneutics by various Sufis. His student Ḥakīm Tirmidhī from Khurasan was the author of a number of treatises on Sufism but is known especially for his *Khatm al-wilāyah* (*Seal of Sanctity*), which is a major early text on this subject. Tirmidhī was one of the first Sufis to discuss doctrinal Sufism (*'irfān*), which became so central with Ibn 'Arabī. The former also developed the theory of the invisible hierarchy consisting of the Pole or Axis (*al-quṭb*), the Helper (*al-ghawth*), and other members of the hierarchy who help to sustain the spiritual activity of human beings here on earth in each generation.

Before leaving this period, it is important to mention that Sufism was spreading gradually at this time elsewhere, for example in Egypt, one of the main arenas of Sufi life during the past millennium, where the influence of both Baghdad and Khurasan could be seen. One of the most remarkable Egyptian Sufis of this period was Muḥammad ibn 'Abd al-Jabbār al-Niffarī (d. 965). He must have possessed an exalted spiritual station for he reached a condition of standing or halting before God and being addressed by Him. These utterances are contained in the *Mawāqif* (*The Book of Spiritual Stayings*) and the *Mukhāṭabāt* (*The Book of Spiritual Addresses*) and are remarkable for their spiritual directness. Niffarī emphasized the importance of prayer and invocation and pointed out that knowledge itself can be a veil if it is not combined with the existential realization of that knowledge. In one of the addresses we read, "To Me belongs the giving: if I had not answered thy prayer I would not have made thee to seek it."[7]

Before going any further it is necessary to mention that the School of Baghdad was usually identified as that of sobriety (*ṣaḥw*) and that of Khurasan as that of intoxication (*sukr*). Actually, every person who has realized fully the truths of Sufism and has entered the Garden of Truth has experienced both intoxication and sobriety. It is impossible to experience the Love of God without becoming intoxicated, as it is impossible to have illuminative knowledge without sobriety. Nor are these two states to be equated simply with love and knowledge for there is intoxication in drinking the wine of gnosis and there is sobriety in beholding the beauty of the Face of the Beloved. When these two schools are characterized as those of sobriety and intoxication, it is a question of emphasis and spiritual style. It cannot be imagined that Bāyazīd, who is considered as the prototype of the intoxicated Sufi, was without the perfection of sobriety any more than one can imagine Junayd, the supreme example of sobriety, to have been devoid of the state of intoxication, even if he did not manifest it outwardly.

THE PERIOD OF CONSOLIDATION AND SYNTHESIS

After over three centuries during which numerous Sufi masters had appeared on the scene, by the tenth century the need was felt to assemble their maxims and teachings along with accounts of their sanctified lives in collections that have remained as classical sources of Sufism to this day. These major works, written mostly by Khurāsānī Sufis, include the *Kitāb al-luma'* (*The Book of Shafts of Light*) of Abū Naṣr al-Sarrāj (d. 988), which includes Sufi prayers, letters, aphorisms, and some hagiography along with the explanation of Sufi terminology; *Kitāb al-ta'arruf* (*The Doctrine of the Sufis*) by Abū Bakr Muḥammad al-Kalābādhī (d. 990 or 994), which is particularly important for early Sufi doctrines; and the *Qūt al-qulūb* (*Nourishment of Hearts*) of Abū Ṭālib al-Makkī (d. 996), which was especially influential in later centuries and was studied by Ghazzālī and Rūmī. To this list must be added two major hagiographic works: the *Ṭabaqāt al-ṣūfiyyah* (*The Classes of the Sufis*) of Abū 'Abd al-Raḥmān al-Sulamī (d. 1021), which is an invaluable source for the history of early Sufism; and *Ḥilyat al-awliyā'* (*The Ornament of the Saints*) of Abū Nu'aym al-Iṣfahānī (d. 1037), which is a monumental work on Sufi hagiography consisting of many volumes.

Efforts at composing works synthesizing the teachings of earlier Sufis continued in the eleventh century. The most famous work of this genre is the *Risālat al-qushayriyyah* (*The Qushayrī Treatise*) by Imam Abū'l-Qāsim al-Qushayrī (d. 1074), read widely to this day in Sufi circles and containing the definitive account of the states and stations that the soul experiences on its journey to the Garden of Truth. Qushayrī, who was also a theologian, jurist, and scientist, belonged to the chain issuing from Sulamī, as did his illustrious Khurāsānī contemporary, Abū Sa'īd Abī'-Khayr (d. 1049), who was one of the most influential figures of Sufism of his day to whom some Sufi quatrains in Persian are attributed.

Until now, all these major treatises were written in Arabic even if many of their authors were Persian. But a colleague of Qushayrī by the name of 'Alī ibn 'Uthmān Hujwīrī (d. circa 1071) wrote the first major work in Sufism in Persian with the title *Kashf al-maḥjūb* (*Unveiling of the Veiled*), a work that has remained popular in Persia and India to this day. Hujwīrī migrated to Lahore, where he died and is buried. Known locally as Dādājī Ganjbakhsh, he is considered as the patron saint of the Punjab and his tomb in Lahore is a major center of pilgrimage in the Indo-Pakistani world. During the annual commemoration of his death it is said that over a million people come to receive his blessings.

Another contemporary, Khwājah 'Abd Allāh Anṣārī (d. 1089), who remains the patron saint of Herat, also wrote extensively in Persian and, moreover, translated Sulamī's work on the classes of Sufis from Arabic into this language. Anṣārī was also a commentator on the Quran and the author of one of the main masterpieces of Sufi literature, the *Manāzil al-sā'irīn* (*The Stations of the Travelers upon the Path*), written in Arabic, on which many later commentaries were composed. But his most popular work is his Persian *Munājāt* (*Supplications*), which are of high literary quality and display the highest purity of intention and sincerity. This work, which was appreciated even by Hindus in India, has become a mainstay of prayer literature in the Persian-speaking world. I can still recall vividly the recitation of some of these supplications on the Tehran radio in the earliest morning hours during the fasting month of Ramaḍān. Here are a few examples:

O God, lift this veil from the way
And abandon us not to ourselves.

O God, from nothing Thou canst bring forth everything,
And amidst everything Thou dost resemble nothing.
Thou, the creator of the world.

O God, with Thy favor there is no place for refuge at
any threshold.
Ahead lies danger, and I have no way back.
Take my hand, for other than Thee I have no refuge.[8]

THE TWO GHAZZĀLĪS

The more public presence of Sufism through the appearance of major works as well as the continuous spread of Sufi practice led to a situation in which Sufism had to be more clearly defined in relation to other aspects of the Islamic religious and intellectual tradition. This event took place in the period that was a watershed in the history of Sufism, a period dominated by the towering figure of Abū Ḥāmid Muḥammad al-Ghazzālī (d. 1111) and, as far as the Persian world and Persian Sufi literature as well as many Sufi orders are concerned, his younger brother, Aḥmad al-Ghazzālī (d. 1126).

After the Prophet of Islam, there is no figure in Islamic history about whom as much has been written in European languages as Abū Ḥāmid, and within the Islamic world itself he continues to be a figure of immense influence. Born in the city of Tus in Khurasan, Abū Ḥāmid and his brother, Aḥmad, were orphaned early in life and brought up in the household of a friend of their father, a friend who belonged to the Sufi tradition. Both brothers, therefore, experienced the reality of Sufism early in life, but they followed different paths yet ultimately not different goals. Abū Ḥāmid was a brilliant student and devoted himself to the study of Islamic Law and theology in Khurasan. Soon he gained great fame as an outstanding scholar and while still in his thirties was offered the chair of Shāfiʿī Law at the illustrious Niẓāmiyyah University in Baghdad, an offer that he accepted. There, while possessing fame, respect, honor, and wealth, he fell into religious doubt to the extent that he became seriously ill. Instead of trying to conceal this doubt, as have many other religious authorities, Ghazzālī, who possessed great sincerity and truthfulness, gave up everything and disappeared from public view in quest of certitude, which he found in Sufism. For years he traveled, usually incognito, in Arabia, Palestine, and Syria, undergoing spiritual discipline. Finally he returned to public life but decided to return finally to Tus, where he taught a small number of choice students and where he died and is buried.

Some have called Abū Ḥāmid al-Ghazzālī the Islamic figure with the greatest spiritual and intellectual impact after the apostolic period. Certainly his influence was immense in Sunni theology, principles of jurisprudence, and even philosophy through his criticism of the Muslim Peripatetics. Here we are concerned only with his significance in Sufism where his achievements were immense. As a leading *'ālim* or scholar in the religious sciences, he had the authority to legitimize Sufism within the exoteric dimension of Sunni Islam. To this day those in the Sunni world who seek to defend Sufism before the attacks of some exoteric scholars appeal to the writings of al-Ghazzālī and his authority.

Al-Ghazzālī also sought to revive Islamic society by breathing the spirit anew into Islamic ethics—reviving the ethics of Islamic society from within rather than through external regimentation, which is the method of so many so-called reformist movements in the modern world. To this end he composed a monumental work in Arabic consisting of forty books and entitled *Iḥyā' 'ulūm al-dīn* (*The Revivification of the Sciences of Religion*), which he himself summarized in his *Kīmīyā-yi sa'ādat* (*Alchemy of Happiness*), written in exquisite Persian prose. The *Iḥyā'* is without doubt the most important work of Islamic ethics. In this book the breath of Sufism brings back to life the ethical teachings of the religion and the inner significance of rites and doctrines of Islam. This text remains popular to this day along with his *al-Munqidh min al-ḍalāl* (*Deliverance from Error*), the masterly spiritual autobiography that has been compared to the *Confessions* of St. Augustine.

If the *Iḥyā'* was meant for the larger public, a number of treatises of al-Ghazzālī dealing with esoteric knowledge were meant only for the chosen few able to understand them. Among these the most famous is the *Mishkāt al-anwār* (*The Niche of Light*), which deals with the symbolism of light in the Quran and *Ḥadīth*. In this and other late works, Ghazzālī turned to a more doctrinal exposition of Sufism and gnosis, preparing the ground for the School of Ibn 'Arabī, to which we shall turn in the next appendix. Ghazzālī also wrote important works on Sufi methods of the exegesis of the Quran, works that were very influential in the long tradition of Sufi commentaries upon the Sacred Text.

Although not a poet in the usual sense of the word, Ghazzālī did compose some fine poems. The following poem, which has become famous and was written originally in Arabic, is said to have been found after his death under his pillow:

> Say unto brethren when they see me dead,
> And weep for me, lamenting me in sadness:
> 'Think ye I am this corpse ye are to bury?
> I swear to God, this dead one is not I.
> I in the Spirit am, and this my body
> My dwelling was, my garment for a time...
> I praise God who hath set me free, and made
> For me a dwelling in the heavenly heights.
> Ere now I was a dead man in your midst,
> But I have come to life, and doffed my shroud.'[9]

The life of the younger brother of Abū Ḥāmid, Aḥmad al-Ghazzālī, is not as well known except that he was a few years younger and grew up in the same household as his brother; but in contrast to Abū Ḥāmid, Aḥmad turned directly to Sufism and is considered by many as the Pole or Axis (*quṭb*) of his day. He studied in Khurasan, where he became celebrated as a Sufi master and also preacher. He was devoted to Ḥallāj and was considered by the later Sufi tradition to have attained a higher rank than his brother in the esoteric hierarchy of Sufism. He also appears in the initiatic chain (*silsilah*) of many Sufi orders.

Aḥmad was not as prolific a writer as his brother, but he left behind a number of Sufi treatises, mostly in Persian. Of these the most important is the *Sawāniḥ* (*Inspirations from the World of Spirits*). According to the author, the Sufi journey beyond this world involves passing through three different levels of being or reality: the heart, the spirit, and the secret. The world of the spirit is, in his terminology, the intermediate level of reality where love of God manifests itself most fully. *Sawāniḥ* in Sufi terminology means in fact the spiritual inspirations experienced by the traveler on the path to God in this intermediary world.

The book therefore deals essentially with the metaphysics of love and in fact marks a new chapter in Sufi writings about love. The first chapter begins with the already cited Quranic verse, "He loves them and they love Him" (5:54), and the whole book may be said to be a commentary upon this verse. Written in poetic Persian prose, this work transformed Persian into almost a sacred language for expressing Sufi doctrines and experiences, symbolically of course, since Arabic is technically the only sacred language of Islam. In any case, in light of the fact that Sufi literature in Persian transformed the cultural and spiritual landscape of much of Asia, one understands the significance of Aḥmad al-Ghazzālī.

TWELFTH-CENTURY SUFISM AFTER THE TWO GHAZZĀLĪS

In the Islamic East

The twelfth century was the beginning of the establishment of the Sufi orders, with whose founders and history we shall deal shortly. But before doing so it is necessary to cite, albeit briefly, several major figures not associated with the well-known orders. In the eastern lands of Islam one can mention Yūsuf Hamadānī (d. 1140), who traced his lineage back to Kharaqānī and Basṭāmī and who was a seminal figure of Sufism in Central Asia. In his teachings he combined classical Sufism with the teachings of the People of Blame (*Malāmatiyyah*), discussed earlier, and gained many disciples in Central Asia. One of his main disciples was Aḥmad Yasawī (d. 1166), who brought many nomadic Turks to Islam and is the father of Turkish Sufi literature. He is the author of the *Ḥikam* (Aphorisms), written in the Turkic dialect of what is known today as Uzbekistan, this being the first Sufi treatise in a Turkic language. His teachings also influenced the Baktāshiyyah Order, which had such a wide dissemination in the Ottoman Empire.

The other main disciple of Yūsuf Hamadānī was 'Abd al-Khāliq Ghujduwānī (d. 1220), the founder of the famous *Ṭarīqa-yi Khwājagān* (The Order of the Masters), from which the Naqshbandī Order came into being. In modern times a number of occultists in the West have sought contact with what they believe are the remnants of this order in faraway places in Central Asia and northern Afghanistan.

One of the most exceptional and tragic figures of this period is another Hamadānī known as 'Ayn al-Quḍāt (d. 1131). A disciple of Aḥmad al-Ghazzālī and a devotee of Ḥallāj, he became a famous scholar at an early age. By the time he was thirty years old, he was chosen as judge. And yet he fell afoul of some exoteric authorities and was put to death at the age of thirty-three. Along with Ḥallāj and Suhrawardī (Shaykh al-ishrāq), he is considered as one of the three most celebrated martyrs of Sufism, his case, like that of the other two, being an exception to the rule that the vast majority of Sufis have lived as respected and usually revered members of their communities. 'Ayn al-Quḍāt is, along with Abū Ḥāmid Ghazzālī, one of the early founders of doctrinal Sufism and theoretical gnosis. His *Tamhīdāt* (*Preludes*) and *Zubdat al-ḥaqā'iq* (*The Essence of Truths*) are among masterpieces of Sufi literature and have both a mystical and a philosophical significance.

Another seminal figure of this century, Shaykh al-ishrāq Shihāb al-Dīn Suhrawardī (d. 1191) was, like 'Ayn al-Quḍāt, an outspoken defender of esoteric doctrines. Born in the small town of Suhraward in western Iran, from which the founders of the Suhrawardiyyah Order who were not related to him also hailed, the young Suhrawardī studied first in Zanjan and then Isfahan, where he entered into Sufism. Later he traveled to Anatolia and Syria, where he was caught in the political turmoil following the Crusades and was put to death in Aleppo. Shaykh al-ishrāq is one of the most important of Islamic philosophers and founder of a new school of philosophy, or theosophy in the original sense of this term, called the School of Illumination, or *ishrāq,* in which Sufism plays a major role. His masterpiece, *Ḥikmat al-ishrāq* (*The Theosophy of the Orient of Light*), bears testimony to this fact. He represents the most important encounter between Sufism and philosophy in Islam.

Certain other Muslim figures combined philosophy and Sufism, including a number of Andalusian philosophers, such as Ibn Masarrah (d. 931) and Ibn Sab'īn (d. 1269), but during later centuries it was especially in Persia, India, and to some extent the Ottoman world where such figures could be found. The most famous of later Islamic philosophers, Mullā Ṣadrā (d. 1640), was very much interested in the integration of philosophy and gnosis, and although he followed a different path, he was deeply influenced by Suhrawardī.

One cannot discuss twelfth-century Sufism without mentioning the Sufi master who was perhaps the most important in the School of

Shiraz, Rūzbahān Baqlī Shīrāzī (d. 1209). This great master, whom Henry Corbin, the twentieth-century French orientalist and philosopher and foremost Western authority on Persian Sufism and Islamic philosophy, calls one of the main *Fedeli d'amore* of Islam (the *Fedeli d'amore* being a circle in Florence during the Middle Ages devoted to the intense love of God, a current to which Dante belonged), wrote of the continuity between human love and Divine Love as well as between earthly beauty and the Beauty of the Face of the Beloved. He wrote a luminous commentary on the theophanic locutions or words of ecstasy of early Sufis, recorded his own spiritual visions in a unique work entitled *Kashf al-asrār* (*The Unveiling of Secrets*), and composed a monumental esoteric commentary upon the Quran. The work that epitomizes his views, however, is *'Abhar al-'āshiqīn* (*The Jasmine of Lovers*), which is one of the supreme testaments to Divine Love in Sufi literature.

There were needless to say also a number of notable Sufis in the Arab East at this time, but we shall deal with them in our treatment of the Sufi orders.

In the Islamic West

As a result of the authority and domination of religious life in the Maghrib (including Andalusia) by scholars (*'ulamā'*) who followed the Mālikī school of law (one of the four existing schools of Islamic Law in Sunnism), Sufism grew later in this area than in the East although in the past several centuries of Islamic history some of the greatest Sufi masters, who still followed Mālikī Law, and most powerful Sufi currents came from this region. In the early centuries Sufism in the Maghrib was deeply influenced by figures from the East. A case in point is al-Ghazzālī, whose influence in the Maghrib was so great that it even affected the political history of that area.

There is a site some fifty miles west of Marrakesh called Sidi Shākir, named after a companion of 'Uqbā ibn Nāfi', who in the seventh century conquered the Maghrib and, according to most historians, brought Islam to that region for the first time. The Berbers of the area believe, however, that both Islam and the reality of what later became known as Sufism were brought to that region, even before 'Uqbā came to that land, by Berbers who had gone to Medina and were received by the Prophet. In any case the site of Sidi Shākir, located in Berber territory, gradually became a great spiritual center where Sufis would gather from the whole of North and West Africa. Tradition among Berbers attributes the beginning of Sufism in the Maghrib to this site and, along with Berbers, to early Arab saints especially the two Mawlay Idrīses buried in Fez and near Meknes.

In any case, in the twelfth century we begin to bear witness to extensive Sufi activity and the appearance of important Sufi writings in the Maghrib; for example, Ibn al-ʿArīf (d. 1141) founded the School of Almeria in Andalusia and authored a famous treatise on spiritual ethics titled *Maḥāsin al-majālis* (*Beauties of Spiritual Gatherings*), which was also read in the East. Among other figures one can mention, Ibn Barrajān (d. 1151) carried out a metaphysical reading of the Quran, and Ibn Qasyī (d. 1151) even established a Sufi state in Algarve in southern Portugal.

As far as the twelfth century is concerned, the most important figure of Maghribī Sufism, called "the Junayd of the West," was Abū Madyān Shuʿayb (d. 1198) from Seville. This central figure of Sufism in North Africa traveled from his original homeland to Morocco and also to the east, to Baghdad, where he is said to have received initiation from ʿAbd al-Qādir al-Jīlānī, the founder of the Qādiriyyah Order. He returned to Morocco, where he became the disciple of ʿAlī ibn Ḥirzihim (d. 1162) of Fez and there familiarized himself with the *Iḥyā'* of Ghazzālī, a work that he loved so much that he required his disciples to read it. He also became the disciple of a famous Berber master, Abū Yaʿzā Yalannūr (d. 1177), who had his Sufi center in the Middle Atlas Mountains. Many currents of Maghribī Sufism met in Abū Madyan, the patron saint of Tlemcen, and also many of the later spiritual currents in the Maghrib emanated from him. He left behind a few short treatises and some beautiful poems, which are still recited in Sufi gatherings in North Africa, especially the *Nūniyyah* (*Poem Rhyming in the Letter Nūn*), which begins with these lines:

> The world confines us when Thou art absent from us,
> And our souls abandon us because of desire.
> Distance from Thee is death and nearness to Thee life,
> Wert Thou to be absent [but the moment of] a breath we
> would die.[10]

Like most Maghribī masters, Abū Madyan wrote little in comparison with many of the great masters of the East, but he left an indelible mark upon the most prolific of all Sufis, Ibn ʻArabī, whom he never met. Abū Madyan's most important direct disciple was perhaps ʻAbd al-Salām ibn Mashīsh (d. 1228), the Pole or Axis of his time and the master of Abū'l-Ḥasan al-Shādhilī, to whom we shall turn soon. Ibn Mashīsh also wrote little and is best known for his supplication on the Prophet that is often recited to this day. His striking tomb on top of the Atlas Mountains is one of the most powerful spiritual centers in the Maghrib.

The confluence of the spiritual influences of the great masters of the twelfth century led to a remarkable revival of Islamic spirituality in the thirteenth century. Every religion includes periods of spiritual revival that mark a kind of return to the golden age of that religion associated with the time of the founder. We see that truth in Christian Europe coincidentally also in the thirteenth century, the age of figures such as St. Francis of Assisi, who was called "the second Christ," as well as St. Bonaventure and St. Thomas Aquinas. Such was also the situation in the Islamic world during the twelfth and the thirteenth centuries. This period may be said to begin with al-Ghazzālī and the founders of Sufi orders and includes such colossal figures as Abū'l-Ḥasan al-Shādhilī (d. 1258), Ibn ʻArabī (d. 1240) and his outstanding student, Ṣadr al-Dīn Qūnawī (d. 1274), Najm al-Dīn Kubrā (d. 1220), the two master Sufi poets of the Persian language, Farīḍ al-Dīn ʻAṭṭār (d. 1220) and Jalāl al-Dīn Rūmī (d. 1273), and the greatest Sufi poet of the Arabic language, ʻUmar ibn al-Fāriḍ (d. 1235), to name some of the major personalities.

As for Ibn al-Fāriḍ, he was an Egyptian who began as a religious teacher but soon turned to Sufism and commenced to compose verses that are considered as peaks of Arabic Sufi poetry. Among his most famous poems is the *Khamriyyah* (*The Wine Song*), which was emulated and commented upon by many later Sufis. His tomb in Cairo remains to this day a place of pilgrimage for lovers of God. It is especially a place that attracts those mesmerized by the incredible beauty of his verses that sing through several symbols of the Divine Love that transcends all finitude.

During the past eight centuries the Islamic world has been nourished mostly by the teachings and spiritual influence of the masters of this period and has seen earlier Sufism mostly through their eyes. This was also the period of the formation of most of the major Sufi orders, to which we now turn.

WHAT IS A SUFI ORDER?

During the early centuries of Islamic history, Sufism was taught by masters who were surrounded by a circle of disciples but without a distinct organization and rules of conduct for the collectivity of disciples as a whole. The circle of Sufis (*al-ḥalqah*) was defined by the master and those who were trained individually by him or her. In the twelfth and thirteenth centuries, however, spiritual and social conditions changed, necessitating a more organized structure. The word *ṭarīqah,* or path to God, gained an added meaning as a brotherhood and sisterhood (women were also allowed as members) with a specific name, rules of conduct, distinct ritual practices, and different emphases. All the orders were nevertheless based on the inner teachings of the Quran and the spiritual model of the Prophet and were made possible through the transmission of initiatic power (*walāyah/wilāyah*) issuing from him and transmitted from master to disciple over the centuries. This chain is called the *silsilah,* and it is absolutely essential for the continuity, legitimacy and orthodoxy of a Sufi order.

A Sufi order is identified by a name derived usually from one of the names or titles of its founder, who received the inspiration and authority from Heaven to start that order. Orders can also have branches, and how these come into being is again based on spiritual and inner causes not evident outwardly. Some orders have survived in a vibrant fashion to this day after many centuries of continuous history; others have become dormant, and yet others have died out. The orders have their gathering (*majlis,* plural *majālis*) and usually their *zāwiyah* or center. Often the master resides in one of these centers, but not necessarily so. Each order has its own litanies (*wird,* plural *awrād*), use of music and sacred dance (*samāʿ*) (or is characterized by the lack thereof), forms of Sufi courtesy (*adab*) and rules of conduct, while the invocation (*dhikr*) is universal in all the orders although even here which Divine Names are invoked and in what sequence differ from one order to another.

In contrast to what many Western scholars wrote in the nineteenth and early twentieth centuries, stating that Sufism was a medieval phenomenon, many of the orders are still very much alive today. To seek to follow Sufism requires finding a functioning order and an authentic master, the only exception being the path of those who are guided by invisible figures of the spiritual world such as Khiḍr. So although the reality of Sufism is not limited to the Sufi orders today, for all practical purposes it is in the orders that one must seek the authentic teachings of Sufism.

The Sufi orders are sacred organizations and are therefore quite naturally hierarchical, the word *hierarchy* itself coming from the Greek and meaning "sacred rule and origin," which implies gradation. The supreme leader and master of an order is usually called the *shaykh* or *pīr,* although other titles are also sometimes used. Most orders, especially those that are widespread, usually have a number of direct and highest representatives of the *shaykh* who are usually called *khalīfah,* meaning vicegerent, or sometimes *nā'ib,* meaning representative. In many cases the *khalīfah* becomes later a *shaykh* himself or herself. In most orders there is also the *muqaddam,* literally the person who has priority, designated by the *shaykh* and like the *khalīfah,* given the permission to initiate people into the order. Then there are *imāms,* whose function it is to organize and direct *majālis* when higher functionaries are not present. This hierarchy does not, however, always coincide with the hierarchy of spiritual stations attained by members of an order, although the designating of functionaries is related to their advancement and spiritual attainment on the path.

THE MAJOR SUFI ORDERS

It is not possible to give an account here of all the Sufi orders stretching over an area from the Atlantic to the Pacific and from the snowy mountain peaks of Central Asia to the tropical jungles of Africa. Our goal here is to say at least something about the major orders that have affected historically (and many continue to affect today) the lives of millions of Muslims throughout the world. To give some order to this exposition we shall go by region, beginning with Iraq, where in the twelfth century the first orders appeared. But since many orders spread beyond the area where they were founded, we shall treat their history in each case even beyond their land of origin.

Iraq

The most universal and oldest of all Sufi orders, in the sense of an organized community of disciples, is the Qādiriyyah, founded by the Persian scholar and saint 'Abd al-Qādir al-Jīlānī, who was born in Gilan but at the age of eighteen came to study in Baghdad, where he became an authority in both Islamic Law and Sufism. He soon became the most luminous spiritual figure of his time, visited by even founders of other Sufi orders from near and far. In fact after the age of the companions of the Prophet, no figure in Islamic history has had the spiritual radiance of 'Abd al-Qādir as far as the whole of the Islamic world is concerned.

A sober Sufi and, like Ghazzālī, an exoteric as well as esoteric authority, 'Abd al-Qādir lived an ascetic life and did not marry until he was more than fifty years old, but then he did marry and had numerous children, who spread his *barakah* far and wide. Still today, his descendants play an important role in the life of the Qādiriyyah Order in many areas of the Islamic world. 'Abd al-Qādir also left behind a number of important Sufi treatises, including the celebrated *Futūḥ al-ghayb* (*Victories of the Invisible*), containing the text of some of his sermons. Translated into Persian by 'Abd al-Ḥaqq Muḥaddith of Delhi (d. 1624), this work became very popular in India. The Qādiriyyah spread throughout the Islamic world, especially from the fifteenth century onward, and there are *zawāyā* (plural of *zāwiyah*) of this order today from Morocco to Malaysia, from Central Asia to South Africa.

The central practice of the Qādiriyyah is the invocation of the Names of God (*dhikr*), and there is emphasis on knowledge and unveiling (*kashf*). And yet in many areas the Qādirīs became associated with extraordinary feats such as piercing their bodies with a spoke, walking on fire, eating sharp razors, and even cutting their stomachs. I shall never forget participating in one of their *majālis* in Sanandaj, capital of the Iranian province of Kurdistan. So extraordinary were the happenings I observed with my own eyes that it was difficult to believe what I was seeing. Such phenomena do demonstrate that there is more to the reality of the human state, including the body, and the world surrounding human beings than meets the eye, but such practices must not be identified with Sufism as such. In fact, most masters have opposed these practices, which take place in a state of Divine Attraction and under the condition of the integration of the physical body into its subtle principle.

'Abd al-Qādir was called the Pole (or spiritual Axis) of his age by Ibn 'Arabī, and later Sufi history gave him the title of *al-Ghawth al-a'ẓam* (the Greatest Help). Numerous miracles were attributed to him, and he figures prominently in later Sufi hagiographies, especially the *Nafaḥāt al-uns* (*Breaths of Familiarity*) of Jāmī (d. 1492). The tomb of 'Abd al-Qādir in Baghdad has remained over the centuries the most important Sufi shrine of that city, which contains, as mentioned, the remains of so many Sufi luminaries. Until the recent turmoil in Iraq, pilgrims used to visit it from as far as Nigeria and Indonesia and lands in between.

A younger contemporary of 'Abd al-Qādir, Aḥmad ibn 'Alī al-Rifā'ī (d. 1182) from southern Iraq, an ecstatic Sufi with great love

for animals, was active independently and also founded a major order, the Rifā'iyyah, which, like the Qādiriyyah, spread over most of the Islamic world from its center in southern Iraq. Only some poems and prayers have survived from his pen, but his spiritual radiance continues to this day. Under the Ayyubid dynasty the order spread into Syria and Egypt and in the thirteenth and fourteenth centuries among the Turks, who caused its dissemination in the Balkans and carried it across the Black Sea to the land of the Golden Horde. In fact, the Rifā'iyyah was the most widespread of the Sufi orders until it was overtaken by the Qādiriyyah in the fifteenth century. In Egypt, however, it continued to have the greatest appeal and is still strong in that land.

The adherents of the Rifā'iyyah have been known everywhere for their unusual feats while in a state of ecstasy, such as riding lions, eating live snakes, walking on hot coals, and plucking out their eyes without being hurt, in order to demonstrate their extraordinary powers. The order, however, is not defined by such practices, any more than is the Qādiriyyah, but is known rather by the Rifā'iyyah's emphasis upon invocation and other spiritual activities. Jāmī in fact calls such extraordinary practices of the Rifā'iyyah aberrations from the Sufi path. The Rifā'iyyah have a loud *dhikr,* which is like a howling sound, so that European travelers who first met its members called them the Howling Dervishes.

Another order founded in Iraq but whose founder hailed from Persia is the Suhrawardiyyah. Its founder, Abū Najīb Suhrawardī (d. 1168), was born and raised in the town of Suhraward in present western Iran but came to Baghdad to study. Beginning as a disciple of

Aḥmad Ghazzālī, he became a Sufi master, writing the famous *Ādāb al-murīdīn* (*Rules for Disciples*) for his followers. But it was his nephew Shihāb al-Dīn 'Umar Suhrawardī (d. 1234), the author of one of the most popular handbooks of Sufism, *'Awārif al-ma'ārif* (*Confessions of Divine Knowledge*), who is the real founder of this order. Given the title of *Shaykh* of *shaykhs* by the Abbasid caliph, he was highly respected as both theologian and Sufi master as well as patron of spiritual chivalry (*futuwwah*). He in fact initiated the caliph al-Nāṣir li-Dīn'i'Llāh into the order of spiritual chivalry, which is an order based on knightly or craft activities (like the Order of the Temple and original Freemasonry in the West) but related to Sufism.

He built the mother *zāwiyah* of the Suhrawardiyyah in Baghdad, where many famous people, including the Persian poet Muṣlih al-Dīn Sa'dī (d. 1292), came to receive initiation. The *'Awārif* was translated into Persian and helped in the propagation of the order eastward. Branches of the order also spread in the Arab and later Ottoman worlds, but the greatest spread of the order occurred in India. This dissemination took place especially through one of the foremost saints of Multan, Bahā' al-Dīn Zakariyyā' Multānī (d. 1262), who was also the master of another celebrated Persian Sufi poet, Fakhr al-Dīn 'Irāqī (d. 1284). The Suhrawardiyyah Order, which emphasized sobriety and strict adherence to the *Sunnah* of the Prophet and explained Sufi practices completely in light of the Quran, was a predominantly aristocratic order that cooperated with government authorities. Many Muslim sultans of India were in fact its members. Some of the members of this order were also in contact with high-caste Hindus, many of whom they brought into Islam.

The Suhrawardiyyah Order was also influential in the creation of other orders. Two of Abū Najīb's disciples became masters of Najm al-Dīn Kubrā (d. 1220), the founder of the Kubrawiyyah Order. Also the Khāksār Order, which is popular in Persia to this day, developed from the Jalāliyyah branch of the Suhrawardiyyah. This order gradually disappeared from most of the area called the Middle East today but still survives in Iraq, its original center, and in India.

Persia and Central Asia

Most Sufi orders in Persia and Central Asia had their spiritual ancestry in Bāyazīd Basṭāmī and the School of Khurasan, which produced so many saints and Sufi poets over the ages. One of the earliest currents that turned later into an order was the Yasawiyyah, which originated with the Persian Sufi Yūsuf Hamadānī. The name of the order comes from Aḥmad Yasawī, who, as mentioned, was one of the earliest Turkic Sufis and played a major role in the conversion of nomadic Turks to Islam. This order was also associated with the *Malāmatiyyah*.

Soon thereafter, the Qalandariyyah Order appeared in the thirteenth century, founded by Jamāl al-Dīn Sāwajī (d. after 1223), which began in Persia and Central Asia but spread to India and elsewhere. Members of this order had a rough appearance, with unruly long hair and beards, and flouted habits of urban dwellers and the prevalent social etiquette. They lived mostly in the countryside, and some displayed psychic powers. In general there was much opposition to them even from some of the other Sufis. The *qalandars* gained some respect, however, when a Sufi poet from Azarbaijan by the name of La'l Shahbāz Qalandar (d. 1274) went to Multan and became one of the great Sufi saints of India. The begging bowl of the Sufis (*kashkūl*) is especially identified with this order.

One of the major orders of the history of Sufism is the Kubrawiyyah, founded by Najm al-Dīn Kubrā (d. 1221). Born in Khwarazm, educated originally in the religious sciences, especially *Ḥadīth,* in Persia as well as in Egypt, he turned to Sufism and was initiated into the Suhrawardiyyah Order. Soon he became a master himself and founded the Kubrawiyyah Order in Central Asia. He gained many eminent disciples, such as Majd al-Dīn Baghdādī (d. 1219) along with his disciple Najm al-Dīn Dāyah (d. 1256) and the outstanding Persian poet Farīd al-Dīn 'Aṭṭār. Probably the father of Jalāl al-Dīn Rūmī, Bahā' al-Dīn Walad (d. 1231) was also his direct disciple. Among the early well-known figures of this order were also Sa'd al-Dīn Ḥamūyah (d. 1252–53), who was an Imami Shi'ite, and the very influential metaphysician and master, 'Alā' al-Dawlah Simnānī (d. 1336), who was moreover a major Sufi commentator upon the Quran. Another notable member of this order is 'Azīz al-Dīn Nasafī (d. after 1281), the author of many enduring Sufi works, and Sayyid 'Alī Hamadānī (d. 1385), who played a major role in the spread of Islam and Sufism in Kashmir. The Dhahabiyyah Order, which is still very much alive in Persia and which produced one of the great twentieth-century saintly figures of that land, Waḥīd al-Awliyā' (d. 1955), is derived from the Kubrawiyyah. This order itself more or less died out in India and Persia but survives in the region of the Pamir Mountains.

The Kubrawiyyah have left many outstanding writings in both Arabic and Persian, starting with the magnum opus of Najm al-Dīn Kubrā, *Fawā'iḥ al-jamāl wa fawātiḥ al-jalāl* (*Aromas of Beauty and Preambles of Majesty*), and Najm al-Dīn Rāzī's *Mirṣād al-'ibād* (*The Path of God's Servants*). These and other works of the order reveal the particular interest of this order in examining the meaning of color symbolism and photism experienced on the Sufi path and the subtle centers within the human macrocosm. Altogether they placed great importance on visionary experiences.

Another major Persian order, the Ni'amtullāhiyyah, was founded by Shāh Ni'mat Allāh Walī (d. 1367), who although born in Aleppo, traveled to Persia, studied in Shiraz, and also journeyed to Samarqand in Central Asia. He later settle in Kerman, which henceforth became the center of the new order established on the basis of the old Ma'rūfiyyah circle. He wrote over 130 works related doctrinally to the teachings of Ibn 'Arabī and had disciples in both Persia and India, where the Bahmanid king of Daccan became his disciple and upon the death of the master built a mausoleum for him in Mahan near Kerman. This site is one of the most beautiful in the Islamic world, combining the *barakah* of the saint with the beauty of nature as well as remarkable architecture and landscaping. The garden of this mausoleum is among the most outstanding in the Islamic world.

Although Shāh Ni'mat Allāh was a Sunni, the order soon became Shi'ite and spread throughout Persia. During the Safavid period it became a rival to the Ṣafawiyyah Order and was finally persecuted to the extent that many of its masters took refuge in Daccan and many of the ordinary members went underground. It was only after the fall of the Safavids that a great master of the order, Ma'ṣūm 'Alī Shāh (d. 1796), returned to Persia and, although eventually martyred, reestablished the order there. Since the nineteenth century the order has prospered in that country with several branches spread in different areas. It is without doubt the most widespread Sufi order of Persia today. During the Iranian Revolution of 1979 some of the masters of the order migrated to Europe, and since then this order has spread in both Europe and America and, through the London *khānqāh,* in West Africa.

After the Qādiriyyah and Rifā'iyyah Orders, no Sufi order has been so widespread and exercised such influence upon the life of the Islamic community as the Naqshbandiyyah. Founded by Bahā' al-Dīn Naqshband (d. 1389), the order soon spread from China to North Africa.

Bahā' al-Dīn was born near Bukhara, where he also studied, where he founded the order, and where he died. Based on the earlier order, *Ṭarīqa-yi Khwājagān* (The Path of Masters), founded by 'Abd al-Khāliq Ghujduwārī, the Naqshbandiyyah Order was essentially a Persian order with Turkish elements integrated into it. From the beginning, the order emphasized the observance of Islamic Law and sought to reform society by bringing rulers and others in authority into its fold. It has been also always a staunch defender of Sunni orthodoxy.

The order established itself firmly in Central Asia before spreading to the part of Persia that is today Afghanistan as well as to Syria. In the sixteenth century it spread to India and soon thereafter into China and the Malay world. It also spread extensively into the Ottoman Empire, among the Kurds in general, and in the Caucasus. The spread of the order was due to a large extent to the efforts of Khwājah 'Ubayd Allāh Aḥrār (d. 1490), who was also a powerful social figure with great wealth. He was much devoted to the teachings of Ibn 'Arabī, to whom we shall turn in the next appendix, and also popularized the *Mathnawī* of Rūmī in Central Asia. Aḥrār had numerous disciples, none more famous than the "Seal of Poets" of the Persian language, 'Abd al-Raḥmān Jāmī, a major Sufi poet and commentator upon Ibn 'Arabī. One of Jāmī's works, the *Lawā'iḥ* (*Gleams*), is the first Sufi text to be translated into classical Chinese.

The great luminaries of the Naqshbandiyyah Order are too many to name completely here. In India they include Aḥmad Sirhindī (d. 1624), who was also an Uwaysī and who founded the Mujaddidiyyah branch of the mother order and who is one of the major figures of the history of Islam in India; Shāh Walī Allāh of Delhi (d. 1762), who is the most famous Islamic thinker that India has produced; and Mīrzā Maẓhar Jān-i Jānān (d. 1781), who strongly encouraged dialogue with Hinduism. Elsewhere one can mention Khālid al-Baghdādī (d. 1827), who revived the order in Syria and Turkey, and some of the great masters of Daghistan such as 'Abd Allāh Dāghistānī (d. 1973). With the advent of Communism the Naqshbandiyyah Order was treated very severely but still survived the Soviet Union and remains active in Central Asia, Daghistan, Chechnya, and Tataristan as well as in the Balkans. It is also still powerful among the Kurds and in Afghanistan. The late grand *muftī* of Syria, Aḥmad Kiftaro (d. 2004), was a Naqshbandī, and the branch of Shaykh Nāẓim of Cyprus has spread to Europe and America.

A near contemporary of Bahā' al-Dīn by the name of Ṣafī al-Dīn Ardibilī (d. 1334) from the northern Persian city of Ardibil also founded a Sufi order, called the Ṣafawiyyah, an order that changed the history of western Asia. In the late fifteenth century his followers gained political power in Azarbaijan, and in 1499 the young head of the order, Shāh Ismā'īl (d. 1524), declared himself king of Persia. With the help of Turkic soldiers, the Safavids established rule over a vast area including parts of Central Asia, the Caucasus, Afghanistan, and Iraq as well as present-day Iran. They declared Twelve-Imam Shi'ism the national religion of the country and established the foundation for the modern Iranian state. The order gradually died out, but it had considerable effect on the later history of several countries in the region and remains one of the most notable examples of the effect of Sufism upon the political life of the Islamic peoples.

India

India is a land in which Sufism has flourished exceptionally well and in many different forms during the past millennium. Islam itself was brought to India to a large extent by various Sufi orders, as one can see in the nature of Indian Islam. There are four major Sufi orders in India: the Qādiriyyah, the Suhrawardiyyah, the Chishtiyyah, and the Naqshbandiyyah. Three of these orders were founded in other regions but spread to India, often with distinctly Indian branches. The Chishtiyyah, however, is solely an Indian order even if its founder was a Persian.

The origin of this order goes back to Mu'īn al-Dīn Chishtī (d. 1236), who was born in the Persian province of Sistan but later studied in Khurasan and Baghdad, where he visited 'Abd al-Qādir al-Jīlānī. Considering himself heir to the teachings of Ḥasan al-Baṣrī and Abū Sa'īd Abī'l-Khayr (d. 1049), this great master of Khurasan, Mu'īn al-Dīn, established the Chishtī Order, which at first spread in Khurasan and Transoxiana but survived only in India, where he finally settled and died. His tomb in Ajmer remains to this day one of the major sites of pilgrimage in the Islamic world.

Mu'īn al-Dīn was followed by a number of eminent Chishtī saints, who, along with Mu'īn al-Dīn himself, were instrumental in establishing Islam in India and whose *barakah* is palpable in that land to this day. One can mention among them Khwājah Quṭb al-Dīn Bakhtiyār Kākī (d. 1235), who became especially popular in Delhi; his successor, Farīd al-Dīn Mas'ūd "Ganj-i Shikar," known popularly as Bābā Farīd (d. 1265), who held discourses with Hindu yogis on the nature of Ultimate Reality; his successor, Niẓām al-Dīn Awliyā' (d. 1325), who was the person most responsible for the crystallization of the Chishtī Order in northern India and whose mausoleum along with that of his disciple, Amīr Khusraw (d. 1325), the greatest Persian poet of India, remains to this day a very important center of pilgrimage; and his successor, Naṣīr al-Dīn of Awadh (d. 1356), another popular saint who suffered much in his lifetime for refusing to cooperate with the sultan on various schemes. The *khalīfah* of Naṣīr al-Dīn, Sayyid Muḥammad ibn Yūsuf al-Ḥusaynī, known as Gīsū Dirāz (d. 1422), became the most famous Sufi saint of the Daccan. The order continued in strength during the Mogul period and was revived under Shāh Kalīm Jahānābādī (d. 1729); it continues its extensive activity throughout India, Pakistan, and Bangladesh to this day. Also a branch of it came to the West in the early decades of the twentieth century and is still active in Europe and America.

The Chishtiyyah Order emphasized poverty and in contrast to the Suhrawardiyyah and Naqshbandiyyah kept away from political authorities. It mingled with low-caste Hindus and played a greater role in bringing Hindus to Islam than any other order. And yet some Chishtī masters, many of whom also had Hindu disciples, carried out dialogue with Hindus on the highest intellectual level, as a study of some of their preserved discourses reveals. The Chishtīs also were always deeply devoted to Sufi music. It is mostly they who transformed North Indian music into a major school of Sufi music. The sitar (meaning "thirty strings" in Persian) is said to have been invented by Amīr Khusraw, and to this day one can hear *qawwālī* at the tombs of the saints of this order. Many Chishtī *khānqāhs* in fact have their own musicians who can perform on the highest professional level. Their role in Indian music is somewhat similar to that of the Mawlawiyyah in Turkish music.

Besides the Chishtiyyah, a number of other specifically Indian orders also saw the light of day, although they were usually branches of earlier orders. One can mention, for example, the Firdawsiyyah Order, an offshoot of the Kubrawiyyah and an order that spread in India and not elsewhere. The order is particularly known for the writings of one of its members, Sharaf al-Dīn Munyarī (Maneri) (d. 1381). His letters to disciples and his *Malfūẓāt* (*Discourses*) are among the most popular Sufi works written in India. Another Indian order is the Shaṭṭāriyyah, which traces its teachings to Imam Ja'far al-Ṣādiq and Bāyazīd Basṭāmī. Founded by Shāh 'Abd Allāh (d. 1485), it spread especially in Bengal and was also influential among the Mogul ruling class. The Mogul emperor Humāyūn is said to have belonged to this order. The order also spread to the Malay world through its members who lived in Mecca and Medina. It is also of interest to note that some Shaṭṭārī masters were interested in integrating certain yogic techniques into the practices of their order.

The Arab East and North Africa

We have already dealt with Iraq, where the first Sufi orders were established. It is now time to turn to the rest of the Arab world, where besides the spread of many of the orders that were founded originally in Persia, Central Asia, and other areas of the Islamic world, local orders were also established, some of which then spread eastward. Among the orders established in North Africa and Egypt, the Shādhilliyyah is perhaps the most important and influential. Only the Qādiriyyah, Rifā'iyyah, and Naqshbandiyyah Orders have had a wider geographic dissemination than it. The founder of the order, Abū'l-Ḥasan al-Shādhilī (d. 1258), is one of the supreme Poles or Axes of Sufism. Born in Morocco, he traveled east in search of a master and then back to Morocco, where he was initiated by 'Abd al-Salām ibn Mashīsh, with whom he stayed for some time. Then he went to the village of Shādhilah in Tunisia, hence his name, al-Shādhilī, although some believe that the name of the order is Shādhdhuliyyah, derived from the title of the master, Shādhdhulī, which means "he whom God has chosen for Himself." It was inside a cave at the outskirts of the city of Tunis that he is said to have had his supreme vision of God.

In any case, he set out from Tunisia following a vision directing him to go eastward. With many of his disciples he moved to Alexandria, where a number of his followers are buried. After participating in a state of blindness in the Seventh Crusade headed by St. Louis, Abū'l-Ḥasan set out with many disciples toward Mecca but died in the desert before reaching the Red Sea. His mausoleum in Humaythara remains to this day a center of pilgrimage to a site surrounded by pristine desert and the presence of nothing but the remains of one of God's greatest saints. He left behind no writings except for a few prayers and litanies (*aḥzāb*), repeated to this day by Shādhilīs all over the world. What he left behind that is much more important than any writing is a spiritual legacy and *barakah* that transformed the history of many lands and the lives of many people during the next eight centuries and that remains alive today. The present book would not have been possible without his specific spiritual influence. Abū'l-Ḥasan al-Shādhilī became the prototype of the sober Sufi master who made his disciples conform to the Law, earn a living, and participate in society while being inwardly detached from the world. He was a master who was drowned in the ocean of Unity (*al-tawḥīd*) while writing little. There is no doubt, however, that his was a path of illuminative knowledge and gnosis (*al-ma'rifah*), as seen by the warm reception that the writings of Ibn 'Arabī and his school have received among the Shādhilīs over the ages.

The immediate successor of Abū'l-Ḥasan, Abū'l-'Abbās al-Mursī (d. 1285), who is interred in Alexandria, also wrote little, but the third master of the order, Aḥmad ibn 'Aṭā' Allāh al-Iskandarī (d. 1309), is the author of many works, the most famous being the *Ḥikam* (*Aphorisms*), which remains very popular even now. His tomb at the edge of the Muqaṭṭam Hills outside of Cairo is visited by Shādhilīs to this day. The Shādhiliyyah Order was brought back to the Maghrib by Ibn 'Abbād of Ronda (d. 1390), who wrote the first commentary upon the *Ḥikam,* while branches of the order spread in Egypt and further east all the way to China. The order also spread rapidly in Morocco and Algeria following in a sense the earlier spiritual currents emanating from Abū Madyan, and the order continued to flourish in the Maghrib, as seen by the appearance of such major figures as Abū 'Abd Allāh Muḥammad al-Jazūlī (d. circa 1470), who, on the basis of the love of the Prophet, revived Sufism in the western lands of Islam and authored the book of litanies, *Dalā'il al-khayrāt* (*The Signs of Benedictions*), the most popular handbook of prayers in the Arab world. Another notable Shādhilī figure was Aḥmad Zarrūq (d. 1493), who sought to revive Sufism by emphasizing the wedding of the Law and the Way. He is the founder of the Jazūliyyah, one of many orders that have branched out of the Shādhiliyyah Order over the centuries.

The major reviver of Shādhilism during the past few centuries is the Moroccan saint Mawlay al-'Arabī al-Darqāwī (d. 1823), who was breathing new life and invigorating Sufism at the very moment when the French, while opposing the Catholic Church at home, were expanding abroad by conquering many countries, including the Maghrib, and supporting anti-Islamic Christian missionary activity. Most of the Shādhilīs in Morocco and Algeria became Darqāwā and remain so to this day. The Darqāwiyyah Order was also the source of several other influential orders, such as the Madaniyyah, which spread to Libya, the Hijaz, and even Sri Lanka; and the Yashruṭiyyah, which spread to Egypt, Palestine, and the Levant and is still very much alive in Lebanon and Syria. The daughter of the founder of the order, Sayyidah Fāṭimah Yashruṭiyyah (d. 1978), is one of the notable Sufi female saints of the twentieth century. One must also mention the 'Alawiyyah Order, founded by the remarkable early twentieth century Algerian saint, Aḥmad al-'Alawī (d. 1934). This extraordinary master had disciples all over the Islamic world all the way to the Malay-speaking areas. Also he was destined to fulfill the prediction of Shaykh Abū'l-Ḥasan al-Shādhilī that one day a branch of the tree of his path would spread to Europe and the West in general, for it was the 'Alawiyyah branch of the Shādhiliyyah-Darqāwiyyah Order that spread in the twentieth century in Europe and established Sufism there for the first time in a serious and permanent manner.

The nineteenth century also witnessed the appearance of another Maghribī figure who had a major role, along with his master, Aḥmad ibn Idrīs, in the revival of Sufism. His name is Muḥammad ibn 'Alī al-Sanūsī (d. 1859). He was of Algerian origin, studied in Fez, and entered the Shādhiliyyah Order and studied with Aḥmad Tijānī without becoming his Sufi disciple. He then went to Mecca, where he studied with important masters, especially Aḥmad ibn Idrīs, becoming his *khalīfah*. After the death of Ibn Idrīs, al-Sanūsī became the *shaykh* of the order. The Wahhābīs, who were very much opposed to Sufism, were on the rise and put many obstacles before him. He therefore left for North Africa, where he founded numerous centers. He died in a desert town near the border of western Egypt.

The Sanūsiyyah Order spread to Algeria, Tunisia, and Libya. The third master of the order and his grandson, Muḥammad al-Mahdī Aḥmad al-Sanūsī (d. 1933), entered the realm of politics and fought against the Italians. Later he went to Turkey to fight on the side of Ataturk against the French. From Turkey he went to Syria and finally Medina, where he died. He wed the order to the political life of Libya, and his cousin later became king of that country. The Sanūsiyyah ruled over the country until their overthrow by Colonel Ghaddafi in 1969. Like the Safavids, they demonstrated the possibility of members of a

Sufi order becoming the actual political rulers of a country, while in many other orders the members shunned political life.

The influence of the Sanūsiyyah in both religious and political spheres is also visible in the spread of one of its branches, the Mīrghāniyyah, or Khatmiyyah, in the Sudan. Founded in Mecca by one of the disciples of Aḥmad ibn Idrīs, Muḥammad al-Mīrghānī (d. 1851), who was sent by his master to Egypt and the Sudan, the Mīrghāniyyah Order spread rapidly. The order opposed the rise to power of the Mahdī of the Sudan and was strongly suppressed for some time, but it was revived in the late nineteenth century and is today the most prominent Sufi order in eastern Sudan, also having many followers in the Horn of Africa, Ethiopia, and Egypt.

The Maghrib also produced other important Sufi orders, especially the Tijāniyyah, which, however, spread mostly in other parts of Africa. The Maghrib did not produce as many writings on Sufism as the East, but it did produce numerous saints and powerful Sufi currents that influenced other parts of the Islamic world. Sufism also played a profound role in the social life of the region until modern times, and even today many of its currents are more powerful and vibrant than in many other regions of the Islamic world.

As for the Arab East, outside of Iraq, Egypt is the most important country as far as founding of orders is concerned. It is a land where Sufism is very much alive to this day and where Sufi practices can even be observed by the larger public in certain mosques. One of the popular Egyptian orders is the Badawiyyah, founded by Aḥmad al-Badawī (d. 1276). Born in Morocco, he settled in Tanta in the Nile Delta, where he established his order and where he is buried. He was an ecstatic Sufi with powerful charisma and is considered the patron saint of Egypt. About the same time, Burhān al-Dīn Dasūqī (d. 1288) founded the Burhāniyyah Order, which is still popular in Egypt and the Sudan. The well-known Egyptian Sufi ʻAbd al-Wahhāb al-Shaʻrānī (d. 1565) was a member of this order.

The other major orders, such as the Qādiriyyah and Naqshbandiyyah, also spread widely in Egypt as well as Syria, as did the Mawlawiyyah Order during the Ottoman period. Egypt has also been a home for the Rifāʻiyyah and Khalwatiyyah over the centuries, not to speak of branches of the Shādhiliyyah. As for Syria, these orders have also been present there over the centuries and, as we shall see in the next appendix, Syria was also the land from which the influence of Ibn ʻArabī and his school spread to the whole of the Islamic world. In the twentieth century the 'Alawiyyah order of Shaykh al-'Alawī spread widely in Syria under the direction of the head of his Damascus *zāwiyah*, Muḥammad al-Hāshimī (d. 1961), who himself became the *shaykh* of the order in Syria.

Sub-Saharan Africa

As far as Sufism is concerned, the destiny of Islamic sub-Saharan Africa has been closely allied to that of North Africa and to some extent Egypt. A case in point is the Tijāniyyah Order, founded by Aḥmad Tijānī (d. 1815). A descendant of the figure many consider the founder of Islam in North Africa, Mawlay Idrīs, and therefore, like Abū'l-Ḥasan al-Shādhilī, a descendant of the Prophet, he was an Algerian who studied in Fez and traveled to the holy cities of Mecca and Medina. He was initiated into the Khalwatiyyah Order in Egypt and even became a *muqaddam* of the order. But as a result of a vision of the Prophet in the oasis of Abī Samghūn in Algeria, he started his own *ṭarīqah* and returned to Fez, where he died and where he is buried. His mausoleum is a major site of pilgrimage especially for members of the order, who usually hail from sub-Saharan Africa. The Tijāniyyah Order spread in the Near East and even Indonesia but became especially important in Senegal, Nigeria, and Mauritania, where to this day it plays a major spiritual, religious, and even political role. One can hardly conceive of any aspect of life in Senegal without taking into account the Tijāniyyah, who in contrast to some other orders do not allow their disciples to enter other Sufi paths. In recent decades the Tijāniyyah have been spreading in East Africa as well, especially in the Sudan. Although its mother *zāwiyah* and the tomb of its founder is in Fez, the order is to all practical purposes a sub-Saharan African order.

Another African order of more recent origin is the Murīdiyyah, founded by Amadou Bamba (d. 1927). Despite its short history, the order is widespread in Senegal and other West African regions and also has many followers in France. The master of the order also attracted a number of Europeans and Americans who joined its ranks. Altogether, Sufism is still very popular in sub-Saharan Africa, especially in countries such as Senegal, Mali, Somalia, and the Sudan. Almost all the major orders have branches in that part of the Islamic world, especially the Qādiriyyah, Rifā'iyyah, and Shādhiliyyah in addition to the Tijāniyyah.

Sufism can hardly be separated from the life of the people who comprised the Ottoman Empire, especially the Turks. Moreover, Sufism in Turkish areas was closely related to Sufi activity in the Caucasus and the Balkans, which were mostly under Ottoman rule. Many of the orders that were established and grew in these areas were originally founded by Persians but are Turkish rather than Persian orders. First among them is the Mawlawiyyah Order, founded by the greatest Sufi poet of the Persian language, Jalāl al-Dīn Rūmī (d. 1273), quoted so often in this book, or to be more precise, by his son, Sulṭān Walad (d. 1312), on the basis of the teachings of his father. Of Persian origin and born in Balkh, Rūmī, the poet whose poems now are the most widely sold in America, spent the last forty years of his life in Konya in Anatolia. His mausoleum remains in Konya to this day and is the "Ka'bah" of the lovers of God who come there from all over the world to pay homage to this universal saint, lover of God, gnostic, and author of the *Mathnāwī* (*Rhyming Couplets*) and *Dīwān-i kabīr* (*The Grand Dīwān*). The latter work is dedicated to the remarkable antinomian Sufi, Shams al-Dīn Tabrīzī (d. 1248), who caused the fire of love to shoot out in flames from the inner being of Rūmī. These two works of Persian poetry, following the tradition of Abū'l-Majd Sanā'ī (d. 1131) and Farīd al-Dīn 'Aṭṭār, brought the Khurāsānī School of Sufi poetry to its peak. These works spread rapidly in Persia and India, where they affected the literature of several local languages such as Sindhi, and became also very popular in the Ottoman world, where most of the educated knew Persian.

Rūmī was highly sensitive to the beauty of music, as mentioned already, and received as inspiration from Heaven the form of the Mawlawī *samā'* based on whirling in the earthly imitation of the rotation of the heavens. The followers of this order were therefore called the Whirling Dervishes by nineteenth-century European travelers when they first observed their spiritual concert and sacred dance. The Mawlawī Order became known for its interiorized music and the most elaborate *samā'* among all the Sufi orders. It influenced deeply classical Turkish music, and the *samā'* can still be observed in Turkey despite the banning of the order by Ataturk. The Mawlawī *samā'* is now also performed in the West, and there is even an American branch of the order that performs the traditional *samā'*.

The influence of the Mawlawiyyah Order in the Ottoman Empire was immense, not only in cultural life but also socially and politically. Many sultans were members of the order, and wherever the Turks went they took the order with them. To this day there are remnants of the *tekkes* of the Mawlawīs in the Balkans as well as Syria, Lebanon, and Egypt. Although severely oppressed by the Turkish Republic, which harbored special animosity against it because of its influence, the order has survived as a living reality in Turkey to this day while the influence of the poetry of Rūmī and the music of the order continue in that country and elsewhere. His poetry remains very popular wherever Persian is read. The Mawlawī Order itself never spread to any appreciable degree in Persia or the Indian subcontinent, but the influence of Rūmī continues to be powerful on Sufism and on general culture in those lands and especially in Persia.

Another order that is almost completely Turkish but whose founder was again Persian is the Baktāshiyyah, founded by Ḥājjī Baktāsh Walī (d. 1338) from Khurasan. The order was organized in Anatolia in the fourteenth century and given its definitive form in the sixteenth century by Bālim Sulṭān, a figure so important that he was called the second master of the order following Ḥājjī Baktāsh himself. The order incorporated certain elements of Christianity and was strongly Shi'ite with devotion to the twelve Shi'ite Imams, especially 'Alī and Ja'far al-Ṣādiq. Some within the order even divinized 'Alī. They also incorporated the science of symbolism of letters, which the extremist movement of the Ḥurūfiyyah had spread in Anatolia. The eclecticism of the Baktāshiyyah is also revealed in their incorporation into their practices of certain shamanic elements and in the belief in the migration of souls.

The Baktāshīs established their mother *zāwiyah* or *tekke* near Kayseri in Anatolia, but their order spread all the way to Albania as well as Iraq and Egypt. Within Turkey they influenced popular piety greatly while gaining special social prominence because of their exclusive religious influence among the Janissaries, who constituted such an important element of the Ottoman army. In 1826 Sultan Mehmet II destroyed the Janissaries, and this in turn led to the destruction of many Baktāshī sites, but the order was revived in the middle of the nineteenth century, especially in the Balkans, with a major center near Tirana in Albania. This order along with others was banned in Turkey by Ataturk, and the Communist takeover of Albania dealt a heavy blow to it there.

Nevertheless, the order continues and the *shaykhs* of the order, called *bābās,* are still found in certain regions of the Balkans and even in Turkey.

A third major Sufi order that first developed in Turkey, that is, the Khalwatiyyah, also had a Persian founder, 'Umar al-Khalwatī (d. 1397) from Gilan. The order was organized by Yaḥyā Shīrwānī (d. 1463) in the Caucasus and spread from there to Anatolia, where it soon became associated with Ottoman politics. The spiritual master of Mehmet the Conqueror, who conquered Constantinople in 1453 and brought the Byzantine Empire to an end, is said to have been a Khalwatī. This order became popular in Turkey with numerous branches and from there spread in the eighteenth century to the Sudan and Ethiopia as well as Southeast Asia. In the nineteenth and twentieth centuries it underwent a remarkable dissemination in Egypt through the influence of Muḥammad al-Ḥifnī (d. 1767). The order also spread into the Balkans, Syria, Lebanon, and North Africa. In the eighteenth century Nūr al-Dīn Jarrāḥī (d. circa 1721) started a branch of the Khalwatiyyah Order named Khalwatiyyah-Jarrāḥiyyah with its center in Istanbul. This order is particularly important because despite the ban on the Sufi orders with the coming of Ataturk, the activities of this order continued and its *tekke* in Istanbul remains spiritually vibrant. Moreover, as a result of the travels to the West and activities of one of its recent *shaykhs,* Muẓaffar Efendi (d. 1985), the order has gained many European and American adherents and in fact has several centers in the West.

From the point of view of practice, this order has always emphasized the spiritual retreat, or *khalwah,* hence its name. Doctrinally it has welcomed the teachings of Ibn 'Arabī, especially the doctrine of the "transcendent unity of being" (*waḥdat al-wujūd*). Also the study and practice of the occult sciences such as divination and alchemy have been widespread among its members. Of all the Turkish orders, this order has had the widest geographical spread throughout the Islamic world.

Through these and other Sufi orders, through a vast corpus of Sufi writings, which contains the peaks of Arabic, Persian, and Turkish literature and especially poetry, not to mention local languages from West Africa to Bengal and Java, and most of all through an ever-present *barakah* emanating from the tombs of great saints and even more important the presence of living spiritual masters, the spiritual dimension of Islam as crystallized in Sufism has provided over the ages and continues to provide a path to the Garden of Truth. This summary history of Sufism reveals the roots of this path in a long tradition going back to the origin of Islam itself. It is hoped that knowledge of the reality and historical development of this spiritual tradition will induce those with the yearning to reach the Truth to walk upon such a path, whether it be Sufi or another authentic tradition whose authenticity can itself be judged by the living Sufi tradition even for those who are not attached to Sufism but who do not possess other means of authentication. The Sufi orders and their teachings are a light upon the path of Muslims seeking proximity to the One but can also be a light for others in quest of the only journey that is ultimately worthy of the human state, a journey that is the very raison d'être of human existence.

Appendix Two

THE TRADITION OF THEORETICAL SUFISM AND GNOSIS

Are they equal, those who know and those who know not?
Quran 39:9

An hour's contemplation is better than a year's adoration.
Ḥadīth

The heart that through gnosis has the light of
  God seen,
Whatever it sees, it first does God see.[1]
Maḥmūd Shabistarī

About the same time that the Sufi orders were taking shape, the doctrinal aspect of Sufism was being crystallized into a body of knowledge consisting of pure metaphysics of the highest order and the application of metaphysical principles to the cosmos and the human state, or cosmology, anthropology, and psychology as these terms are understood in the traditional sense. This body of knowledge is not philosophy, as this term is usually used today, although it had profound impact on later Islamic philosophy. Nor is it theology, although many Muslim theologians, both Sunni and Shi'ite, have embraced it over the ages. It is in reality gnosis or theosophy if these terms are understood in their original sense. It is what I have called elsewhere a *scientia sacra,* a sacred and an illuminative knowledge attainable through noesis and intellection combined with spiritual training. Almost all its true masters over the ages have been outstanding Sufis and/or esoterists, but not all Sufis have been its adherents, and also many who studied this science over the centuries were not active practitioners of Sufism. In chapter two we dealt with truth as understood in Sufism. Gnosis or doctrinal Sufism, whose tradition will be briefly outlined in this appendix, is an intellectual crystallization of that truth in the form of an organized science and a distinct intellectual discipline that corresponds in many ways to the writings of a Śankara in Hinduism or an Eriugena in the Christian tradition.

Usually contrasted to practical Sufism (*al-taṣawwuf al-'amalī*), theoretical and doctrinal Sufism (*al-taṣawwuf al-naẓarī* and *'ilmī*) or gnosis (*al-ma'rifah* in Arabic and *'irfān* in Persian) is associated most of all with the name of the incomparable thirteenth-century Andalusian Sufi sage, Muḥyī al-Dīn ibn 'Arabī. He did not establish an ordinary *ṭarīqah* like the Qādiriyyah or Shādhiliyyah, although there is definitely an Akbarian current in later Sufism, the name "Akbarian" coming from the title of Ibn 'Arabī as Shaykh al-akbar, that is, the greatest master. This current is seen within many other Sufi orders that embraced his teachings. In fact, one could say that with the possible exception of al-Ghazzālī, there is no single intellectual figure more influential than Ibn 'Arabī during the last eight centuries of Islamic history.

This theoretical gnosis (known also as doctrinal Sufism) does not mark progress over earlier Sufism but is a crystallization in more explicit terms of the *ma'rifah* attained by earlier Sufi masters, this event having been made necessary by the spiritual and intellectual needs of the Islamic community under new historical conditions. Earlier Sufis had spoken more or less through allusions to the reality of the Garden of Truth while Ibn 'Arabī and his followers provided a full map of the nature of the Garden along with the means of reaching it. In any case, in a book devoted to the Garden of Truth it is also necessary to deal with this tradition, whose knowledge in many ways complements that of the Sufi orders. This tradition has had its opponents and detractors over the centuries, among some exoteric scholars of the Law, theologians, philosophers, and even certain practitioners of Sufism who have emphasized that it is not necessary to master the writings associated with this tradition in order to follow the Sufi path and attain sanctity. This assertion is true, but nevertheless the tradition of theoretical gnosis, which contains a metaphysics of the highest order, has remained a vibrant reality to this day, not only because it is true but also because it has been the indispensable guide for many on their journey to the One.

A BRIEF HISTORY OF THE TRADITION OF THEORETICAL GNOSIS

The Earliest Foundation

Before turning to theoretical gnosis itself, its subject matter, and its significance today, it is necessary to provide a brief history over the ages in the Islamic tradition of the expressions of this Supreme Science, which itself stands beyond history and temporal development, being at the heart of the *philosophia perennis* as understood by traditional authorities, and not bound in its essence by the local coloring of various epochs and places. Of course, the wisdom with which this Supreme Science deals has always been and will always be, but it has received distinct formulations in the framework of various traditions. In the Islamic tradition this knowledge was handed down, albeit not in explicit form and externally but in a principial manner by the Prophet to a number of his companions, chief among them 'Alī, and in later generations to the Sufi masters and the Shi'ite Imams. Besides being transmitted orally, this knowledge was often expressed in the form of allusions, elliptical expressions, symbolic poems, and the like.

Gradually from the tenth century onward some Sufis, such as Ḥakīm Abū 'Abd Allāh Tirmidhī, began to write more systematically on certain aspects of Sufi doctrine. During the century after him Abū Ḥāmid

Muḥammad Ghazzālī wrote on divine knowledge in the *Iḥyā'* and in such shorter treatises as *al-Risālat al-laduniyyah* (*Treatise of Knowledge of Divine Proximity,* only attributed to him according to some scholars), and he also wrote the already-mentioned esoteric and gnostic commentary on the Light Verse of the Quran titled *Mishkāt al-anwār* (*Niche of Lights*). Shortly afterward, 'Ayn al-Quḍāt Hamadānī dealt with the subject of divine knowledge and a philosophical exposition of certain Sufi teachings in his *Maktūbāt* (*Letters*) and *Tamhīdāt* (*Dispositions*) while in his *Zubdat al-ḥaqā'iq* (*The Best Essence of Truths*) he criticized the existing rationalistic currents in the thought of some philosophers and pointed to another way of knowing, which is none other than gnosis. These figures in turn prepared the ground for Ibn 'Arabī, although he is a colossal and providential figure whose writings cannot be reduced to historical influences of his predecessors.

Many have rightly considered Ibn 'Arabī the father and founder of theoretical gnosis or doctrinal and theoretical Sufism. This remarkable figure was born in Murcia in the Andalusian province of Almeria. He carried out his early studies in Seville and other major centers of Islamic Spain, within which he traveled extensively as a young man. At an early age he also met many Sufi saints and masters and already by the age of sixteen had theophanic visions. His meeting at this age with the venerable master of discursive philosophy, Ibn Rushd (Averroës), in which he predicted the latter's death, is one of the peaks of Islamic intellectual history. As the result of a vision, Ibn 'Arabī left his land of birth for the east, journeying for some time in the Maghrib, where he absorbed the spiritual heritage of Abū Madyan, and then to Cairo, where he was not well received. He therefore left Egypt for Mecca, where he composed his magnum opus, *al-Futūḥāt al-makkiyyah* (*The Meccan Illuminations*). He finally settled in Damascus, where he wrote the *Fuṣūṣ al-ḥikam* (*Bezels or Ringstones of Wisdom*) and where a number of important disciples assembled around him. In this city he died, and his mausoleum in the northern part of the city remains a major site of pilgrimage to this day.

Although the seminal figure in the tradition of gnosis, Ibn 'Arabī did not write works concerned only with pure metaphysics and gnosis. His writings also deal extensively with Quranic and *Ḥadīth* commentary, the meaning of religious rites, various traditional sciences, including the science of the symbolic significance of letters of the Arabic alphabet, ethics, law, and many other matters, all of which are also of an esoteric and gnostic nature.

Ibn 'Arabī was, moreover, a major poet, in fact, as already mentioned, one of the greatest Sufi poets of the Arabic language. One of his most significant poetic works is the *Tarjumān al-ashwāq* (*Interpreter of Desires*), wherein he expounds the highest meaning of love. To demonstrate that in Sufism knowledge is not separated from love, in one of the poems of this work he, who was the proverbial exemplar of the path of gnosis and illuminative knowledge in Islam, calls his religion the religion of love. In verses that have become justly famous even in the West he sings:

> Receptive now my heart is for each form;
> For gazelles pasture, for monks a monastery,
> Temple for idols, Ka'bah to be rounded,
> Tables of Torah and script of Qur'ān.
> My religion is love's religion: where'er turn
> Her camels, that my religion is, my faith.[2]

memorize

Discussion here is confined to works of Ibn 'Arabī and his school that are devoted completely to theoretical gnosis and metaphysics, works that deal directly with the Supreme Science of the Real. Otherwise, every work of Ibn 'Arabī and his school is related in one way or another to gnosis or *ma'rifah,* as are numerous writings of many other Sufis. The groundbreaking work of Ibn 'Arabī on the subject of gnosis, and a work that is foundational to the whole tradition of theoretical gnosis in Islam, is the *Fuṣūṣ al-ḥikam,* along with certain sections of *al-Futūḥāt al-makkiyyah* and a few of his shorter treatises, including *Naqsh al-fuṣūṣ* (*Exposing the* Fuṣūṣ), which is Ibn 'Arabī's own commentary upon the *Fuṣūṣ.*

In any case, the *Fuṣūṣ* was taken by later commentators as the central text of the tradition of theoretical gnosis or doctrinal Sufism. Many of the major later works of this tradition are in fact commentaries upon this text, which Ibn 'Arabī believed was inspired directly by the Prophet. The history of these commentaries, many of which are "original" works themselves, stretching from the thirteenth century to this day, is important for understanding this tradition and also reveals how widespread was the influence of this tradition, from Morocco to the Malay world and China. Unfortunately, despite so much scholarship carried out in this field during the past few decades, there is still no thorough history of commentaries upon the *Fuṣūṣ,* any more than there is a detailed history of the tradition of theoretical gnosis and/or Sufi metaphysics itself.

Ibn 'Arabī's teachings were first disseminated from Damascus. Some of his immediate students who were particularly drawn to pure metaphysics and gnosis, with a number also having had training in Islamic philosophy, began to interpret the master's teachings and especially his *Fuṣūṣ* in a more systematic and philosophical fashion, thereby laying the ground for the systematic formulation of that Supreme Science of the Real with which the tradition of theoretical gnosis is concerned. The first commentator upon the *Fuṣūṣ* was Ibn 'Arabī's immediate student and Qūnawī's close companion, 'Afīf al-Dīn al-Tilimsānī (d. 1291), who commented upon the whole text but in summary fashion. It is of interest to note that he also wrote a commentary upon the *Kitāb al-mawāqif* of al-Niffarī. But the most influential propagator of the Murcian master's teachings in the domain of theoretical gnosis and metaphysics and the person who gave the systematic exposition that characterizes later expressions of theoretical gnosis is Ṣadr al-Dīn Qūnawī (d. 1274). This most important student of Ibn 'Arabī did not write a commentary on the text of the *Fuṣūṣ,* but he did write a work titled *al-Fukūk* (*Openings*), which explains the titles of the chapters of the *Fuṣūṣ* and was considered by many later Sufis and gnostics as a key to understanding the mysteries of Ibn 'Arabī's text. Qūnawī is also the author of a number of other works of a gnostic (*'irfānī*) nature, chief among them the *Miftāḥ al-ghayb* (*Key to the Invisible*), a monumental work of theoretical gnosis that, along with its commentary by Shams al-Dīn Fanārī known as *Miṣbāḥ al-uns* (*The Lamp of Familiarity*), became one of the premier texts for the teaching of theoretical gnosis especially in Persia.

Qūnawī trained a number of students who themselves became major figures in the tradition of theoretical gnosis. But before we turn to them, it is necessary to mention a poet who was a contemporary of Ibn 'Arabī and who played an exceptional role in the later history of this tradition. This poet is 'Umar ibn al-Fāriḍ (d. 1235), whose *al-Tā'iyyah* (*Poem Rhyming in* Tā') is considered as a complete exposition of the doctrines of *'irfān* expressed in sublime poetry and the subject of several commentaries that are themselves seminal texts of gnosis. There were also many important Persian poets such as Fakhr al-Dīn 'Irāqī (d. 1289), Awḥad al-Dīn Kirmānī (d. 1238), Shams al-Dīn Maghribī (d. 1406–07), Maḥmūd Shabistarī (d. circa 1318), the author of the *Gulshan-i rāz* (*The Secret Garden of Divine Mysteries*), one of the greatest works of Persian Sufi poetry, and 'Abd al-Raḥmān Jāmī, whom we have already mentioned, who followed Ibn 'Arabī's teachings. There are also many Turkish poets and those from the Subcontinent who expressed Ibn 'Arabian teachings in the medium of poetry. The poetry of these figures, however, does not belong strictly to doctrinal texts of the tradition of theoretical gnosis with which we are concerned here, although some of the commentaries on their poetry do, such as *Sharḥ-i gulshan-i rāz* (*Commentary upon the* Gulshan-i rāz) of Shams al-Dīn Lāhījī (d. before 1494) and also some poetic texts such as *Ashi''at al-lama'āt* (*Rays of Light*) and *Lawā'iḥ* (*Gleams*) of Jāmī.

Returning to Qūnawī's students, as far as the subject of this essay is concerned, the most notable and influential for the later tradition was first of all Sa'īd al-Dīn Farghānī (d. 1296), who collected the commentaries of his master in Persian on the *Tā'iyyah* and on their basis composed a major work in both Persian and Arabic (which contains certain additions) with the title *Mashāriq al-darārī al-zuhar* (*Orients of Radiant Stars*) and *Muntaha'l-madārik* (*The Utmost Limit of Perception*), respectively. Second, one must mention Mu'ayyid al-Dīn Jandī (d. 1300), the author of the first extensive commentary upon the *Fuṣūṣ,* which also influenced the very popular commentary of his student 'Abd al-Razzāq Kāshānī (d. 1330). Both of these men also wrote other notable works on theoretical gnosis, such as the Persian treatise *Nafḥat al-rūḥ wa tuḥfat al-futūḥ* (*The Breath of the Spirit and the Gift of Spiritual Illuminations*) of Jandī and the Arabic *Ta'wīl al-qur'ān* (*Esoteric Hermeneutic of the Quran*) of Kāshānī, which has been also mistakenly attributed to Ibn 'Arabī himself. This work illustrates a whole genre of writings that explain the principles of gnosis and metaphysics on the basis of commentary upon the inner levels of meaning of the Quran. During this early period, when the school of theoretical gnosis was taking shape, there were other figures of importance associated with the circle of Ibn 'Arabī and Qūnawī although not the students of the latter, such as Sa'd al-Dīn Ḥamūyah and his student 'Azīz al-Dīn Nasafī, who wrote several popular works based on the doctrine of *waḥdat al-wujūd* (the transcendent unity of being) and *al-insān al-kāmil* (*Universal Man*), which are pivotal to Ibn 'Arabī's teachings. It is not possible, however, in this short historical review to deal with all such figures.

Although our goal in this appendix is to provide a survey of the tradition of doctrinal or theoretical Sufism and gnosis, it is necessary to say a few words about what Ibn 'Arabī's doctrinal teachings involve, although these have been treated in another manner in the main text of this book. The central teaching of Ibn 'Arabī concerns the doctrine of unity, which is also the heart of the message of the Quran. But for him the assertion of this unity means not only that God is one but that ultimately Reality is one. This is what is called the doctrine of "the transcendent unity or oneness of being," with which we have already dealt and which is the hallmark of his school and of much of Sufism in general. This single Reality manifests all the levels of existence through reflections of Its Self-Determinations upon what he and other Sufis call the mirror of nothingness. Everything in the cosmos is the result of this reflection or theophany (*tajallī*). Ibn 'Arabī also discusses the doctrine of human nature in this context. The human being, both male and female, contains potentially all levels of existence within and is the mirror in which God contemplates Himself. The reality of this archetypal human being, who is called by Ibn 'Arabī the Universal or Perfect Man (*al-insān al-kāmil*), is contained potentially in every human being but is actualized only within the being of prophets and the greatest saints of not only Islam but all authentic religions. On the basis of these two doctrines, Ibn 'Arabī develops an elaborate cosmology, sacred psychology, eschatology, epistemology, and prophetology—all bound together by the doctrine of *waḥdat al-wujūd*. He even deals with the inner meaning of alchemy, astrology, and other so-called occult sciences on the basis of the metaphysical principles that he elucidates. Furthermore, he explicates the meaning of "the imaginal world" and its reality within us related to the power of "creative imagination," which is so important in the spiritual life.

The Arab World

From the early foundation of this school in Syria and Anatolia, the teachings of Ibn 'Arabī spread to different regions of the Islamic world. In summary fashion we shall deal with some of the most important figures belonging to this tradition in each region of the Islamic world. Let us begin with the Arab world, proceeding from west to east. As we have seen, in the Maghrib a very strong Sufi tradition has been preserved over the centuries, but as mentioned, Maghribī Sufism, although devoted to gnosis in its purest form, as we see in such figures as Abū Madyan, Ibn Mashīsh, and Abū'l-Ḥasan al-Shādhilī, was not given to long theoretical expositions of gnosis as found in the East. Most works from this region were concerned with the practice of the Sufi path and explanation of practical Sufi teachings. One had to wait for the eighteenth century to find in the works of Aḥmad ibn 'Ajībah (d. 1809–10) treatises that belong to the genre of theoretical gnosis. But the oral tradition based on Ibn 'Arabian teachings was kept alive in this region, as we see in the personal instructions and also written works on Sufism of such celebrated twentieth-century Sufi masters of the Maghrib as Shaykh al-'Alawī and Shaykh Muḥammad al-Tādilī (d. 1952). Maghribī works on gnosis tended, however, to be usually less systematic and philosophical in their exposition of gnosis than those of the East.

A supreme example of Ibn 'Arabian teachings emanating from the Maghrib is found in the writings of the celebrated Algerian prince (*amīr*) and Sufi master 'Abd al-Qādir al-Jazā'irī (d. 1883), who taught the works of Ibn 'Arabī in Damascus, to which he was exiled by the French after being captured on the battlefield in Algeria after a long struggle. Amīr 'Abd al-Qādir also composed a number of independent works on gnosis, such as the *Kitāb al-mawāqif* (*The Book of Halts,* as it is usually translated into English). To this day the text of the *Fuṣūṣ* and the *Futūḥāt* are taught in certain Sufi centers of the Maghrib, especially those associated with the Shādhiliyyah Order, which has continued to produce over the centuries its own distinct genre of Sufi literature going back to the prayers of Abū'l-Ḥasan al-Shādhilī and especially the treatises of the third Pole or Axis of the order, Ibn 'Aṭā' Allāh al-Iskandarī. In later centuries these two currents, the first issuing from early Shādhilism and the second from Ibn 'Arabian gnosis, met in many notable figures of Sufism from the Maghrib as well as other regions.

There was greater interest in theoretical gnosis and Sufism in the eastern part of the Arab world as far as the production of written texts is concerned. Strangely enough, however, Egypt, which has always been a major center of Sufism, is an exception. In that ancient land there has always been more interest in practical Sufism and Sufi ethics than in speculative thought and doctrinal Sufism although Akbarian teachings spread to Mamluk Egypt in the thirteenth century. There were also some popularizers of Ibn 'Arabī's teachings in Egypt, perhaps chief among them 'Abd al-Wahhāb al-Sha'rānī, whose well-known works present a more popular version of the *Futūḥāt* and *Fuṣūṣ*. He tried also to link Shādhilī teachings with those of Ibn 'Arabī. Fewer notable commentaries on classical texts of gnosis are found, however, in Egypt than in many other lands. Theoretical gnosis was, nevertheless, taught and studied by many Egyptian figures. In this context it is interesting to note that even the modernist reformer Muḥammad 'Abduh (d. 1905) turned to the study of Ibn 'Arabī later in life. However, opposition to these writings has remained strong to this day in many circles in that country, as one sees in the protests in front of the Egyptian Parliament some years ago on the occasion of the publication of the new edition of the *Futūḥāt* by Osman Yahya, who had edited the text critically.

In the Yemen there was great interest in Ibn 'Arabian gnosis in the School of Zabīd, especially under the Rasūlids up to the fifteenth century. Ismā'īl al-Jabartī (d. 1403), Aḥmad ibn al-Raddād (d. 1417–18), and 'Abd al-Karīm al-Jīlī (d. 1428) were particularly significant figures of this school in the Yemen. Al-Jīlī, who was originally Persian but resided in the Yemen, is particularly important because of his magnum opus, *al-Insān al-kāmil* (*The Universal Man*), a primary work used to this day from Morocco to India as a text for the instruction of theoretical gnosis and Sufism. It is a more systematic exposition of the teaching of Ibn 'Arabī.

In the eastern Arab world, one finds in greater Palestine and Syria continuous interest in theoretical Sufism and gnosis and the writing of important commentaries on Ibn 'Arabī, such as that of 'Abd al-Ghanyī al-Nābulusī (d. 1731) on the *Fuṣūṣ*. Also, the defense by Ibrāhīm ibn Ḥasan al-Kūrānī (d. 1690), a Persian Kurdish scholar who resided in Mecca, of the gnosis of Ibn 'Arabī had much influence in Syria and adjoining areas. Although, as in Egypt and elsewhere, many jurists and theologians in Syria going back to Ibn Taymiyyah (d. 1328) and also students of Sa'd al-Dīn al-Taftāzānī (d. 1389) opposed the doctrines of Ibn 'Arabian gnosis, this school remained very much alive and continues to survive to this day in that region. One of the most remarkable contemporary Sufis who died in Beirut just a few years ago, the woman saint Sayyidah Fāṭimah al-Yashruṭiyyah, whom we already mentioned, gave the title *al-Riḥlah ila'l-Ḥaqq* (*The Journey to the Truth*) to her major work on Sufism on the basis of a dream of Ibn 'Arabī.

Ottoman Turkey

Turning to the Turkish part of the Ottoman world, we find a continuous and strong tradition in the study of theoretical gnosis going back to al-Qūnawī himself and his circle in Konya. Foremost among these figures after the founding of this school are Dā'ūd Qayṣarī (d. 1350) and Shams al-Dīn Fanārī (d. 1431). A student of Kāshānī, Qayṣarī wrote a number of works on gnosis, including his commentary on the *Tā'iyyah* of Ibn al-Fāriḍ, but chief among them is his commentary upon the *Fuṣūṣ,* which is one of the most thorough and remains popular to this day. He also wrote an introduction to this work called *al-Muqaddimah* (*The Introduction*), which summarizes the whole cycle of gnostic doctrines in a masterly fashion and has been itself the subject of many commentaries, including fairly recent glosses by Ayatollah Khomeini and a magisterial commentary by Sayyid Jalāl al-Dīn Āshtiyānī (d. 2005).

As for Fanārī, besides being a chief judge (*qāḍī*) in the Ottoman Empire and a major authority on Islamic Law, he was the author of what many Turkish and Persian students of gnosis consider as the most advanced text of *'irfān,* namely the *Miṣbāḥ al-uns.* It is strange that today in Bursa where he is buried, as elsewhere in Turkey, he is known primarily as a jurist and in Persia as a gnostic. In addition to these two major figures, one can mention Bālī Efendī (d. 1553), well-known commentator of Ibn 'Arabī, and many other Sufis who left behind notable works on theoretical Sufism and gnosis up to the twentieth century. In fact, the influence of this school in the Ottoman world was extensive, including in such areas as Bosnia, which produced outstanding gnostics such as 'Abd Allāh of Bosnia (d. 1644), and is to be found in many different types of Turkish thinkers into the contemporary period. Among the most famous of them is Ahmed Avni Konuk (d. 1938), who wrote a four-volume commentary on the *Fuṣūṣ;* his contemporary Ferid Ram (d. 1944), who was at the same time a gnostic, philosopher, and political figure and the author of several works on Ibn 'Arabian gnosis; and Ismail Fenni Ertugrul (d. 1940), a philosopher who used the teachings of Ibn 'Arabī to refute the errors of modern Western philosophy, especially materialism. His writings contributed greatly to the revival of interest in metaphysics in twentieth-century Turkey.

Muslim India

We have been moving eastward in this brief historical survey, and logically we should now turn to Persia and adjacent areas, including Shi'ite Iraq, which has been closely associated with Persia intellectually since the Safavid period, as well as Afghanistan, which also belongs to the same intellectual world as Persia. Because, however, of the central role played in Persia in the cultivation of theoretical gnosis or *'irfān-i naẓarī* during the past few centuries, we shall turn to it at the end of this survey and first direct our attention farther east to India, Southeast Asia, and China.

Although a thorough study has never been made of all the important figures associated with the School of Ibn 'Arabī and theoretical Sufism and gnosis in the Indian subcontinent, the research that has been carried out so far reveals a widespread influence of this school in that area. Already in the fourteenth century Sayyid 'Alī Hamadānī (d. 1385), the Persian Sufi who migrated to Kashmir, helped to spread Ibn 'Arabī's ideas in India. He not only wrote a Persian commentary on the *Fuṣūṣ* but also composed a number of independent treatises on *'irfān*. A century later 'Alā' al-Dīn 'Alī ibn Aḥmad Mahā'imī (d. 1432) not only commented upon the *Fuṣūṣ* and Qūnawī's *Nuṣūṣ* (*Texts*) but also wrote in Arabic several independent expositions of gnosis of a more philosophical nature. These works are related in approach to later works on theoretical gnosis written in Persia. He also wrote an Arabic commentary upon Shams al-Dīn Maghribī's *Jām-i jahānnamāy* (*The World-Revealing Cup*), which some believe received much of its inspiration from the *Mashāriq al-darārī* of Farghānī. It is interesting to note that Maghribī's poetry, which like that of many other poets such as Kirmānī, 'Irāqī, Shabistarī, Shāh Ni'mat Allāh Walī, and Jāmī, was based on basic gnostic theses such as *waḥdat al-wujūd,* was especially appreciated by those followers of the School of Ibn 'Arabī in India who were acquainted with the Persian language, as the poetry of Ibn al-Fāriḍ was appreciated among Arab as well as Persian, Turkish, and Indian followers of that school who knew Arabic.

Notable exponents of theoretical gnosis in India are numerous, and even the better known ones cannot all be mentioned here. But it is necessary to mention one figure who is probably the most profound master of this school in the Subcontinent. He is Muḥibb Allāh Ilāhābādī (also known as Allāhābādī) (d. 1648). Author of an Arabic and even longer Persian commentary on the *Fuṣūṣ* and also an authoritative commentary on the *Futūḥāt,* Ilāhābādī also wrote independent treatises on *'irfān.* His writings emphasize intellection and sapience rather than only spiritual states, which many Sufis in India as elsewhere claimed as the sole source of divine knowledge. The significance of the works of Muḥibb Allāh Ilāhābādī in the tradition of theoretical gnosis under consideration in this chapter and his later influence in India are immense. He marks one of the major peaks of the school not only in India, but in the whole of the Islamic world.

The central thesis of Ibn 'Arabian gnosis, that is, *waḥdat al-wujūd,* had a life of its own in India. While certain Sufis, such as Shaykh Aḥmad Sirhindī, opposed its usual interpretation, it was embraced by many Sufis, including such great saints as Gīsū Dirāz and Niẓām al-Dīn Awliyā' and many of their disciples. One can hardly imagine the history of Sufism in the Subcontinent without the central role played by *'irfān-i naẓarī.* Even notable Indian philosophers and theologians such as Shāh Walī Allāh (d. 1762) of Delhi wrote works highly inspired by this school, and its influence continued into the twentieth century, as we see in some of the works of Mawlānā Ashraf 'Alī Thanwī (d. 1943). Moreover, once the philosophical School of Illumination (*ishrāq*) of Suhrawardī and the Transcendent Theosophy or Philosophy (*al-ḥikmat al-muta'āliyah*) of Mullā Ṣadrā reached India, there were many interactions between these schools and the school of *'irfān,* as we also see in Persia itself. Also the very fact that a body of knowledge similar to *'irfān* existed in Hinduism in the school of Advaita Vedanta brought about many dialogues and discourses of a gnostic nature between the two traditions in a special spiritual and intellectual ambience.

Southeast Asia

Turning to Southeast Asia and the Malay world, we encounter a unique phenomenon, namely the role of the School of Ibn 'Arabī, sometimes called *wujūdiyyah,* in the very formation of Malay as an intellectual language suitable for Islamic discourse. Ḥamzah Fanṣūrī (d. 1592), the most important figure of this school in that region, was a major Malay poet and played a central role in the development of Malay as an Islamic language while he also had a command of both Arabic and Persian. He was, moreover, a master of the doctrines of the School of Ibn 'Arabī. He was followed in his attachment to this school by Shams al-Dīn

Sumātrānī (d. 1630). Although this school was opposed by certain other Malay Sufis, such as Nūr al-Dīn Rāniri, and most Malays paid more attention to the operative rather than the doctrinal aspect of Sufism, the school of theoretical Sufism and gnosis continued to be studied in certain places in the Malay world and even today there are circles in Malaysia, Singapore, and Indonesia where the teachings of this school are followed and many of the classical texts continue to be studied.

China

A word must also be said about China. Until the seventeenth century, Chinese Muslims who dealt with intellectual matters in general and Sufism in particular did so on the basis of Arabic and Persian texts. It was only in the seventeenth century that they began to use classical Chinese and to seek to express Islamic metaphysics and philosophy in the language of neo-Confucianism. Henceforth, there developed a significant body of Islamic thought in Chinese that is being systematically studied only now. It is interesting to note that two of the classical Islamic works to be rendered the earliest into Chinese are, first, the *Lawā'iḥ* of Jāmī, which is a masterly summary of *'irfān* in Persian, translated by Liu Chih (d. circa 1670) as *Chen-chao-wei* (*Displaying the Concealment of the Real Realm*) and, second, the *Ashi''at al-lama'āt* also by Jāmī and again, as already mentioned, dealing with *'irfān,* translated by P'o Na-chih (d. after 1697) as *Chao-yüan pi-chüeh* (*The Mysterious Secret of the Original Display*). Also the first Chinese Muslim thinker to expound Islamic teachings in Chinese, that is, Wang Tai-yü (d. 1657 or 1658), who wrote his *Real Commentary on the True Teaching* in 1642 and several later works, was steeped in the same *'irfānī* tradition. The school of theoretical gnosis therefore has been destined to play a major role in the encounter on the highest intellectual level between the Chinese and the Islamic traditions during the past few centuries.

Persia

Persia was to become one of the main centers, if not the central arena, for the later development of theoretical gnosis. The circle of Qūnawī was already closely connected to the Persian cultural world, and many of its members, including Qūnawī himself, wrote some treatises in Persian. Qūnawī's student Fakhr al-Dīn 'Irāqī is considered one of the greatest poets of the Persian language. Among other early members of the school were Sa'd al-Dīn Ḥamūyah; his disciple 'Azīz al-Dīn Nasafī, who wrote on gnosis in readily accessible Persian; Awḥad al-Dīn Balyānī (d. 1288) from Shiraz, whose famous *Risālat al-aḥadiyyah* (*The Treatise on Unity*) was for a long time attributed to Ibn 'Arabī; and 'Abd al-Razzāq Kāshānī, who, as mentioned, is a major figure of the school of theoretical gnosis and a prominent commentator upon the *Fuṣūṣ*. From the fourteenth century on in Persia we see, on the one hand, the continuation of the school of theoretical gnosis through the appearance of prose works in both Arabic and Persian, either in the form of commentaries upon the *Fuṣūṣ* and other seminal texts of this school or as independent treatises. On the other hand, we observe the deep influence of this school in Sufi literature, especially poetry. A supreme example is the *Gulshan-i rāz* of Maḥmūd Shabistarī, which as mentioned is one of the greatest masterpieces of Persian Sufi poetry and which summarizes the principles of Ibn 'Arabian gnosis in verses of celestial beauty. That is partly why its extensive commentary by Muḥammad Lāhījī in the fifteenth century is such a major text of theoretical gnosis. Here, however, we are concerned only with the prose and systematic works of theoretical gnosis and Sufism and not the poetical tradition, but the nexus between the two should not be forgotten, as we see in the works of 'Irāqī, Shāh Ni'mat Allāh Walī, Jāmī, and many others.

Another important event that took place in the fourteenth century and that left its deep influence upon the history of the school during the Safavid, Qajar, and Pahlavi periods was the integration of Ibn 'Arabian gnosis into Shi'ism, which possesses its own gnostic teachings, to which scholars refer as *'irfān-i shī'ī* (Shi'ite gnosis). These two outwardly distinct schools are inwardly connected and go back to the original esoteric and gnostic dimension of the Islamic revelation. It was most of all Sayyid Ḥaydar Āmulī (d. 1385) who brought about a synthesis of these two branches of the tree of gnosis, although he also did make certain criticisms of Ibn 'Arabī, especially concerning the question of *walāyah/wilāyah*. Many others walked in his footsteps. Āmulī was at once a major Twelve-Imam Shi'ite theologian and a Sufi devoted to the School of Ibn 'Arabī. His *Jāmi' al-asrār* (*The Sum of Divine Secrets*) is a pivotal text for the gnosis of Ibn 'Arabī in a Shi'ite context. He was also the author of a major commentary upon the *Fuṣūṣ* as well as independent metaphysical treatises. The later development of theoretical gnosis in Persia, as well as the School of Transcendent

Theosophy of Mullā Ṣadrā cannot be fully understood without consideration of Āmulī's works.

The fourteenth to the fifteenth century marks a period of intense activity in the field of theoretical gnosis and the School of Ibn 'Arabī in Persia. Commentaries upon the *Fuṣūṣ* continued to appear. The first in Persian was most likely that of Rukn al-Dīn Mas'ūd Shīrāzī, known as Bāhā Ruknā (d. 1367). But there were many others by such figures as Tāj al-Dīn Khwārazmī (d. circa 1435), Shāh Ni'mat Allāh Walī, Ibn Turkah Iṣfahānī (d. 1432), and Jāmī. This extensive activity in the domain of gnosis associated specifically with the School of Ibn 'Arabī took place in addition to, on the one hand, the flowering of the Sufism of the School of Khurasan and Central Asia and profound gnostic teachings, mostly in poetic form, of figures such as 'Aṭṭār, Rūmī, and perhaps the greatest poet of the Persian language, Muḥammad Shams al-Dīn Ḥāfiẓ (d. 1389) and, on the other hand, the Kubrawiyyah School founded by Najm al-Dīn Kubrā. We can hardly overemphasize the metaphysical importance of the Khurāsānī and Central Asian schools, but in this appendix we shall not deal with them, being concerned only with *'irfān-i naẓarī* in its association with the School of Ibn 'Arabī.

Among the gnostic figures of this period, Ṣā'in al-Dīn ibn Turkah Iṣfahānī stands out as far as his later influence is concerned. The author of many independent treatises on metaphysics and the traditional sciences, he also wrote a commentary upon the *Fuṣūṣ* that became popular. But the work that made him one of the pillars of the school of theoretical gnosis in Persia during later centuries is his *Tamhīd al-qawā'id* (*The Disposition of Principles*). This masterly treatment of the cycle of gnosis became a popular textbook for teaching the subject in Persia especially during the Qajar period and has remained so to this day, as one sees in the extensive recension of it by the contemporary Persian philosopher and gnostic 'Abd Allāh Jawādī Āmulī.

The figure who was given the title of the Seal of Persian Poets, that is, 'Abd al-Raḥmān Jāmī from Herat, was also in a sense the seal of this period in the history of theoretical gnosis in Persia. Also, in a sense, he synthesized within his works the two distinct currents of Islamic spirituality that flowed from Ibn 'Arabī and Rūmī. Jāmī belongs to the poetic tradition of Rūmī while being also the author of a number of commentaries upon the works of Ibn 'Arabī, such as the famous *Naqd al-nuṣūṣ* (*Glancing upon the Texts*). He also authored summaries of the teachings of this school in works already mentioned, which are used as texts for the teaching of *'irfān* to this day.

The spread of Twelve-Imam Shi'ism in Persia during the Safavid period transformed the scene as far as the study and teaching of *'irfān* were concerned. During the earlier part of Safavid rule, many Sufi orders flourished in Persia whereas from the seventeenth century onward, because of special religious and social causes, opposition grew to Sufism associated with *khānqāhs* especially among most of the class of Shi'ite scholars (*'ulamā'*), who henceforth chose to speak of *'irfān* rather than *taṣawwuf.* Although other types of Sufi and gnostic writings appeared during this period written by members of various Sufi orders, such as the Dhahabīs, and *'irfān-i shī'ī* also flourished in certain circles, few new works on the subject of theoretical gnosis appeared during this period in comparison to the previous era.

The main influence of the School of Ibn 'Arabī came to be felt through the writings of Mullā Ṣadrā, who was deeply influenced by Shaykh al-Akbar and quoted from him extensively in his *al-Asfār al-arba'ah* (*Four Journeys*) and elsewhere. But technically speaking, the School of Mullā Ṣadrā is associated with *ḥikmat* and not *'irfān,* although Mullā Ṣadrā was also a gnostic and deeply versed in Ibn 'Arabian teachings. But he integrated elements of this teaching into his *al-ḥikmat al-muta'āliyah* (*The Transcendent Theosophy or Philosophy*) and did not write separate treatises on pure gnosis in the manner of an Ibn 'Arabī or Qūnawī. It is highly significant that Mullā Ṣadrā did not leave behind a commentary on the *Fuṣūṣ,* like that of Kāshānī or Qayṣarī, or write a treatise like *Tamhīd al-qawā'id* of Ibn Turkah although he was well acquainted with this book. Nor do we find major works devoted purely to theoretical gnosis or *'irfān-i naẓarī* by his students such as Fayḍ Kāshānī, who was also a gnostic, or Lāhījī. The school of *'irfān-i naẓarī* certainly continued during the Safavid era, but the major intellectual thrust of the period lay in creating the School of Transcendent Theosophy, which had incorporated major theses of *'irfān* such as the transcendent unity of being (*waḥdat al-wujūd*) into its philosophical system, but which was distinct in the structure of its doctrines, manner of presentation, and method of demonstration from *'irfān.* Specialists in later Islamic thought distinguish between *'irfān* and *ḥikmat* by stating that the subject of *ḥikmat* is "being conditioned by negation" (*wujūd bi-sharṭ-i lā*) while the subject of *'irfān* is totally nonconditioned Being (*wujūd lā bi-sharṭ*). The first means being in itself, rejecting all conditionality, and the second, being totally non-conditioned, including being devoid of negation of conditionality.

In any case, as far as Persia is concerned, one had to wait for the Qajar period in the nineteenth century to see a major revival of the teaching of *'irfān-i naẓarī* and the appearance of important commentaries on classical texts of this tradition. This revival occurred along with the revivification of the teachings of the School of Mullā Ṣadrā, and many masters of this period were both *ḥakīm* and *'ārif,* while *'irfān* continued to influence philosophy deeply. The first major figure to mention in the context of the school of *'irfān* during the Qajar period is Sayyid Raḍī Lārījānī (d. 1853), who was a student of Mullā 'Alī Nūrī in *ḥikmat,* but we know less of his lineage in *'irfān.* He is said to have possessed exalted spiritual states and was given the title of "Possessor of the States of the Inner (*bāṭin*) World" by his contemporaries. We know that he taught the *Fuṣūṣ* and *Tamhīd al-qawā'id* in Isfahan and was considered a saint as well as master of *'irfān-i naẓarī.*

Sayyid Raḍī's most important student was Āqā Muḥammad Riḍā Qumsha'ī (d. 1888–89), whom many Persian experts on *'irfān* consider as a second Ibn 'Arabī and the most prominent commentator upon gnostic texts such as the *Fuṣūṣ* since the time of Qūnawī. Āqā Muḥammad Riḍā studied in Isfahan but later migrated to Tehran, which became from the middle part of the nineteenth century onward perhaps the most significant locale for the teaching of *'irfān-i naẓarī* for the next century. There he taught and trained many important students in both *'irfān* and *ḥikmat.* He also wrote a number of major glosses and commentaries on such works as the *Tamhīd al-qawā'id* and Qayṣarī's commentary on the *Fuṣūṣ* as well as some of the works of Mullā Ṣadrā, in addition to independent treatises. Like so many masters of *'irfān-i naẓarī,* Āqā Muḥammad Riḍā was also a fine poet and composed poetry under the pen name Ṣahbā. Unfortunately, much of his poetry is lost. It is also of great significance to note that Āqā Muḥammad Riḍā emphasized the importance of spiritual practice and the need for a spiritual master parallel with the study of theoretical gnosis.

One of Āqā Muḥammad Riḍā's important students was Mīrzā Hāshim Ashkiwarī Rashtī (d. 1914), commentator upon *Miṣbāḥ al-uns,* who took over the circle of instruction of *'irfān* in Tehran after Āqā Muḥammad Riḍā. He was in turn teacher of such famous *ḥakīms* and *'ārifs* of the past century as Mīrzā Mahdī Āshtiyānī (d. 1953), Mīrzā Aḥmad Āshtiyānī (d. 1940), my own teacher, Sayyid Muḥammad Kāẓim

'Aṣṣār (d. 1975), and Muḥammad 'Alī Shāhābādī (d. 1951). Although in his later life he entered the realm of politics and departed from the traditional gnostic understanding of *walāyah/wilāyah,* Ayatollah Ruhollah Khomeini (Rūḥ Allāh Khumaynī) was a student of Shāhābādī and deeply interested in the School of Ibn 'Arabī for many years.

The extensive political fame and influence of Ayatollah Khomeini (d. 1989) has prevented many people in the West and even within the Islamic world from paying serious attention to his gnostic works. Whatever one may think of his political views, there is no doubt that on the basis of his many works on *'irfān,* he has a place in any objective treatment of the long history of theoretical gnosis outlined in a summary fashion above. Although he also studied the *ḥikmat* of the School of Mullā Ṣadrā, his great love remained *'irfān* of the School of Ibn 'Arabī, which in some of his earlier writings he combined with the tradition of *'irfān-i shī 'ī.*

It is perplexing that although later in life he entered fully into the arena of revolutionary politics, earlier in his life Ayatollah Khomeini was very much interested not only in theoretical gnosis but also in operative Sufism with its ascetic dimension and emphasis on detachment from the world. What made him depart from the life of an *'ārif* and his models such as Qumsha'ī and Shāhābadī, who kept aloof from the life of this world and politics, to enter the realm of such extensive and revolutionary political action as he did seems hard to understand. But that is the subject for another day. Suffice it to say here that the key to this riddle should perhaps be sought in the stages of humanity's journeys (*asfār*) to God mentioned by Mullā Ṣadrā, in whose thought Khomeini was also an expert. As mentioned earlier in this book, at the beginning of the *Asfār,* Mullā Ṣadrā explicates the stages of the journey as follows: the journey from creation (*al-khalq*) to God (*al-Ḥaqq*), the journey in God, the journey back from God to His creation, and finally the journey in creation with God. It is both surprising and unusual that Ayatollah Khomeini applied these stages to his own life in such a way that he thought he was already in the fourth stage of the journey when he began his tumultuous political life. This has had no precedence in Islamic history as far as one of the traditional religious scholars, or *'ulamā',* or Sufis are concerned. In any case, his career is an unprecedented and perplexing case of the relation between esoterism and political life acted in a new mode, and very different from the establishment of the Safavid and Sanūsiyyah dynasties by Sufi orders.

The tradition of *'irfān-i naẓarī* continues to this day in Persia. After the generation of such figures as 'Allāmah Ṭabāṭabā'ī (d. 1983), another of my teachers, who was a major gnostic without writing any commentaries on Ibn 'Arabī, and also one of the important masters of *'irfān,* Sayyid Muḥammad Kāẓim 'Aṣṣār, notable figures have appeared upon the scene such as Sayyid Jalāl al-Dīn Āshtiyanī, Ḥasan-zādah Āmulī, and Jawād Āmulī, of whom the latter two still teach at Qom. Āshtiyanī's commentary upon the introduction of Qayṣarī to the *Fuṣūṣ,* mentioned above, as well as a number of his other commentaries, such as those on *Tamhīd al-qawā'id* and *Naqd al-nuṣūṣ,* are major commentaries upon texts of theoretical gnosis, while the recent commentary by Ḥasan-zādah Āmulī on the *Fuṣūṣ,* titled *Mumidd al-himam dar sharḥ-i fuṣūṣ al-ḥikam* (*Protractor of Intention in the Commentary upon the Bezels of Wisdom*), reveals the living nature of this school in Persia, as does Jawād Āmulī's recension of *Tamhīd al-qawā'id.*

WITH WHAT DO THEORETICAL SUFISM AND GNOSIS DEAL?

Having provided a brief history of the school of gnosis and before turning to the significance of theoretical gnosis and doctrinal Sufism today, it is necessary to summarize again at the end of this discourse the subjects that Supreme Science treats, many of which have already been dealt with in one way or another in earlier chapters of this book. And before delineating the subjects made known through theoretical gnosis, one needs to know how one can gain such a knowledge. I dealt with the subject of salvific knowledge in chapter two. Here I will only mention again that the knowledge of the Supreme Reality or the Supreme Substance is itself the highest knowledge and constitutes the very substance of principial knowledge. As Frithjof Schuon, one of the foremost contemporary expositors of gnosis and metaphysics, has said, "The substance of knowledge is Knowledge of the Substance."[3] To make the issue clear it is necessary to recall that this knowledge is contained deep within the heart/intellect or the Garden of Truth within, and gaining it is more of a recovery than a discovery. It is ultimately remembrance, the Platonic *anamnesis.* The faculty associated with this knowledge is the intellect (*al-'aql*), the *nous,* not to be confused with reason. To function correctly, the intellect within us in most cases needs that objective manifestation of the intellect that is revelation. In any case, its attainment always requires intellectual intuition, which is ultimately a Divine gift, and the ability to "taste" the Truth. In the Islamic tradition this supreme knowledge or gnosis is associated with such qualities as *dhawq* (taste), *ḥads* (intuition), *ishrāq* (illumination), and *ḥuḍūr* (presence). Those who are able to understand gnosis must possess certain intellective gifts, not to be confused with powers of mere ratiocination. Also, as should be clear from our earlier discussion, in Islam gnosis has always been related to the inner meaning of the revelation and its attainment of the initiatic and esoteric power of *walāyah/wilāyah,* about which so many Muslim gnostics from Ḥakīm Tirmidhī and Ibn 'Arabī to Sayyid Ḥaydar Āmulī and from Āqā Muḥammad Riḍā Qumsha'ī to Muḥammad 'Alī Shāhābādī have written with differing interpretations. It should be added here that although theoretical gnosis can be mastered through instruction and one's own intellectual powers, its full realization is possible only through spiritual practice and not through theoretical understanding divorced from spiritual realization.

Turning now to the subjects with which theoretical gnosis and doctrinal Sufism deal, I must mention that it is not my intention here to expound details of its teachings, but only to discuss the subjects of concern to this school and in fact to Islamic metaphysics as a whole. The supreme subject of gnosis may be said to be the Supreme Principle or Reality, which is absolute and infinite and not even bound by the condition of being absolute and infinite. It corresponds to what Meister Eckhart calls the Godhead and others have called the Ground of Being. The gnostics often write that it is Absolute Being without even the "limitation" of absoluteness. It is in fact the Reality that is both Beyond-Being and Absolute Being. Later gnostics called the supreme subject of this science *wujūd-i lā bi-sharṭ-i maqsamī,* that is, the totally unconditioned Being, which is itself beyond all conditionality and the ground for all divisions and distinctions of being. Gnosis, therefore, deals not only with ontology or the science of being, but with a metaphysics that is grounded beyond Being in the Supreme Reality of which Being as usually understood is the first Self-Determination. It begins with the Divine Essence (*Dhāt*), which is above all limits and determinations and which is often referred to in Sufism as *al-Ḥaqq* (the Truth). It also deals with multiplicity within the Divine Order, that is, the Divine Names and Qualities, which are still in the Divine Order but are so many Self-Determinations and Self-Disclosures of the Supreme Essence in a reality that already partakes of multiplicity.

This Supreme Science (*al-'ilm al-a'lā*) or *scientia sacra,* that is, gnosis, also deals with manifestations of the Principle (or God, in religious language), with all the levels of universal and cosmic existence from the archangelic to the material, viewing all that exists in the cosmic order in light of the Principle. All creation is seen in its relation to God. Gnosis then descends from the Divine Order to the realm of manifestation and deals with cosmology as a science of the cosmos in relation to the Principle, as a form of knowledge that provides maps to guide and orient us who are situated in the confines of cosmic existence to the Metacosmic Reality. This Supreme Science also deals of necessity with the human state in all its width, breadth, depth, and height. It contains a most profound "science of the human state," which one could call an anthropology if this term were understood in its traditional and not modern sense, as well as a "science of spirit" within us, or pneumatology, which is absent from the modern worldview but found in traditional psychology. Finally, gnosis deals with the Principle and all the levels of manifestation from the point of view of the unity that dominates over all that exists and that is especially central to the Islamic perspective. As already mentioned, one might say that Islamic metaphysics or gnosis is dominated by the two basic doctrines of the "transcendent oneness or unity of being" (*waḥdat al-wujūd*) and the Universal Man (*al-insān al-kāmil*), which includes not only a gnostic anthropology but also a symbolic cosmology on the basis of the correspondence between the microcosm and macrocosm.

Theoretical gnosis is also concerned in the deepest sense with the reality of revelation and religion. The question of the relation between gnosis and esoterism, on the one hand, and the formal and exoteric aspect of religion, on the other, is a complicated one into which we cannot enter here. What is clear is that in every traditional society gnosis and esoterism have been inextricably tied to the religious climate in which they have existed. This is as true of Luria and Jewish esoterism as it is of Śankara and Hindu gnosis as well as everything in between. In any case, in this appendix, which deals with gnosis in the Islamic tradition, we need to emphasize the deepest concern of the gnostics, like Sufis in general, with the realities of religion and explanation of its teachings on the most profound level, as we observe in many well-known Sufi treatises on the inner meaning of the Quran, and also of the Islamic rites as well as on the central Islamic doctrine of Unity (*tawḥīd*).

Theoretical gnosis is concerned on the intellectual level in one way or another not only with the practical aspects of religion but also with basic Islamic doctrines such as creation, prophecy, eschatology, and even Divine Law. Islamic masters of gnosis speak of both the why and the how of creation. As I mentioned in earlier chapters, they speak of "creation *in* God" as well as "creation *by* God". They expound the doctrine of the immutable archetypes (*al-a'yān al-thābitah*) (corresponding in many ways to the Platonic ideas) and the breathing of existence upon them associated with the Divine Mercy, which brings about the created order. They see creation itself as the Self-Disclosure of God. They also discuss the renewal of creation (*tajdīd al-khalq*) at every moment. Furthermore, theoretical gnosis speaks extensively about the end as well as the beginning of things. The deepest explanation of Islamic eschatology based on the Quran and *Ḥadīth* is found in such writings as the *Futūḥāt al-makkiyyah* of Ibn 'Arabī.

In all traditional religions and cultural climes gnosis also provides the basis for the science of forms, including artistic forms, and makes comprehensible the language of symbolism, as we see in Hindu treatises on the metaphysics of art, Chinese treatises on the tao of painting, or the profound exposition of Islamic aesthetics and the science of symbolism in so many Sufi works, such as the *Mathnawī* of Rūmī. Although dealing at the highest level with the Formless, it is gnosis and metaphysics that can provide the basis for the science of symbols, especially in a world where the "symbolist spirit" has been lost. If Islamic treatises on theoretical gnosis do not usually deal explicitly in a separate section with forms and symbols, they do expound the principles of this science, which can then be applied when necessary. Besides the poems of Rūmī, the writings of Ibn 'Arabī are replete with such examples. Such masters elucidate the science of spiritual hermeneutics (*ta'wīl*) as well as apply it to diverse religious and artistic forms, symbols, and myths, including of course those found in the Quran itself.

Let us now summarize what constitutes the reality of gnosis as understood in the Islamic tradition. Gnosis when realized is illuminative and unitive knowledge. It is also a *theoria* or vision of the Garden of Truth, and therefore it is natural that theoretical gnosis be concerned with knowledge as such, primarily sacred knowledge and knowledge of the Sacred but also with the grades and the hierarchy of knowledge. It is true that most traditional philosophies, including the Islamic, also deal with this issue, but it is only in works on theoretical gnosis that one finds the most universal treatment of this subject, including of course supreme knowledge, which is gnosis itself. Theoretical gnosis or *scientia sacra* is also the metaphysics that lies at the heart of perennial philosophy understood traditionally. It has been sometimes called theosophy, as this term was understood before its modern distortion, and is also related to what is called by some mystical theology and mystical philosophy in Western languages. In the Islamic tradition it has provided the ultimate criteria for the judgment of what constitutes *philosophia vera.* It has been foundational in the development of both traditional philosophy and the traditional sciences and is key to the deepest understanding of all traditional cosmological sciences, including the "hidden sciences" (*al-'ulūm al-khafiyyah* or *gharībah*). As we have seen, the later traditional schools of philosophy that have persisted in the Islamic world to this day, chief among them the School of Illumination founded by Suhrawardī and the Transcendent Theosophy/Philosophy established by Mullā Ṣadrā, are closely associated with *'irfān.* One might in fact say that while after the Middle Ages and the Renaissance in the West philosophy became more and more wedded and also subservient to modern science, as we see so clearly in Kant, in the Islamic world philosophy became ever more closely associated with *'irfān,* from which it drew its sustenance and whose vision of reality served as basis for philosophizing. One needs only read the works of Mullā Ṣadrā, such as his *al-Shawāhid al-rubūbiyyah* (*Divine Witnesses*), to ascertain the truth of this assertion. Many of the works of the later Islamic philosophers lie at the borderline between *ḥikmat* and *'irfān* although, as already mentioned, the two disciplines remain quite distinct from one another.

THEORETICAL GNOSIS AND ENTRY INTO THE GARDEN OF TRUTH

As stated earlier, in the traditional Islamic world theoretical gnosis was not only opposed by certain, but certainly not all, jurists, theologians, and philosophers, it was also opposed by certain Sufis who claimed that gnosis is the result of what is attained through spiritual states and not through reading books on gnosis. Titus Burckhardt, one of the foremost authorities on traditional metaphysics and the perennial philosophy in the twentieth century and the person who opened the door for the understanding of Ibn 'Arabī in the West, once told me that when he first went to Fez as a young man, one day he took the *Fuṣūṣ* with him to a great teacher to study this basic text of *ma'rifah* or *'irfān* with him. The teacher asked him what book he was carrying under his arm. He said it was the *Fuṣūṣ*. The teacher smiled and said, "Those who are intelligent enough to understand the *Fuṣūṣ* do not need to study it, and those who are not intelligent enough are not competent to study it anyway." The master nevertheless went on to teach the young S. Ibrāhīm (Titus Burckhardt) the *Fuṣūṣ*, but he was alluding to the significance of realized gnosis and not only its theoretical understanding, a knowledge that once realized delivers us from the bondage of ignorance, being by definition salvific knowledge. Burckhardt went on to translate a summary of the *Fuṣūṣ* into French, a translation that played a groundbreaking role in introducing the school of theoretical gnosis and Ibn 'Arabī to the West. In fact, although the magisterial exposition of gnosis and metaphysics by traditional masters such as René Guénon, Frithjof Schuon, Burckhardt, and others was directly related to inner inspiration and intellection, Islamic esoterism, as well as teachings of non-Islamic origin, it was also inextricably linked (in a more particular manner) with the tradition of *'irfān* discussed in this appendix

Of course, one does not become a saint and enter the Garden of Truth simply by reading texts of *'irfān* or even understanding them mentally. One has to realize their truths and "be" what one knows. Nevertheless, the body of knowledge contained in works of theoretical gnosis and doctrinal and theoretical Sufism are a most precious science, which must be cherished as a gift from Heaven. This vast body of writings from Ibn 'Arabī and Qūnawī to Āqā Muḥammad Riḍā Qumsha'ī and Amīr 'Abd al-Qādir and in the contemporary period from Mawlānā 'Alī Thanwī and Sayyid Jalāl al-Dīn Āshtiyānī to Ḥasan-zādah Āmulī contain a body of knowledge of vast richness, a knowledge that alone can provide the deepest answers to the most acute contemporary intellectual, spiritual, and even practical questions. Its very presence helps human beings avoid the mental errors that surround us today, errors whose consequences now threaten our very existence. But above all, this living tradition can provide for not only Muslims but also non-Muslims capable of understanding it the Supreme Science of the Real, the vision of the Garden of Truth whose realization and attainment is the highest end of human existence and the goal of the spiritual path. The teachings of gnosis are a fruit of the vision of the Garden and can therefore lead to that vision which precedes, for those with an intellectual bent, the actual march upon the path to the Garden. The experience of the Garden of Truth is the realization of the teachings of gnosis that are expounded on the theoretical level. It is for those who understand such teachings to transform *theoria* into actual experience, the description of the Beloved into Her embrace.

> I am the bird of the spiritual Garden, not of this world of dust;
> For a few days, they have a cage of my body made.
>
> *Rūmī*

NOTES

ONE WHAT IT MEANS TO BE HUMAN

1. Trans. Martin Lings, *Sufi Poems: A Medieval Anthology* (Cambridge, UK: Islamic Texts Society, 2004), 88.
2. *Ḥadīth qudsī,* a saying in which God speaks through the mouth of the Prophet, but the saying is not part of the Quran.
3. Trans. Martin Lings, in *Muhammad: His Life Based on the Earliest Sources* (Cambridge, UK: Islamic Texts Society, 1991), 69 (with a slight modification).
4. Rūmī, *Selected Poems from the Divan-e Shams-e Tabrizi,* coll. and trans. R. A. Nicholson (Bethesda, MD: Ibex Publisher, 2001), 124–25. My translation is based directly on the Persian and differs somewhat from Nicholson's. Furthermore, in the last verse I have used an alternative reading found in some manuscripts but not in the one adopted by Nicholson. This sonnet does not appear in the Furūzānfar edition of the *Dīwān,* and some scholars believe that it is attributed to him and not by him. But there is also no proof that it is not by him. Moreover, this sonnet is one of the most famous poems associated with the name Rūmī over the centuries.
5. Trans. Martin Lings, *Sufi Poems,* 86.

TWO TRUTH

1. Trans. Martin Lings, *Sufi Poems: A Mediaeval Anthology*, 28.
2. Trans. Abu Bakr Siraj Ed-Din in his *The Book of Certainty* (New York: Samuel Weiser, 1974), 12.
3. *Gulshan-i rāz,* in *Sharḥ-i gulshan-i rāz,* ed. 'Alī Qulī Maḥmūdī Bakhtiyār (Tehran: 'Ilm Press, AH 1377), 722.
4. Trans. Lings, *Sufi Poems,* 64.
5. From the translation of T. Weir, *Journal of the Royal Asiatic Society* (1901), 809 (with slight modification). This treatise, attributed to Ibn 'Arabī but actually by another master of gnosis, 'Abd Allāh al-Balyānī, is among the most famous in Sufi literature on the doctrine of the oneness of being.
6. *Dīwān* of Nāṣir-i Khusraw, ed. Sayyid Naṣr Allāh Taqawī (Tehran: Amīr Kabīr Press, AH 1355 [solar]), 4.
7. Trans. Lings, *Sufi Poems,* 1.
8. Rūmī, *Mathnawī,* ed. Mohammad Estelami (Tehran: Zawwār Press, AH 1346 [solar]), 2:160.

THREE LOVE AND BEAUTY

1. Quoted by Ibn 'Arabī in his collection of sacred *ḥadīths,* in his *Divine Sayings: The Mishkāt al-Anwār of Ibn 'Arabī,* trans. Stephen Hirtenstein and Martin Notcutt (Oxford: Anqa Publishing, 2004), 64 (translation slightly modified).
2. A *ḥadīth* transmitted by 'Alī ibn Abī Ṭālib, trans. Abu Bakr Siraj Ed-Din, *The Book of Certainty,* 93.
3. Rūmī, *Mathnawī,* ed. Mohammad Estelami, 1:5.
4. *La Divina Commedia,* ed. and ann. C. H. Grandgent, rev. Charles S. Singleton (Cambridge: Harvard University Press, 1972), 930.
5. Ḥāfiẓ, *Dīwān,* published as *Dars-i Ḥāfiẓ,* ed. Mohammed Estelami (Tehran: Sukhan Press, AH 1382 [solar]), *ghazal* 317, p. 815.
6. Awḥad al-Dīn Kirmānī, *Heart's Witness,* trans. Bernd Manuel Weischer and Peter Lamborn Wilson (Tehran: Imperial Iranian Academy of Philosophy, 1978), 167 (translation somewhat modified).
7. Kirmānī, *Heart's Witness,* 168 (my translation).
8. From the *Mathnawī,* 5:372, trans. R. A. Nicholson, *Rumi: Poet and Mystic* (Boston: Unwin Paperbacks, 1978), 45.

FOUR GOODNESS AND HUMAN ACTION

1. Rūmī, *Mathnawī,* 1:1821–24, trans. R. A. Nicholson, *Rumi: Poet and Mystic* (Boston: Unwin Paperbacks, 1978), 141.

2. Rūmī, *Mathnawī,* 1:1821–24, trans. Nicholson, *Rumi: Poet and Mystic,* 152.
3. Rūmī, *Mathnawī,* ed. Mohammad Estelami, 1:3735ff.
4. Sa'dī, *Gulistān,* in *Kulliyāt-i Sa'dī,* ed. Muḥammad 'Alī Furūghī,(Tehran: Amīr Kabīr Press, AH 1365 [solar]), 46.

FIVE HOW DO WE REACH THE GARDEN OF TRUTH?

1. *Mathnawī* 4:761 (my translation).
2. Ḥāfiẓ, *Dīwān,* published as *Dars-i Ḥāfiẓ,* ed. Mohammed Estelami, *ghazal* 129, v. 5, p. 383.
3. An abbreviated version of one of my own poems from *Poems of the Way* (Oakton, VA: Foundation for Traditional Studies Press, 1999), 21.
4. This poem is from the *Dīwān* of Shaykh Aḥmad al-'Alawī (d. 1934), one of the most notable Sufi masters of recent centuries with disciples in nearly every Muslim country as well as in the West. It is translated by Martin Lings in his *A Sufi Saint of the Twentieth Century* (Berkeley and Los Angeles: University of California Press, 1973), 224.
5. *Dīwān-i Shams,* ed. Badī' al-Zamān Furūzānfar (Tehran: Amīr Kabīr Press, AH 1363 [solar]), vol. 5, *ghazal* 2133, p. 12.
6. Frithjof Schuon, "The Mystery of the Prophetic Substance," *In the Face of the Absolute* (Bloomington, IN: World Wisdom Books, 1989), 223.
7. Translated by Annemarie Schimmel in her *Mystical Dimensions of Islam* (Chapel Hill: University of North Carolina Press, 1975), 110.
8. Ḥāfiẓ, *Dīwān,* ed. Estelami, *ghazal* 80, p. 269.
9. Based on the translation by Martin Lings, *A Return to the Spirit* (Louisville, KY: Fons Vitae, 2006), 72.
10. *Mathnawī,* ed. Estelami, 1:606. In some manuscripts there is a variant according to which the second verse would be, "Thou art Absolute Being and our existence." I prefer the second reading but have translated the poem as it appears in the edition of the *Mathnawī* being used in this book.
11. Trans. Martin Lings, *Sufi Poems: A Mediaeval Anthology*, 38.
12. Frithjof Schuon, *Adastra and Stella Maris* (Bloomington, IN: World Wisdom Books, 2003), 16.

SIX ACCESS TO THE CENTER

1. Ḥāfiẓ, *Dīwān,* published as *Dars-i Ḥāfiẓ,* ed. Mohammed Estelami, *ghazal* 49, p. 197.
2. *Gulshan-i rāz,* in *Sharḥ-i gulshan-i rāz,* ed. 'Alī Qulī Maḥmūdī Bakhtiyār, 73.
3. Ḥāfiẓ, *Dīwān,* ed. Estelami, *ghazal* 11, p. 96.

APPENDIX ONE THE SUFI TRADITION AND THE SUFI ORDERS

1. Shabistarī, *Gulshan-i rāz,* in *Majmū'a-yi āthār,* ed. Samad Muwaḥḥid (Tehran: Taḥūrī Press, AH 1365 [solar]), 68.
2. Trans. Martin Lings, *Sufi Poems: A Mediaeval Anthology*, 2.
3. From the *Ḥilyat al-awliyā'* of Abū Nu'aym al-Iṣfahānī, quoted by Annemarie Schimmel in her *Mystical Dimensions of Islam* (Chapel Hill: University of North Carolina Press, 1975), 46.
4. Trans. Lings, *Sufi Poems,* 18.
5. Schimmel, *Mystical Dimensions of Islam,* 69.
6. From the *Kitāb al-luma'* of Abū Naṣr al-Sarrāj, trans. Schimmel, *Mystical Dimensions of Islam,* 49.
7. Arthur J. Arberry, ed. and trans., *The Mawāqif and Mukhāṭabāt of Muḥammad Ibn 'Abdi' L-Jabbār Al-Niffarī* (London: Luzac, 1978), 169 (p. 199 of the Arabic text). (I have somewhat modified the translation.)
8. Khwājah 'Abd Allāh Anṣārī, *Munājāt: The Intimate Prayers,* trans. Lawrence Morris and Rustam Sarfeh (New York: Khaneghah and Maktab of Maleknia Naserali-Shah, 1975), 53, 63, and 41.
9. Trans. Lings, *Sufi Poems,* 56.
10. Vincent Cornell, *The Way of Abū Madyan: The Works of Abū Madyan Shu'ayb* (Cambridge, UK: The Islamic Texts Society, 1996), 156.

APPENDIX TWO THE TRADITION OF THEORETICAL SUFISM AND GNOSIS

1. Shabistarī, *Gulshan-i rāz,* in *Majmū'a-yi āthār,* ed. Ṣamad Muwaḥḥid, 70.
2. Trans. Martin Lings, *Sufi Poems: A Mediaeval Anthology*, 62.
3. To quote the original French, "La substance de la connaissance est la Connaissance de la Substance." Frithjof Schuon, *Formes et substance dans les religions* (Paris: Dervy-Livres, 1975), 35.

GLOSSARY OF TECHNICAL TERMS

Note: The Arabic article *al-* has been deleted except where it is grammatically necessary.

'abd: *servant, slave, bondsman*

adab: *correct comportment, courtesy, literary culture, appropriate manner*

Aḥad: *the One (a Name of God)*

al-aḥādīth al-qudsiyyah: *sacred sayings, traditions of the Prophet of Islam in which God speaks in the first person but these sayings are not parts of the Quran*

ahl al-ṣuffah: *people of the bench, in reference to a bench that was placed in front of the mosque of the Prophet in Medina and the most revered members of the early Islamic community would often sit on it*

ahl-i dil: *people of the heart, one of the names used for Sufis*

a'lā: *most exalted, most elevated*

Allāh: *the Supreme Name of God in Arabic*

'ālam al-ghayb: *the absent world, the invisible world*

'ālam al-shahādah: *the manifested world, the visible world*

'ālim: *scholar, the person who has knowledge (usually understood as knowledge of religion)*

'Alīm: *the Knower (a Name of God)*

'amal: *action, practice*

'amalī: *practical, operative*

amīr: *prince, ruler*

'aql: *intellect, reason*

'ārif: *gnostic, possessor of unifying knowledge*

'ārif[u] bi'Llāh: *the person who knows God by God*

asfār (*sing.* safar): *journeys interpreted in Sufism as the various stages of the journey of the soul to God, in God and in creation with God*

asmā' (*sing.* ism): *names (usually in reference to the Names of God)*

asrār (*sing.* sirr): *secrets, mysteries (usually understood as Divine Mysteries)*

Ātman: *the Supreme Self (according to Hindu doctrines)*

avātaric: *related to the avātar, a divine incarnation or descent*

awrād (*sing.* wird): *litanies (used by Sufis)*

āyah: *symbol, sign, portent, verse of the Quran*

'ayn al-yaqīn: *the eye of certainty*

'ayn thābit (*pl.* al-a'yān al-thābitah): *immutable archetype*

bābā: *father, title of masters in the Baktāshī Sufi order*

baqā': *subsistence*

barakah: *grace*

basmalah: *abbreviation of "In the Name of God, the All-Good, the Infinitely Merciful"*

basṭ: *expansion*

bāṭin: *inward, esoteric*

Bāṭin: *the Inward (a Name of God)*

bhakti marga: *the path of love and devotion (in Hinduism)*

Bismi'Llāh al-Raḥmān al-Raḥīm: *"In the Name of God, the Infinitely-Good, the All-Merciful," the formula with which all chapters of the Quran except one begin and with which Muslims begin various activities in their lives*

darwīsh: *a follower of Sufism*

dhākir: *invoker, the person who remembers God*

Dhāt: *the Essence (of God)*

dhawq: *taste*

dhikr: *invocation, remembrance, mention*

fanā': *annihilation*

al-faqr al-muḥammadī: *Muḥammadan poverty, one of the names used for Sufism*

faqīr: *poor, in Sufism the spiritually poor, a follower of Sufism*

faqr: *poverty, spiritual poverty*

farsh: *the carpet, allusion to the lowest level of existence*

Fātiḥah: *the Opening, the first chapter of the Quran*

al-fayḍ al-aqdas: *the most sacred effusion or emanation*

al-fayḍ al-muqaddas: *sacred effusion or emanation*

fikr: *meditation, thought*

firdaws: *garden, Paradise, the Garden*

fiṭrah: *primordial nature, original nature*

futuwwah: *spiritual chivalry*

ghayb: *hidden, nonmanifest, invisible, absent*

gharībah: *hidden, occult, unfamiliar*

ghazal: *a form of poetry found in many Islamic languages similar in form to the sonnet*

ḥabīb: *friend, intimate*

Hādī: *the Guide (a Name of God)*

ḥadīth: *a saying or tradition of the Prophet; in Shi'ism the sayings of the Imams are also included as a special category of* ḥadīth

Ḥadīth: *the collection of the sayings of the Prophet*

ḥads: *intellectual intuition*

hāhūt: *Divine Presence at the level of the Essence*

ḥajj: *pilgrimage to Mecca*

ḥakīm: *sage, wise person, philosopher, physician*

ḥāl: *spiritual state*

ḥalqah: *circle (in reference to Sufi gatherings where male disciples usually sit or stand in a circle)*

ḥamd: *praise*

al-ḥamd^{u} li'Llāh: *praise be to God (a common Islamic utterance)*

ḥaqq: *truth, verity*

Ḥaqq: *the Truth (a Name of God)*

ḥaqīqah: *truth, verity*

al-ḥaqīqat al-muḥammadiyyah: *Muḥammadan Reality*

ḥijāb: *veil*

ḥikmat: *theosophy, philosophy (of later Islamic schools), wisdom*

al-ḥikmat al-muta'āliyah: *transcendental theosophy or philosophy*

himmah: *ardor, spiritual aspiration*

ḥubb: *love, devotion*

hubūṭ: *fall (in general in reference to humanity's fall from the Edenic state)*

ḥuḍūr: *presence*

ḥusn: *beauty*

hylé: *prime matter (in Greek philosophy)*

'ibādah: *worship*

iḥsān: *virtue, beauty, goodness*

ikhlāṣ: *sincerity*

ilāhīs: *Sufi songs as they are known especially in the Turkish world*

'ilm: *knowledge, science*

'ilm al-yaqīn: *the science of certainty*

īmān: *faith*

al-insān al-kāmil: *the Universal Man, the Perfect Man*

irādah: *will, intention*

'irfān-i naẓarī: *theoretical gnosis, theoretical or doctrinal Sufism*

'irfān-i shī'ī: *Shi'ite gnosis*

inābah: *contrition, penitence*

'irfān: *gnosis*

'irfānī: *gnostic*

ishrāq: *illumination*

islām: *submission (to God)*

'ishq: *love, ardent devotion, intense love*

'ishq al-ḥaqīqī: *true love*

al-'ishq al-majāzī: *metaphorical love*

jabarūt: *the archangelic world*

jalāl: *majesty*

jallabah: *long woolen dress still worn by Muslims especially in North Africa*

jalwah: *splendor, effulgence, external radiance*

jamāl: *beauty*

jannat al-Dhāt: *the Paradise of the Divine Essence*

jawānmardī: *spiritual chivalry*

jihād: *exertion*

jinn: *a class of psychic beings mentioned in the Quran, a demon*

jñāna: *illuminative knowledge in Hinduism*

Karīm: *The Generous (a Name of God)*

karāmah: *generosity*

karma yoga: *the path of approaching God through action or karma according to Hinduism*

kashf al-maḥjūb: *the unveiling of the veiled*

kashkūl: *begging bowl used by certain Sufis*

khalīfah: *vicegerent, vice-regent, representative*

khalwah: *spiritual retreat*

khānqāh: *Sufi center*

khayāl: *imagination*

khiḍr-i rāh: *guide on the spiritual path*

khalq: *creation, to create*

lāhūt: *the Divine Presence at the level of the Divine Names and Qualities*

layl: *night*

līlā: *divine play associated with the creation of the world in Hinduism*

liwā' al-ḥamd: *the flag of praise*

maḥabbah: *love, devotion*

madhkūr: *the invoked, the remembered*

majdhūb: *attracted by God*

majlis (*pl.* majālis): *gathering of Sufis*

makhāfah: *fear, reverential fear of God*

malakūt: *the spiritual world, the angelic world*

malāmah: *blame*

ma'nā: *meaning*

manzil (*pl.* manāzil): *place of descent, station*

maqām (*pl.* maqāmāt): *spiritual station*

ma'rifah: *principial knowledge, gnosis*

ma'shūq: *the beloved*

mathnawīkhānī: *the special art of reciting the Mathnawī of Jalāl al-Dīn Rūmī*

mawqif (*pl.* mawāqif): *place of halting, spiritual staying*

mawlā: *master*

māyā: *the creation power of Ātman, which also veils It and brings about the illusion of separate cosmic existence, according to the nondualistic school of the Vedanta*

mi'rāj: *the Nocturnal Ascent of the Prophet from Mecca to Jerusalem and from there to the Divine Presence; spiritual ascent*

muftī: *religious authority who can issue religious edicts*

muḥaqqiq: *one who is immersed in the realization of the Truth, verifier*

mulk: *the world that surrounds humanity here below on this earth*

mullā: *a title given in Persian to a religious scholar*

muqaddam: *a designate of a Sufi master who is able to initiate aspirants and guide them on the path under the direction of the master*

murād: *the reality or the person who is sought, the Sufi master*

murīd: *seeker, the person who wills to reach the truth, the disciple in Sufism*

murshid: *spiritual master, guide*

musīqā'l-andalus: *Andalusian music (of Morocco)*

muslim: *a being who is surrendered to God, Muslim*

nā'ib: *representative*

nafas al-Raḥmān: *the breath of the Compassionate*

nafs: *soul, ego, self, psyche*

al-nafs al-ammārah bi'l-sū': *that part of the soul that incites to evil*

nashīd: *Sufi song*

nāsūt: *the human world*

nubuwwah: *prophecy*

Om (Aum): *sacred sound symbol in Hinduism, considered the primordial word through which everything came into existence*

pardīs: *garden*

pashmīnah-pūsh: *wearer of wool (in reference to Sufis)*

pīr: *spiritual master*

qabḍ: *contraction*

qāḍī: *judge*

qalandar: *wandering darwīsh*

quṭb: *the Pole or spiritual Axis of the age*

qawwālī: *special form of Sufi singing associated with the Indo-Pakistani Subcontinent*

Rabb: *the Lord (a Name of God)*

rāg: *a mode in Indian music*

raḥmah: *compassion, mercy*

Raḥmān: *the All-Good, the Compassionate (a Name of God)*

Raḥīm: *the Infinitely Merciful (a Name of God)*

rajul (*pl.* rijāl): *man, any human being male or female who has advanced on the path*

riḍā: *contentment*

Riḍwān: *the most exalted Paradise*

rijāl al-ghayb: *absent or invisible persons (men)*

Rūḥ: *the Spirit*

ṣabr: *patience*

ṣafā: *purity*

ṣaḥw: *sobriety*

saki: *from the Arabic word sāqī, meaning pourer of drink (allusion to the spiritual master in Sufism)*

sakīnah: *Divine peace*

salaf: *ancestors, those who have come before*

salām: *peace*

ṣalāh: *the canonical prayers that Muslims are obliged to perform five times a day*

sālik: *traveler upon the spiritual path*

samā': *Sufi concert, audition*

samsāra: *the world of change, corruption, and death, according to Buddhism*

ṣifāt: *qualities (in particular Divine Qualities)*

al-ṣirāṭ al-mustaqīm: *the straight path, the path of ascent (in Sufism)*

silsilah: *chain, the initiatic chain in Sufism*

ṣūrah: *form*

Ṣhekinah: *Hebrew equivalent to the Arabic sakīnah, meaning divine peace*

Sharī'ah: *Divine Law*

shaṭḥiyyāt (sing. shaṭḥ): *theophanic sayings, words of ecstasy*

shukr: *gratitude, thankfulness*

suḥbah: *discourse of the Sufis*

sukr: *intoxication, drunkenness*

ṣulḥ-i kull: *universal peace, total peace*

sunnah: *traditions or wont of the Prophet*

śunyata: *void, the void (in Buddhism)*

sūrah: *name of the chapters in the Quran*

tābi'ūn: *followers, the generation after the Prophet*

taḥaqquq: *realization*

tajallī: *theophany*

tāj-i faqr: *the crown of spiritual poverty*

takhalluq bi-akhlāq[i]'Llāh: *becoming imbued with the Qualities of God*

ṭalab: *yearning (more specifically for God and the spiritual life)*

taqwā: *reverential fear (of God), asceticism, mindfulness*

ta'aqqul: *intellection*

tark: *abandonment*

tark-i tark: *abandonment of abandonment*

ṭarīq: *path (in reference to Sufism)*

ṭarīqah (*pl.* ṭuruq): *Sufi path, Sufi order*

ṭarīqah ila'Llāh: *the path to God*

taṣawwuf: *Sufism*

al-taṣawwuf al-'ilmī: *theoretical or doctrinal Sufism*

taslīm: *submission*

ta'ayyun: *determination, entification*

tay'īd: *affirmation, support*

ta'wīl: *spiritual hermeneutics*

tawakkul: *reliance (upon God)*

tawbah: *repentance*

tawḥīd: *oneness, unity*

waḥdat al-wujūd: *transcendent oneness of being, unity of being*

walāyah/wilāyah: *initiatic power (in Sufism)*

wara': *scrupulousness, chasteness (in religious matters)*

wujūdiyyah: *the school of the primacy and unity of being*

Wadūd: *the Loving (a Name of God)*

Walī: *Guardian, Ruler, Friend (a Name of God); saint, friend of God*

yaqīn: *certainty, certitude*

Ẓāhir: *the Outward (a Name of God)*

ẓāhir: *outward, external, exoteric*

zāwiyah (pl. zawāyā): *Sufi center*

zuhd: *asceticism*

zuhhād: *ascetics*

SELECTED BIBLIOGRAPHY OF WORKS IN ENGLISH

Böwering, Gerhard. *The Mystical Vision of Existence in Classical Islam*. New York: de Gruyter, 1980.

Burckhardt, Titus. *An Introduction to Sufism*. Translated by D. M. Matheson. Wellingborough, Northamptonshire, UK: Crucible, 1990.

Chittick, William. *The Sufi Path of Knowledge*. Albany: State Univ. of New York Press, 1989.

———. *Sufism: A Short Introduction*. Oxford: One World Publications, 2000.

Chodkiewicz, Michel. *An Ocean Without Shore: Ibn 'Arabī, the Book, and the Law*. Translated by David Streight. Albany: State Univ. of New York Press, 1993.

———. *Seal of the Saints: Prophethood and Sainthood in the Doctrine of Ibn 'Arabī*. Translated by Liadain Sherrard. Cambridge: Islamic Texts Society, 1993.

Corbin, Henry. *Alone with the Alone: Creative Imagination in the Sufism of Ibn 'Arabī*. Princeton, NJ: Princeton Univ. Press, 1997.

———. *The Man of Light in Iranian Sufism*. Translated by Nancy Pearson. Boulder, CO: Shambhala, 1978.

Cornell, Vincent. *Realm of the Saint*. Austin: Univ. of Texas Press, 1998.

Ernst, Carl. *The Shambhala Guide to Sufism*. Boston: Shambhala, 1997.

Lewisohn, Leonard, ed. *The Heritage of Sufism.* 3 vols. Oxford: One World Publications, 1999.

Lings, Martin. *Sufi Poems: A Mediaeval Anthology.* Cambridge, UK: The Islamic Texts Society, 2004.

———. *A Sufi Saint of the Twentieth Century.* Berkeley and Los Angeles: Univ. of California Press, 1971.

———. *What Is Sufism?* Boston: Unwin Books, 1981.

Michon, Jean-Louis, and Roger Gaetani, eds. *Sufism: Love and Wisdom.* Bloomington, IN: World Wisdom Books, 2006.

Nasr, Seyyed Hossein, ed. *Islamic Spirituality.* 2 vols. New York: Crossroad Publications, 1987, 1991.

———. *Sufi Essays.* Chicago: ABC International, 1999.

Schimmel, Annemarie. *As Through a Veil.* New York: Columbia Univ. Press, 1982.

———. *Mystical Dimensions of Islam.* Chapel Hill: Univ. of North Carolina Press, 1975.

Schuon, Frithjof. *Sufism: Veil and Quintessence.* Bloomington, IN: World Wisdom Books, 2006.

———. *Understanding Islam.* Bloomington, IN: World Wisdom Books, 1998.

INDEX

history *(continued)*
of "Sufi," 170–71; transcending, 98, 164–66; the two Ghazzālīs, 181–84. *See also* Sufi orders; theoretical gnosis
Howling Dervishes, 192
human body, 11, 51–53, 98–102, 191, 192
human love, 63–68
human microcosm, 51–52
humility, 126–27
ḥusn, 71
hypocrisy, 132–33, 148

I-Thou dichotomy, 101
Ibn al-Fāriḍ, 'Umar, 188
Ibn 'Arabī, Muḥyī al-Dīn: association with Dhū'l-Nūn, 173; on contemplation of female beauty, 74; on creation of the mirror, 43; father and founder of theoretical Sufism, 210–16; on the Five Divine Presences, 50; historical influence worldwide, 217–21, 223–25; on perfect servanthood, 12; on recitation of the Quran, 114; as supreme master, 30, 39, 188; *Tarjumān al-ashwāq* (poem), 213; on the veil of God, 44. *See also Fuṣūṣ;* theoretical gnosis
Ibn Mashīsh, 'Abd al-Salām, 188
Ibn Turkah Iṣfahānī, Ṣā'in al-Dīn, 224
Ibrāhīm ibn Adham, 177
Ihyā' 'ulūm al-dīn (al-Ghazzālī), 126, 182, 212
immutable archetypes, 8, 11, 44, 63, 64
India, 146, 197–99, 220–21
initiatic death, 18, 22–23
initiatic guidance (*walāyah/wilāyah*) of, xv, 23, 56, 105–11, 150–51, 223
integration and totality, 99–102, 117–18
intellect, 9–11, 35, 52–53, 85–86
intoxication (*sukr*), 114, 117, 177, 179
Iraq, 191–93
'irfān-i naẓarī. See theoretical gnosis
Islam/Islamic world and teachings: belief in initiation by the Prophet, 107; cross symbolism in, 20; essential to Sufi practice, 109, 111, 113–14, 157; fall from primordial state in, 54, 92; fundamentalism and modernism in, xvi, 154–56; imitation of the Prophet in, 121; influence of Sufism on, xv–xvi, 146, 150, 153–56, 231; Muḥammadan Reality, 38, 122, 123, 128; Muslim extremists, 88, 129; pilgrimages to Sufi shrines, 151–52; prayer rites, 14–16, 100, 104; *Sharī'ah* (Sacred Law of Islam), 4–5, 20, 56, 97, 113–14; spiritual hermeneutics (*ta'wīl*), 49; teaching of doctrine, 33–34

Jāmī ('Adb al-Raḥmān Jāmī), 67, 224–25
Ja'far al-Ṣādiq, 169–70
Jesus Christ: as alpha and omega, 45; on being not of this world, 118; on disciples, 111; on forgetting the Divine Reality, 22; on freedom through Truth, 30; Lord's prayer, 97, 101; on loving others, 62, 92; on multiple spiritual paths, 31; on peace, 132; on seeking, 156
jihād, 24, 88, 97
Judaism, 107, 149, 158
al-Junayd, Abū'l-Qāsim, 174

Kashf al-maḥjūb (Hujwīrī), 180
Khāksār Order, 193
khalq, 128–29
Khalwatiyyah Order, 206
Khamriyyah (poem; Ibn al-Fāriḍ), 188
Kharaqānī, Abū'l-Ḥasan, 135, 224
al-Kharrāz, Abū Bakr, 173–74
Khiḍr, 107–8, 112, 190
Khomeini, Ayatollah, 219, 227
Kirmānī, Awḥad al-Dīn, 76
Kitāb al-luma' (al-Sarrāj), 179
Kitāb al-ta'arruf (al-Kalābādhī), 179
knowledge (*ma'rifah*): as highest station, 133; illuminative, 9–11, 52–53, 231; as main gate to the Garden, 82, 86, 98; relation to action, 90–91; relation to love, 60, 69; self-knowledge, 4–7, 11–12, 23–24, 51; Sufism as path of, 30, 79; of the Truth and deliverance, 57–58; unitive knowledge, 128, 133, 135, 216, 230, 231
Kubrawiyyah Order, 193–95, 224
Laylā and Majnūn, 67–68

literature, 142–45
"Love-Death Song" (song; Wagner), 66
love (*'ishq*): action in truth with,

91–93; and compassion, 90, 91, 94–95; complementarity to beauty, 70; divine, 63–64, 68–69, 172; as highest station, 133; human, 63–68; as main gate to the Garden, 82, 86, 98, 101; as purpose of creation, 43; related to charity and nobility, 127; relation to knowledge, 60, 69; role in spiritual life, 60–64, 69–70. *See also* beauty

Maghrib, 186–88, 217
majdhūb, 107
majlis, 115–16
Malay, 144, 146, 221–22
Manāzil al-sā'irīn (Anṣārī), 180
manifested order. *See* creation and manifested order
Manṣūr al-Ḥallāj. *See* Ḥallāj
Massignon, Louis, 21, 175
master. *See* Sufi master
materialists, 7, 219
Mawlawiyyah Order of Rūmī, 116, 146, 204–5
meaning of life: attainment of Truth, 30–31; doctrine of the Universal Man, 20–22; entry into the Garden of Truth, 4–6, 13, 158–59; initiatic death and the, 22, 23; servanthood as worship, 12–13
meditation (*fikr*), 114–15
memory, 5–6, 8, 9, 11, 76
Menuhin, Yehudi, 145
metaphysics, 35–36, 39, 46, 126, 141–42, 149–50. *See also* theoretical gnosis
microcosm-macrocosm correspondence, 51–52
mi'rāj, 122–23
mirror symbolism, 13, 21, 24, 43, 44, 216
modernism, 154–56
Moses, 30, 107–8
Muḥammadan Reality, 38, 122, 123, 128
al-Muḥāsibī, al-Ḥārith, 174
Mullā Ṣadrā (Ṣadra al-Dīn Shīrāzī), 185
multiplicity, 40
Munājāt (Anṣārī), 180–81
murīd and *murād,* 112, 120
Murīdiyyah Order, 203
music, 115–17, 124–25, 145–46, 204
Muslims. *See* Islam/Islamic world
mutaṣawwif, 117

nafs, 92
Nahj al-balāghah ('Alī), 167
Names of God. *See* Divine Names and Qualities
Naqshbandiyyah Order, 195–97, 199, 202
Nāṣir-i Khusraw, 49
nature, 46–47
New England Transcendentalists, 156
Ni'amtullāhiyyah Order, 195
al-Niffarī, Muḥammad ibn 'Abd al-Jabbār, 178–79
nihilists, 7
nobility, 126, 127
North Africa, 199–203
Nūniyyah (poem; Abū Madyan), 187
al-Nūrī, Abū'l-Ḥusayn, 174–75

oneness or unity of being, 37–41
orders. *See* Sufi orders
Ottoman Empire, 204–5, 219

pantheism, 38, 40
Paradise, xv
Path (*Ṭarīqah*): function of the spiritual master, 107–11; in Islam (*Sharī'ah*), 5, 20, 56, 104–5; as path of ascent, 20; process of remembrance, 5, 53; role of other traditions in the, 105–6; role of the disciple, 111–13; Truth as beginning and ending, 58; as vertical and horizontal, 158–59; *walāyah/wilāyah*, xv, 23, 56, 105–11, 150–51, 223. *See also* stations
patience (*al-ṣabr*), 131–32
Paul (apostle), 82
peace (*al-salām*), 77–79
People of Blame (*Malāmatiyyah*), 133, 147–48, 184
Perfect Man. *See* Universal or Perfect Man
Persia, 193–97, 220, 222–28
Persian arts, 142, 143, 146
philosophy, 232
Pir Inayat Khan, 157
Plato, 8, 71–72, 228
Plotinus, 72, 101
poetry, 32, 116, 142–45, 213, 223. *See also* Rūmī
Poles of Sufism, 173
politics, 201–2
poverty (spiritual; *faqr*), 13, 19, 121–22, 132